# Rethinking Organizational Change

*Rethinking Organizational Change: The Role of Dialogue, Dialectic & Polyphony in the Organization* makes an important scholarly contribution to our understanding of dialogue applied to the management of change. Muayyad Jabri offers an involved assessment of the differences between 'dialogue' and 'dialectic' and an intriguing invitation to rely on both for managing creative interventions into the change process. The book provides a surplus of new insights that will help to promote scholarly work in the area of managing change and to develop a more creative practice associated with the processes of managing change.

The call for polyphony facilitates a crossover from sameness to diversity and from univocal to multivocal representations. In reading patterns of managing change, whether from within or across organizational borders, it is found that a vital part of the reading is, at present, 'unreadable' because we lack involved knowledge of how diversity and polyphony are interrelated. This book seeks to change this; based on a rendition of Mikhail Bakhtin's anthropological concept of polyphony applied to organizational change. The reader is treated to a cutting-edge discussion of a variety of contemporary ontological and epistemological themes centered on process, dialectic, dialogue and social construction.

**Muayyad Jabri** is an Associate Professor at the Graduate School of Business University of New England Business School, Australia.

# Routledge Studies in Organizational Change & Development

# Rethinking Organizational Change

The Role of Dialogue, Dialectic & Polyphony in the Organization

**Muayyad Jabri**

Routledge
Taylor & Francis Group

NEW YORK AND LONDON

First published 2016
by Routledge
711 Third Avenue, New York, NY 10017

and by Routledge
2 Park Square, Milton Park, Abingdon, Oxon OX14 4RN

First issued in paperback 2018

*Routledge is an imprint of the Taylor & Francis Group,
an informa business*

*Library of Congress Cataloging-in-Publication Data*
Names: Jabri, Muayyad, author.
Title: Rethinking organizational change : the role of dialogue, dialectic & polyphony in the organization / by Muayyad Jabri.
Description: New York : Routledge, 2016. | Includes bibliographical references and index.
Identifiers: LCCN 2015035948 | ISBN 9781138837928 (cloth : alk. paper) | ISBN 9781315734774 (ebook)
Subjects: LCSH: Organizational change—Management. | Communication in organizations.
Classification: LCC HD58.8 .J3273 2016 | DDC 658.4/06—dc23
LC record available at http://lccn.loc.gov/2015035948

ISBN 13: 978-1-138-34004-6 (pbk)
ISBN 13: 978-1-138-83792-8 (hbk)

Typeset in Sabon
by Apex CoVantage, LLC

For Wendy, Nadia, Estefan, and Joseph

# Contents

# Tables and Figures

**TABLE**

**FIGURES**

# Preface

This book is based on a rendition of Mikhail Bakhtin's anthropological concept of polyphony applied to organizational change. The reader is treated to a cutting-edge discussion of a variety of contemporary themes centered on process, dialectic, dialogue, and plasticity. Why Bakhtin? Bakhtin's thought is a source of inspiration. His notion of utterance and his distinction between monologue and dialogue have an important role to play in the face of the monologues of managerialism and the rigidity of dialectics. This book's title therefore mentions "rethinking polyphony" because it enacts and maintains that polyphony, applied to organizational settings, means multiple voices that are unmerged into a single or unified perspective.

I think the scholarly concept of this book began when I first came across the work of Mikhail Bakhtin, some years back. Bakhtin greatly valued the existence of others. As the title of this book—*Rethinking Organizational Change: The Role of Dialogue, Dialectic & Polyphony*—suggests, Bakhtin was careful to distinguish between language as a self-constrained system, which he identified as a codification, and "a feeling for utterance." The former is centered on a Cartesian separation. It is about positing the self against objectifying truth and upon much of the ideology on which managerialism is based. A "feeling for utterance" is Socrates's notion that we all contribute to forming each other's sense of truth.

Applied to change, polyphony is about people having a say in the way change is managed. It is not the same as cacophony. Polyphony elegantly explains how people are given the opportunity to put their case excitedly and to argue their views on how change is managed with exuberance and energy, as they include their lived experiences and felt meanings in the presentation of their case.

Bakhtin's work is centered on appreciating the excess of meaning achieved through the other. As utterances are exchanged, they become owned not only for oneself but also by the other and for the other. In a way, this appreciation already meant that the other was more important in managing change than I had suspected.

I saw Bakhtin's notion of polyphony as providing an olive branch to reconsider the task ahead of us, showing that there can be more than one way of thinking about change and changing. That is one reason why I see polyphony as the touchstone for creating a dialogic sense of truth. All this made me think that polyphony is much more important than I myself had realized in all the years I have been teaching and researching the subject of organizational change.

The call for polyphony facilitates a crossover from sameness to diversity and from univocal to multivocal representations. In reading patterns of managing change, whether from within or across organizational borders, we find that a vital part of the reading is, at present, 'unreadable.' This is because we lack involved knowledge of how polyphony and the *simultaneity* of voice and representations are being undermined by the way the logic of managerialism is embraced in managing the change effort. The point about managerial logic and its ideology is not the content of the ideological system *per se* as much as locating ways through which system controls are sustained based on single consciousness.

Indeed, the image of an organization striving to become polyphonic draws attention to an important point, namely that change, in itself, belongs to *no one*. Change is a co-constructed and socially-determined effort that is played and performed in dialogue. The resentment between managerialism and polyphony emerges from both Bakhtin and Voloshinov's genuine efforts to shed light on how the ideology of managerialism can perpetuate control over managerial groups and professions. These insights, in fact, negate a viewpoint that Bakhtin shunned the full political implications of his polyphony by overestimating the importance of a dialogic sense of truth in combatting monoglossic forms.

The work of Bakhtin constitutes a rebuttal of the monoglossic tendencies exhibited through the pursuit of managerial dialectic, as such insights are crucially important in the management of change. That is because they also bring on board matters concerned with consensus, often sought in decision-making. I highlight the critical reach of Bakhtin's work when analyzing the notion of the consensus that often accrues when monologic perspectives dominate the way change is managed. That is, when managers and organizational leaders invite contributions from employees towards a plan of action, or some strategy, but in reality want employees to vote 'yes' to some predetermined option.

In time, the search for a more involved reading of change and changing led me to consider how polyphony could occur by bringing the thinking of Bakhtin into a dialogical relationship with that of the French philosopher Catherine Malabou. In writing this book I have, therefore, relied on ideas from both Bakhtin and Malabou about plasticity to formulate an interpretation of functions and decision-making for creative renewal of organizations, achieved by coupling malleability of forms with polyphony and simultaneity of voice.

As an overarching theme, the drive for both polyphony and plasticity is timely given the burgeoning interest in the quest for the real self, embodiment, and the problems associated with the spread of managerialism. Indeed, the world scene today is dominated by a drive for social representation, inclusion, and a growing recognition of the fact that the task of changing, in itself, belongs to no one and that change needs to be managed through a more malleable mode of changing based on the capacity to transgress one's own limits as well as become the other. In making the implicit comparison between polyphony, plasticity, and managerialism much more explicit, I endeavor to reflect on the pitfalls of managerial dialectic and other organizational practice, and also to expand our search for plasticity and plastic readings in the way change is treated.

There is no point in sitting around and thinking about voice and the other without plastic readings because that is where polyphony in its dialogic sense of truth is internally compromised. Not surprisingly, once the frontier of dialectics is consolidated, once a stage is set for organizational life to be subordinated by that of dialectics, there will be no point in advocating polyphony in the presence of rigid structures centered on rules of monologic (managerialist) modes of thinking.

In configuring the frontier, there are both internal and external forces pushing towards managerialism and maintenance of the status quo. This usually results in strengthening of the frontier, through reliance on more dialectics, rules and reviews, moving towards a monologic sense of truth, where human approaches are considered subordinate to science.

Plasticity has a crucial role in getting an organization to continue changing and to see 'what is' coming. It provides the ground for transforming organizations into polyphonic places. The book is not, however, about the dualism between dialogue and dialectics. It is not meant to show their role as equal rivals. Instead, the aim is to show the need for a plastic reading to help change leaders shape the direction of change and the possibilities of plastic readings in giving, receiving, and destroying ways of thinking about change. What a plastic reading does, then, is illuminate and retrieve simultaneity of lived experiences of people to illuminate the issues at hand.

A plastic reading provides a means of understanding the limits of normative modes of thinking and of managerialism. Building on the interrelationships between dialogue and plasticity, we will consider how communication, learning, and the embodiment of the change effort are conceived around each other. Some of the questions asked include:

- What is polyphony?
- How is polyphony informed by Malabou's notion of plasticity?
- How is polyphony informed by dialogue and excess of meaning?
- How can we enhance knowledge and learning in organizational settings?
- How can we promote polyphonic modes of communicating change?
- How can we promote the embodiment of the change effort?

All these questions drew me closer to polyphony and then slowly into the relationship between polyphony and plasticity; both play an important role in enhancing and embellishing the process through which polyphonic change is achieved.

I hope that "*Rethinking Organizational Change: The Role of Dialogue, Dialectic & Polyphony in the Organization*" provides a surplus of new insights that will help to open new research frontiers in both organization studies and managing organizational change.

Muayyad Jabri

# Acknowledgments

I would like to acknowledge the warm support of my colleagues and friends at Manchester Business School and the University of New England, Australia. I thank my undergraduate and postgraduate students who, over the years, have engaged me in thinking about the connections between dialogue, polyphony, and the management of change. I also wish to thank Frederick W. Kelly S.J., Mary-Louise Conway, Alison Sheridan, Melissa Leffler, David Boje, Amal Jabri, Julie Wolfram Cox, Mark Dibben, Allyson Downs Adrian, Rune Todnem By, and Philippe Lorino for their support and encouragement.

Very special thanks go to the series editor Bernard Burnes, David Varley, Brianna Ascher, and the copyediting and production teams at Routledge. I wish to thank Routledge anonymous reviewers. I acknowledge the permission of the Bodleian Libraries, The University of Oxford, Shelfmark: MS. Ashmole 304, fol. 31 v. I thank the University of Minnesota Press for granting the authorization to reprint excerpts from Mikhail Bakhtin, *Problems of Dostoevsky Poetics*, edited and translated by Caryl Emerson (University of Minnesota Press, 1984). I thank Palgrave Macmillan for permission to use of excerpts from my 2012 book *Managing Organizational Change: Process, Social Construction and Dialogue*. Every effort has been made to trace all copyright holders, but if any have been inadvertently overlooked, the publishers will be pleased to make the necessary arrangements at the first opportunity.

# 1 Managing Change and the Role of Polyphony

*I realize myself initially through others: from them I receive words, forms and tonalities for the formation of my initial idea of myself.*

Mikhail Bakhtin (1986, 138).

This book applies Russian philosopher Mikhail Bakhtin's (1895–1975) anthropological concept of 'polyphony' to organizational change. Bakhtin's notion of 'utterances' and his distinction between 'monologue' and 'dialogue' help us to change the way that we think about organizations. The idea of dialogue is particularly important in combatting the focus on the monologues of managerialism and the rigidity of dialectics. It gives us new ways of thinking about how we can manage organizational change.

We begin by highlighting the importance of utterances in organizational change. Whether interpreting workplace changes in general or one's immediate workplace in particular, we share our utterances with others as they share theirs. Utterances carry an enormous weight and have a profound effect. Through utterances, we obtain new meanings as we interpret change. Having highlighted the importance of utterances, this chapter then introduces the work of Mikhail Bakhtin and his notion of dialogue.

Mikhail Mikhailovich Bakhtin was a Russian philosopher who lived in anonymity for most of his life. According to Clark and Holquist (1984), it was only in his late years that he drew world attention as a prominent philosopher and theorist of art and philosophy of language. Bakhtin's major work was written almost one year after the October Revolution of 1917 (Clark and Holquist 1984). Bakhtin was an active member of the so-called Bakhtin Circle, a twentieth century school of Russian thought and philosophy addressing the role of language and other matters concerned with aesthetics and literature. According to Clark and Holquist (1984), the Bakhtin Circle began in Petrograd. Members of the circle included Valentin Voloshinov (1895–1936) and Pavel Medvedev (1891–1938). Bakhtin suffered from ill health and was sentenced to labor camps, because his thinking was at variance with the official Communist Party lines. He was sent in 1930 to Kazakhstan (Clark and Holquist 1984). Bakhtin's exile lasted four years and resulted in his left leg being amputated because of frostbite (Clark and Holquist 1984).

Bakhtin's work on dialogue presents us with a wide spectrum of themes that have found their way into several fields of knowledge including philosophy, literary theory, education, religious thought, aesthetics, anthropology, and human sciences. The recent interest in the work of Mikhail Bakhtin among management and organization studies scholars has developed since the materiality of 'language' became the centerpiece for constructing, rather than representing, reality. Because of its openness and resourcefulness as well as its variety of aspects and concepts, Bakhtin's ideas about dialogue, polyphony, and other concepts, including surplus of meaning, are increasingly emerging as a very rich source for various approaches within organization studies. The core of Bakhtin's theory is a number of concepts that are shaped and reshaped by each other, as we shall see shortly.

Such concepts continue to borrow from each other. To fully appreciate Bakhtin's concept of dialogue, we must also understand his idea of polyphony. In general terms, the word 'polyphony' means the simultaneous interweaving of several melodic lines, usually soprano, alto, tenor, and bass. It encompasses intricate combinations of several melodies or a variety of voices (fugue), sometimes merging them and sometimes keeping them separate. Even though Bakhtin's ideas of polyphony emerged from music and literature, they prove very useful for reflecting on change.

Bakhtin (1984, 6) defined polyphony as "a plurality of independent and unmerged voices and consciousnesses." The main characteristic of polyphony is, therefore, that of consciousnesses having their own social property which come together. Utterances continue to resonate with voice ideas, giving way to new surpluses of meaning. As utterances come together, spontaneity of events occur. Spontaneity is about glimpses achieved during an exchange of utterances, which provide the 'aha' or 'eureka' moment, calling for embodiment of some new immediate improvement. This can be understood as a glance in a rear view mirror, but one that brings the future to the present.

In music, polyphony is a series of musical notes that have a distinct rhythm in which several musical notes are combined to form a distinct unit. Polyphonic music is that in which two or more musical notes are produced concurrently: the term derives from the Greek words for 'many sounds.' As in a choir, every participant brings their own melody, voice, and style in a way that contributes to the harmony of the multi-voiced whole. Polyphony has also been used to describe the intertwining or interweaving of voices.

Applied to a texture or surface level, the word 'polyphony' describes the way in which the object is created from different constituents. For example, in the art of carpet design, different colors and/or textures of thread can be interwoven to create the design. The intertwining of threads produces a polytexture, with its own colors and themes.

Applied to organizational life, we will use the term polyphony to mean the way in which several voices, parties, and structures interact and where each representation is intertwined with the others relative to its own role or function. An effort is exerted in a combined way to produce an output.

The effort itself is continuous and has its own direction. It is ongoing and creative, leading to a state of becoming.

Polyphony can help us reflect on how we manage and lead organizations, as well as in contesting ideologies held by those charged with managing and leading the change effort. We will explore what polyphony means for managing change, with specific reference to Bakhtin's idea of the 'excess of meaning' achievable through the more involved sharing of utterances from the perspective of the 'other.'

## THE NATURE OF CHANGE

The Greek philosopher Heraclitus is reported to have said: "You cannot step into the same river twice," to which his student is reported to have responded: "Not even once, since there is no same river." The philosopher was emphasizing that experiencing change is an *ongoing* process, and his student's response underlined this by emphasizing 'changing,' rather than just 'change.'

The metaphor of the river directs attention to the process (flow) aspect of ongoing change. Some say that change is the only constant in organizational life (Elving 2005), while others point out that even change changes. Both assertions are right, of course, because change is a steadfast phenomenon we all live and move through. Our experience is expressed as ongoing thoughts or utterances, whether word, phrase, or sentence, and whether directed to ourselves or others.

Using the metaphor of the river again, it might be said that every river has its own context, which is constituted by its banks, topography, and terrain. As the external and internal forces associated with the river change, so too does its context. The same is true of change: every change has its own peculiar context, and every context is in a continuing state of flux.

At the heart of change is the notion that all things flow in a continuous process of becoming (Whitehead 1956), demonstrating the continuity of our utterances as a "ceaseless becoming process" (Rescher 1996). Our awareness, sensations, and feelings are all crucial even though we do not see them. Henri Bergson (1859–1941), awarded the Nobel Prize for Literature, noted:

> The point is that usually we look at change but we do not see it. We speak of change, but we do not think about it. We say that change exists, that everything changes, that change is the very law of things: Yes, we say it and we repeat it; but those are only words, and we reason and philosophize as though change did not exist.
>
> (Bergson 1946, 131)

Every process, e.g., downsizing, represents change, and takes place in time. It involves the generation of recurring thoughts or consciousness and utterances. These thoughts, in turn, affect our lives and the lives of other members of the organization, as they also think with the intention of creating change.

Consider the words used to describe the insecurity people feel when they discover that their organization is about to be downsized and that they face the prospect of being made redundant. Consider the challenges faced as one organization merges with another. Consider the words used by those who are suddenly required to use a new gadget or follow a new procedure in their work. All these utterances are discourses with the self, with neighbors, and with others. They shape and co-shape the fabric of the changes we inhabit. Each individual plays a part in constructing this fabric. Since the process affects the lives of organization members, we cannot go on assuming that we are on our own and that each of us is the only person constructing change. Others are also involved but in their own way.

How does one come to appreciate the recurring aspects of such constructions? As we will see in this chapter, this can be approached in more than one way, or from more than one perspective. For example, Bakhtin (1981) considered the role of polyphony in ensuring that people are represented in determining the direction change should take. Gergen (2008, 145–46) considered "coordinated action" achieved through its social supplement. Taylor and Van Every's (2000, xi) approach was through thinking of the "organization as an emergent reality." It is through such varying perspectives that we can learn to manage and lead continuous change.

## UTTERANCES

An utterance can be a word or a sentence, spoken or written, including to oneself. It is a real unit of speech because it reflects a real speech situation (Bakhtin 1986). Each utterance is infused with intentions. A word uttered is necessarily a word infused with the speaker's awareness of his or her listener, and of the influence of other speakers they have heard. This notion of the speaker becoming aware of the addressee and vice versa allows utterances to inter-animate each other, even in silence. Bakhtin used the concept of utterance to include the notion of talking to oneself internally or externally, as well as conversation with others.

In each speech act, an utterance is an expression of subjective experience. It is firmly situated within a context and so it gets framed within the space or the situation. Voloshinov (1986, 97) described an utterance as "a fact of the social milieu." At any given point in time, there is a particular change situation, and this ensures that the meaning attached to a word uttered at a particular time is different from the meaning attached to that same word under other conditions. Whether communicated externally or internally in silence, utterances are active expressions of meaning. An utterance eventually generates another. Utterances, therefore, can produce what might be called a 'stretch of interaction' in given social contexts.

According to Bakhtin, there is a constant dialogue between change recipients: a situation in which every utterance predicts and relationally changes the one that follows it. Through speech, people experience an endlessly internalized exchange of utterances. Recognition of the undecidable, unfinalizable nature of utterances permits an understanding of change being shaped and reshaped through shifting identities, and of the interlocking relationship between change and individuals' accounts of change. These accounts are never complete and final. This is what Bakhtin (1981) described as "carnival:" identity is fluid, playful, intermingling, and ambiguous. For Bakhtin (1981), no single interpretation, meaning, or definition of an identity achieved through narrative can stand as more than a momentary manifestation.

## BAKHTIN AND DOSTOEVSKY

Bakhtin brought his notion of polyphony into focus after considering the work of the Russian novelist Fyodor Dostoevsky, in his *Problems of Dostoevsky's Poetics*. In his preface to the book, Bakhtin (1984, 3) noted that he considered Dostoevsky to have created "a completely new type of artistic thinking . . . called polyphonic." For Bakhtin, polyphony was exemplified through Dostoevsky's artistic style of novelistic writing, in which he accorded his characters the opportunity to showcase their perceptions and ways of coping with the world around them. Clark and Holquist (1984) explained that the most important attribute that Bakhtin saw in Dostoevsky's work was that "the nature of human beings is dialogic," that no one is left out in the process of creating polyphony, and that polyphony achieves its meaningfulness through the view that human beings are dialogic.

Dostoevsky allowed each character to draw a self-portrait. He used a representational structure in which every character presents themselves as a foreground figure. Based on this style of writing, Bakhtin described polyphony as a place or field where individuals' subjectivities are shared in time and where the actors come to engage in their own joint authorship of the reality they inhabit.

In *The Brothers Karamazov*, for example, where Dostoevsky is often described by critics as truly excelling in showcasing the authorial voice of his characters, we have a murder mystery that unfolds in a series of love affairs involving the father, Karamazov, and his three sons, Alyosha, Ivan, and Dimitri. Each character has his own distinct way of speaking and presents his own views of the world. Every character brings their own perspective on events.

Dostoevsky allows Alyosha to show his own reason and to express himself freely in ways that are truly different from the views held by his brother, Ivan. Neither view necessarily chimes with the views held by the author:

> "I understand it all too well, Ivan: to want to love with your insides, your guts–you said it beautifully, and I am terribly glad that you want

so much to live," Alyosha exclaimed. "I think that everyone should love life before everything else in the world."

"Love life more than its meaning?"

"Certainly, love it before logic, as you say, certainly before logic, and only then will I also understand its meaning. That is how I've long imagined it."

(Dostoevsky 1990, 231)

Dostoevsky enabled his characters to speak in their own voices. In his introduction to the translation from the Russian of *The Brothers Karamazov*, Pevear noted:

> Dostoevsky composed in voices. We know from his notebooks and letters how he gathered the phrases, mannerisms, verbal tics from which [his characters] would emerge, and how he would try out these voices, writing many pages of dialogue that would never be used in the novel.
>
> (Pevear 1990, XV)

Bakhtin commented on this feature of Dostoevsky's work by noting that "self-consciousness" is the main distinguishing feature that is brought forward and given weight. Boundaries are permeable and so as utterances are exchanged, they become owned not only by the speaker but also by and for the hearer, or 'other.' That is when consciousness moves away from being solely a property of the individual to something more social as well.

Bakhtin described Dostoevsky as doing everything possible to allow his heroes to fully express their viewpoints, in ways in which every utterance depends on its response and, most importantly, where excess of meaning results from the exchange. Bakhtin (1984, 6) noted: "[Dostoevsky] creates not voiceless slaves, [. . .] but *free* people, capable of standing *alongside* their creator, capable of not agreeing with him and even of rebelling against him" (italic in original).

## SUMMARY

What is so peculiar about all this and why does Dostoevsky want to let his characters do all the talking? He really wants to give authority back to them whilst also accepting that not all of them will agree. He wants to treat people not as objects in a conversation but as subjects, with a view of some artistic visualization that is translated into conversations. What they say might contradict the author's values and viewpoint. He wants to pull away and let them explore their own perspectives and share their ideas. He does not want to keep them voiceless, or take over, and so each comes with a viewpoint, even though it contradicts the author's beliefs.

## THE CALL FOR POLYPHONY

Polyphony is generally viewed as rebellion in the history of music. Polyphony is based on the interweaving of many voices, some of which might contradict each other, and bring different melodies. It is about differentiated voices brought together and yet treated as separate and distinct. Even though polyphony is a musical and literary concept, the scope for forging it in organizational life is high. Individuals within organizations each have their own voices, independent and yet with a relationship to others, and expressed with different rhythm or style. Polyphony describes a way of managing change as collections of voices, some in harmony and others in conflict or counterpoint, or using the same tune but a different pitch. It is, therefore, about people having a say in the way change is managed. Clark and Holquist (1984) noted that the notion of polyphony is used to emphasize a style of writing composed of many points of view, some of which may result in contradictions and each of which is valid, and can seem equally justified.

Polyphony is not the same as cacophony. Polyphony is where people are given the opportunity to put their case excitedly and to argue their views on how change is managed with exuberance and energy, including their lived experiences and felt meanings in the presentation of their case. Cacophony, by contrast, is where voices cannot be heard individually. It is the situation where voices are clashing, resulting in noise but no harmony.

What is important is not only how the change leader sees the change recipients, but how they see the leader and themselves, and how they relate to each other. The emphasis is on how the rules and norms appear to organization members and how they see or define their roles, rather than on how the organization defines or sees its members. This means that for an organization to be polyphonic, the construction of change would itself need to be embodied in a sense of self that wanted to relate to others.

## BAKHTIN'S NOTION OF SELFHOOD

To understand polyphony, we must explore Bakhtin's notion of selfhood. Bakhtin greatly valued the existence of others. His treatment was centered on appreciating the uniqueness of people. His idea of the self is the dialogic achieved through utterances in which the self surrenders its surplus to the other. The individual obtains the excess of meaning through social interaction. Under polyphony, excess of meaning is developed through the exchange of utterances.

> Bakhtin's dictum that "the self is an act of grace, a gift of the other" (quoted in Clark and Holquist 1984, 68) has important implications for the way we manage change. That is because polyphony is about seeing the other from
>
> (*Continued*)

"outside," namely from a different angle. This different angle, or "outside-ness," as Bakhtin called it, explains our selfhood and why such selfhood is in fact '*the gift of the other*' given to us as we go about relating to the other and otherness.

Bakhtin developed his polyphonic theory based on the work of Dosto-evsky. In his analysis of Dostoevsky as a novelist whose work has had a last-ing influence on literature, Bakhtin (1984) argued that Dostoevsky's novels were structured to give the characters full access to their own ways of seeing the world around them. In short, "self-analysis" or "self-consciousness" is only achieved through others. Self-analysis is "interrogated and provoked into revealing and representing itself" (Bakhtin 1984, 65) through the eyes of the other.

Nielsen (2002) described Dostoevsky's characters as people who are truly fond of their own self-analysis and desire to share their self-analysis with others around them, listening to what the other is experiencing and/or what they have to say. There is a dependence between the characters and yet within that, they are willing to treat the voice of the other as independent. There is contestation but also the sharing of realities even though such reali-ties might be very different. They are, therefore, aware not only of their own self-analysis, but also of their own external setting, including the awareness of the other.

In short, each and every character presented her or his view indepen-dently of the other. They shared their views, or consciousness, with each other even though they differed. For Bakhtin (1984, 6) what emerged out of such difference was not a consensus, as in "a single objective word, illu-minated by a single authorial consciousness; rather *a plurality of conscious-nesses, with equal rights and each with its own world*" (italic in original). Importantly, such a state does not have to be based on agreement but a state of awareness that everyone is different in the way they express their con-sciousness in their utterances.

For Bakhtin, polyphony was also about not leaving anything of any real consequence outside the voice of the other, and bringing everyone into contact with what is being said. Bakhtin (1984, 73) noted that "whenever someone's 'truth' is presented in a given novel, it is introduced without fail into the *dialogic field of vision* of all other major heroes of the novel." Hence A understands what B is saying and why, and vice versa. There are many truths and yet everyone understands them perfectly. Everyone is fond of listening to everyone else's voice but with attention to their difference.

Polyphony has appeal because it elegantly explains how ideas can exist as embodied concepts and be shared among organization members. It involves presenting each idea as a reality. The polyphony brings all these ideas to the foreground, rather than leaving them ignored or undiscussed. Each idea is brought forward and contemplated by the character itself. The portraits relate to each other without being merged.

The insights and ideas of individuals, when shared through utterances, have a liberating effect. Applied to organizations, uttering insights in exchange with others enables the individual to move away from isolation, and by sharing their embodied concepts or images, towards a situation where they can see for themselves how their embodied insights, or consciousness "teems with the consciousness of others" (Clark and Holquist 1984, 241).

For Bakhtin, consciousness had its own field or dialogic space of vision, the space where utterances are exchanged and opinions shared. This space creates awareness of what everyone else is saying and the reasons for that but without having or expecting any defined state of genuine agreement or consensus to be reached.

What happens within that field of vision can be polyphonic in the sense that every word will have a sort of a 'reactionary' response to any attempt aimed at locking or confining it within the limits of a single consciousness, that is, expressing it as an authoritative discourse, based on the singularity of some specific monologic experience. Bakhtin (1984, 36; italic in original) noted that, "The important thing in Dostoevsky's polyphony is precisely what happens *between various consciousnesses*, that is, their interaction and interdependence."

To change and be willing to manage change means to take part in accepting the social awareness of others. If change agents, or change leaders, want to gauge the reality of change in a realistic way, they need to strengthen their subjectivity, or consciousness, *and* that of others. What characterizes the field of vision lies at the heart of having to provide people (characters in the change effort) with both strategic and operational levels of perceived autonomy, to allow them to come up with their own utterances based on how they have already embodied their own experiences and the world around them. This will be the only way through which further consciousness (subjectivity) and sociality could come to bear on the efforts needed for change to take root.

## POLYPHONY AS METAPHOR

Metaphors provide a way of linking two phenomena to highlight common ground. Derived from the Greek *metapherein*, 'metaphor' refers to meaning being carried over from one concept to another. As a figure of speech, metaphors use an idea or image to replace another, to suggest a resemblance or analogy between them. They are often used to make communications more accessible, and play an important role in the impact of messages. For example, by using polyphony in music as a way of describing a change process, we harness the imagery of polyphony as the many voices of organization members, to obtain a vivid view of the meaning in terms of empowerment, social representation, and inclusiveness.

Bakhtin's analogy of polyphony is rendered more vivid and imaginative by his relating it to musical composition combining several melodies or voices without merging them into one. As a metaphor, polyphony relates the orchestration of organizations with that of music as a performance. Organization members are enabled to participate, to become more self-conscious, and, at the same time, be willing to relate to what others have to say, without necessarily feeling the threat that their voices are forced to merge.

In the opening pages of *Problems of Dostoevsky's Poetics*, Bakhtin (1984, 3) wrote of Dostoevsky "as one of the greatest innovators in the realm of artistic form." He noted that such artistic form extends beyond the limits of the novel to other spheres, including the way we relate to the world by communicating and building relations.

Bakhtin (1984, 4) wrote of Dostoevsky as "first and foremost an artist (of a special type, to be sure)" and considered that his artistic thinking was polyphonic. All his characters and their viewpoints were ideologically independent, providing each character with the opportunity to argue their own ways of thinking against their own views as well as those of every other character. For Bakhtin (1984), this was what made Dostoevsky's novelistic style of writing and composition so polyphonic, in the sense that every character was given the full freedom to come up with his or her own viewpoint, put it forward, and juxtapose it with others.

According to Bakhtin (1984), the essence of polyphony lies precisely in keeping voices independent of each other in a way that reflects the consciousness of the individual character. Each voice is unique in its own way. They are taken one by one, rather than combined. For Bakhtin, this is the most important condition in moving beyond the monologism of a worldview where separate plot lines or points of view are combined into one.

## POLYPHONY AS A SOCIAL CONSTRUCT

Polyphony is related to the processes through which meanings and affirmations are constructed. For a genuine state of polyphony to exist in an organization, certain conditions need to be met:

- Every point of view must play a truly essential role in the conversation.
- Every point of view (identity) must be a living thing.
- A point of view must be full of meaning.
- Every point of view must be an embodied human voice.
- There must be no artificial consensus between voices.

It is particularly important that voices are not forced into consensus and lined up with some desired situation. Instead, they are received into a responsive exchange and, as such, combined in a unity of a higher order (Bakhtin 1984), involving dialogue.

A higher order of understanding is one that actively invites, expects, and encourages points of views to be explored in an effort to capitalize on their insights from more than one angle and at more than one level. It is the sort of exploration that results in a surplus of seeing. Such a surplus develops in a back-and-forth manner as people exchange utterances and as words are transposed across levels and situations (Jabri 2005). It prevents the temptation to aggregate and summarize points of view and enhances the exchange of utterances, enabling individuals to get a glimpse of how others feel as free subjects, and experience their own consciousness in terms of differing realizations, points of view, remarks, and perceptions.

What unfolds in Dostoevsky's works is not a number of characters managing the organization in a single objective world that is illuminated by a single plot (strategy) driven by singularity and fixation. Instead, it is a "plurality of consciousnesses with equal rights and each with its own world" (Bakhtin 1984, 7). For Bakhtin, the essence of polyphony was more than one sound, a plurality of independent and unmerged voices with each voice having its own rights and each with its own world. Basically, it is about showcasing the melodic notes in each part and creating some rhythmic distinction between them.

## POLYPHONY VERSUS MONOLOGUE

The essence of polyphony is that each human voice remains independent. Bakhtin warned against summarizing or trying to merge or group them as one. He noted "in place of the unity of an event, in which there are several autonomous participants, one ends up instead with the empty unity of an individual act of will" (Bakhtin 1984, 21). Any 'summary' or the use of rhetorical statement amounted, in his view, to a reduction of representations into nothing but a monologic mode.

Bakhtin warned against merging voices and the direct combination of separate elements of reality or separate plot lines. Combining separate elements would result in a state of combining people (separate consciousnesses, identities) into structures based on some unified state that is largely driven by aggregation. For Bakhtin, there was always a sideways glance at what the other is saying, based on utterances that are made in anticipation of the other's active response. Bakhtin's view of the self is in fact not fully autonomous or substantive, as much as it is relational. Utterances are made because of what we take ourselves and the other to be.

Trying to merge voices (consensus) also means getting several autonomous characters into a sort of unity confined to a single act. This does little but serve monologic control and command, serving as a mouthpiece for the person in charge. When put into practice, such unity is likely to be short-lived, because it is based on pseudo-consensus (Jabri, Adrian, and Boje 2008) of separate elements of reality, or separate plot lines. Sooner or later, those who have been asked to merge their voices, sections, or departments will be less ready to bring their realizations and inherent capabilities to bear. They will unite in name only, remaining separate by avoiding any issue that would overlap or bring about the need for responsiveness. A forced unity of merged voices would result in squeezing plurality into a framework of a single perspective.

Monologism is often done in a subtle way, which can be both insidious and dangerous. You can go into a meeting and all you see is a group of people agreeing with what the leader is saying. Although everyone is nominally in agreement, they may not agree in substance. Here we have a field of vision where a person cannot really express their views and is, therefore, characteristic of pseudo-consensus. People hide behind a pseudo-consensus and pretend everything is fine and they are all in agreement.

There is a problem in the way consensus is handled. Consensus implies the need for freedom and so it is insufficient to highlight the role consensus plays by merely acknowledging it. Consensus, as with free speech, is a wonderful thing for organizations to take on board. But it suffers from one very serious deficiency. It offers an opportunity for self-serving bias, in the sense that to survive and play the game, a person might profess adherence to explanations, dominant beliefs, opinions, and feelings that they themselves might not hold. Many people are good at reaching consensus based on the power of rules and norms of the game. Does that not make consensus largely monologic, or single-voiced?

Jabri, Adrian, and Boje (2008) differentiated between two views of decision-making processes, one that focuses on conversations enhancing monologic collectivized thinking, and another that sees all conversations among people as dialogic. Current views of the role of conversations in change management continue to have a *grammatical* view of the communication process—a view where form and meaning are determined by constant relations. Such a view is carried out in practice through an ongoing search for consensus and the presentation of common ground among group members. There is no 'meeting of minds,' so it remains a proclaimed state of the situation until tested, and that is when things fall apart, and change fails to take root. We therefore distinguish between consensus-as-monologue and consensus-as-dialogue. Under the former, the notion of a single speaker is emphasized (expectations of response are low). Under the latter, consensus becomes saturated with the self as the other (polemic, but born between people). Bakhtin's dialogic theory focuses on the surplus of meaning obtained from diverse points of view inhabiting a variety of speech genres.

Using dialogue, we (and the organization) start to be more open to change as we assume the creative content of other consciousnesses and as we aspire to a post-human extension with creative content of consciousness as a social property. Voloshinov (1986, 95; italic in original) noted that *"any utterance . . . is only a moment in the continuous process of verbal communication.* But this continuous verbal communication is, in turn, itself only a moment in the continuous, all-inclusive, generative process of a given social collective."

Voloshinov's statement on consciousness having a social property sheds a new light on how managerialism is often practiced. In fact, it shows how consensus is often made to appear as it if has a social property, when, in fact, it has no genuine agreement but one that accrues from a monologic perspective (single consciousness of the person in power). Managers and organizational leaders might very well invite contributions from employees towards a plan of action, or some strategy, but in reality want employees to vote 'yes' to some predetermined course.

Bakhtin suggested that much of the consensus we often achieve is largely the result of false but very well staged conversations based on singularity of consciousness and absence of genuine involvement. Consensus, in reality, often hides large differences between people (Jabri, Adrian, and Boje 2008). There is no 'meeting of minds,' either in whole or part. A genuine consensus is eventful but only in a monologic way, and may only appear when people are getting tired of arguing. This sort of consensus affirms lack of the independence between those engaged in a conversation, where there is no internal freedom.

A 'make believe' consensus may be endorsed and so treated as a fine accomplishment or even an achievement, until it is tested as and when change is implemented and that is when things fall apart (change fails to take root as background resistance starts to build up). People often feel quite threatened by change and so they do not wish to engage; one way to close a meeting or focus group session would be to show consensus and to *'escape'* the meeting happily and on good terms with each other. This is "I own meaning but will let it go" rather than "we own meaning." It is ego-centric even where it prefers to remain silent or anonymous for fear that anything it says will distract from building consensus or might attract more work for itself. It is here that we see the true nature of the social missing from building genuine agreement. There is, definitely, an ugly side to monoglossia, for there is no dialogue, only a plurality of people, a collection of minds, a full merging of voices of those attending. More importantly, there is no even-ness (spontaneity and flow of nonlinear moments) and the reason for the lack of creative exchange of utterances is the coherence of the meeting as purely linguistic and bounded by consensus.

We all have examples of organizations that have ended because it was too late for them to be destroyed in time to save their heritage. Enron Corporation, for example, was an organization of 20,000 staff, and one of the world's largest energy and natural gas providers, with revenues of nearly $111 billion (Newman, 2007). Its demise was largely due to an institutionalized consensus driven by systematic dialectic that led to a scandalous fraud.

A counter-narrative against polyphony could easily be mounted by noting that, too often, organizations have to endure forced unity by merging voices and entities, on the grounds of urgency: the need for unity and standards can often override the benefits of polyphony. Admittedly, this will always remain a contested issue, but the point that Bakhtin (1984) made is that such 'unity' would need to be non-final and hence subject to a higher order of unity because it would need to remain subject to an unfolding context.

We know from music that homophony is distinct from polyphony. The former is about two or more parts of music moving together in harmony, and the latter is about more than one melody, more than one section, more than one division, in which all have varying capabilities, but contribute to organizational efforts that are distinct and have the potential to be combined in a higher order of unity.

Polyphony is not about an immediate (solo) action aimed at merging and achieving unity. Instead, it is about unity of simultaneity in a process of becoming. That becoming is not dialectic. Rather, it is achieved based on a dialogic sense of truth involving consciousness as a social property. Bakhtin (1984) noted that he meant the comparison between polyphony and homophony as a graphic analogy. Indeed, the image of an organization striving to become polyphonic, or even declaring itself as polyphonic, draws attention to an issue which arises when change is declared and an organization is structured and managed solo even though change, in itself, belongs to *no one*. Change is a co-constructed and socially-determined effort that is played and performed in dialogue. The similarity with polyphony might be somewhat unlikely or, even, for some, far-fetched. However, in embracing the challenge of change, I make this implicit comparison mainly to reflect on organizational practice and also to expand our search for styles and ways of managing change.

An example of the perils of summarizing is the way in which feedback is often conducted in practice. Organizations frequently rely on voice audits and engagement surveys to identify 'average' perceptions in the hope of arriving at a collective viewpoint of organization members. However, almost all such perceptions lose their meaning once merged and aggregated. Organizations pursue aggregation, thinking that they are capturing and promoting the sharing of collective ideals when, in fact, all they are doing is squeezing plurality into monologic modes of unity of analysis, not knowing, or perhaps not caring, that such aggregation amounts to a merger of voices.

Many leaders continue to believe that aggregated profiles will be sufficient and ignore the importance of independent thoughts and perceptions. Even more significantly, some assume that the *word* finds fulfilment in the process of aggregating responses, independent of interaction with the minds of others. Self-consciousness is a sort of consciousness of separation whereby the collective is aggregated and given lip service. The problem of managing change, however, is one of managing interdependence and creating settings where collaboration can flourish. This is a major dilemma for change management: how to handle values centered on self-expression, and the growth of complex problems demanding dialogue.

## BAKHTIN'S NOTES ON POLYPHONY

A polyphonic view of change communication leads us to focus on what organization members are saying rather than what the person in charge thinks or would like organization members to say for the plot to develop along the desired line. With communication being critical to the effective adoption of change methodologies (Kakabadse et al. 2011), we must ask ourselves how we should view organization members, how we want them to communicate, and whether or not we are willing to listen to their defiance. Bakhtin (1984, 6) commented that: "Dostoevsky, like Goethe's Prometheus, creates not voiceless slaves (as does Zeus), but free people, capable of standing alongside their creator, capable of not agreeing with him and even of rebelling against him."

Bakhtin (1984) argued that because Dostoevsky's characters are free people, one cannot examine his novels in terms of the usual analysis of plot development. Jabri, Adrian, and Boje (2008) drew inspiration from Bakhtin and argued that change management has, for too long, focused on monologic implementation of predetermined plans for changing (i.e., how to develop the 'best plot'). Instead, change agents need to consider their anthropology and ask themselves whether the people in their organizations are the *objects of* communication or *subjects in* communication: how one communicates depends entirely on which approach is taken.

## THE ROLE OF CONVERSATIONS

A conversation is basically an exchange between two or more people. In conversations, each of us communicates with the other. Much of the emphasis in conversation is on recursive talk. That is where the 'output' or utterance returns to form itself as an 'input,' to increase meaning. Any form or perspective involving some aspect of social construction is bound to involve some element of recursive talk, producing a new output as if there is a contrasting condition or some kind of in-between form of talk, an interim form emerging in time as the conversation unfolds.

There are always features in conversation that correspond to dialogue, as well as to dialectics. Hans-Georg Gadamer (1979) talked about conversation as a process where responsive exchange takes place:

> [It] is a process of two people understanding each other. Thus it is a characteristic of every true conversation that each opens himself to the other person, truly accepts his point of view as worthy of consideration and gets inside the other to such an extent that he understands not a particular individual, but what he says. The thing that has to be grasped is the objective rightness or otherwise of his opinion, so that they can agree with each other on a subject.
>
> (Gadamer 1979, 347)

According to Bakhtin (1984, 293), "life is by its very nature dialogical." This suggests a close link between dialogue and the conversations we all have every day. To be in conversation is to be with the other. We only get a feel for the mood of a conversation by listening and reflecting on what is being said. Not every conversation is dialogic. We can be in a conversation and yet remain aloof from the other person.

The principles of dialectics and of deduction and reasoning are those of many organizations. Deduction and reasoning are not exclusive. Both ways of thinking and action run through management. A dialectical reasoning is supported by monologic tendencies through which rules and procedures are laid out, often in a way that shuts out the very people who are doing the coordination.

Monologism can infect organizations even when they are sincerely trying to change. One can understand the need for both transparency and closed door discussions. Outsourcing is one area where full disclosure can be premature. But then, holding back from giving light remains an issue. It has a monologic reason where a top-down mode infused with a short-term political gain is seen to be the safest and most secure mode for urgent decision-making. This is also widespread where redundancies or outsourcings are in a secret pipeline. Change, including where the call is made for decisions to be made behind closed doors, can easily become the breeding ground of monologic infection.

Change and transparency can be difficult. The reasons for staying monologic can neutralize the will to include others. Often, the case is made that decisions need to be made along with risk management. This will usually mean declaring all other matters to be peripheral or secondary to the act of disclosure. Advocates for closed door policies call on everyone to be aware of the risks involved on the grounds that staying monologic needs to be considered alongside the possibility of information resulting in misinterpretation, or a backlash. They often mask their top-down modes by convincing people that their feedback will be taken into account and acted upon, promoting empowerment and feedback in a language that avoids confrontation. All this enables them to initiate change under the veneer of dialogue.

To talk about dialogue and dialectics, we need to know that language functions not only as a system of words that enhances our communication by including the views of others, but also in ways that involve accepting that with many voices involved, there are no immediate right-or-wrong perspectives. There is more than one perspective backed by an intention to express points of view.

To accomplish polyphony, a certain level of patience is needed. Seikkula and Olson (2003) noted that polyphony needs to have the double purpose of holding people long enough, that is, a tolerance of uncertainty, so that those who have been distanced from sharing their views can be given a voice by others in the network. Such tolerance might involve a willingness to bring stories on board even though some of them might be incoherent, in the sense that not everyone is willing to accept the themes that lie behind them.

## POLYPHONY VERSUS DESCARTES

One treatment of selfhood is based on the concept of the 'certainty of the mind'—*cogito ergo sum* ("I think, therefore I am")—described as 'Cartesian' after René Descartes, a French philosopher of the seventeenth century. Descartes emphasized connecting the cognition of the person with one's own existence, meaning that each individual comes to consciousness through his or her own existence in the world and that consciousness is achieved through cognitive capacities of the mind (Descartes 1969). There is a subject-object dichotomy (subject-world) where self-sufficiency takes precedence over any relation with the body and/or dialogue with some other. In the place of a Cartesian explanation, Bakhtin saw selfhood as immersed in what is largely social and relational and his emphasis on sociality makes the notion of embodiment central.

With his emphasis on '*I think, therefore I am*' and the importance he attached to the substantive existence of the subject, Descartes had a tendency to glorify the self as *self-sufficient*, hence coherent, self-contained, and unitary and as having the autonomy to manage and cope on its own (Descartes 1969). There is a sort of self-sufficiency that subdues or even suppresses the body. That is because the 'I' is a unitary 'I:' an 'I' that can manage and control through an objective set of rules and policies that exists somewhere 'out there,' in isolation from some other (Pondy and Mitroff 1979).

In Cartesian thinking, the mind is responsible for all our cognition and mental representation, and so the emphasis is on separating the mind from everything else. Everything else, including every other human being, is external. That position has been questioned, with a view to clarifying and extending our understanding of its limitation. The questioning appears to be on solid ground in probing why the mind is separate from the body. It asks why we are being separated from the world around us, and why our estimation of the distance between us and 'them' is being so exaggerated.

An alternative to the Cartesian view of the world has been proposed through the work of Merleau-Ponty on the phenomenology of body and space and his notion of embodiment. That aspect was also considered by Bakhtin, through his notion of embodiment applied to sociality and inter-subjective utterances. Bakhtin (1993, 47; italic in original) noted that "As a disembodied spirit, I lose my compellent, ought-to-be relationship to the world, I lose the actuality of the world. Man-in-general does not exist; *I* exist and a particular concrete *other* exists."

Dufva (2004, 141) explained that Merleau-Ponty developed the phenomenology of the body with the aim of "passing the Cartesian abyss between mind and body." Merleau-Ponty (1964, 3–5; quoted in Dufva 2004, 141) put it as: "the perceiving mind is incarnated, and it is the body that is our point of view on the world." According to Dufva (2004, 141), to say that mind is incarnated or embodied means the same as "saying that it also has an intimate connection with the world." We therefore grasp that we are embodied in our own experiences and they in us. In other words, there is mutuality connecting the body with the mind. We are located heart and soul in our experiences, which assume our body. From the perspective of embodiment, our experiences of strategy, structure, and systems should be treated as embodied, rather than as objective responses or external entities. Unfortunately, it is often the case that such entities are treated as fully external, and, therefore, taken as independent of our own existence and our own social construction of them and what they mean to each of us (Jabri 1997).

Many years ago, the British philosopher Alfred North Whitehead cautioned against an important concept he called the "fallacy of misplaced concreteness" (Whitehead 1956, 72). This refers to our tendency to reduce the organization in thought and language to a material system based on interrelated entities, and then to assume that this representation of such entities is organizational reality. This fallacy can also be captured by the idea that the organization is not simply a combination of strategy, structure, and systems working together.

We may ask, then, why does the early vision of strategy, structure, and systems working together have such wide appeal? Why should management consultants and other change agents retain a commitment to the idea of fit or misfit? The most likely reason rests largely on a *fallacy of misplaced concreteness*. That is, the emphasis on treating an entity as stable and enduring has become so compelling that many practitioners dedicate themselves to a view of the organization based on 'being' rather than 'becoming.'

An objective mode sees change as something that can be looked at in ways that separate knowing and being (Cunliffe 2004). In practical terms, this often means managing change by relying on a set of principles and guidelines based on 'I think, therefore I am,' rather than as a relational process in which people can see that change is co-constructed in the context of their talk and conversations: 'We think, therefore we are,' or maybe 'We are, therefore we think and talk together.' If the dominant mode is change as an objective reality, then it is less likely that so-called 'responsive exchange' will occur.

Here we have a problem in the way we go about managing organizations, which stems from treating them as entities. Structures are considered pivotal. Objects on their own are desired to become more fixed over time. Relations presuppose objects but objects do not presuppose relations. Structures do not presuppose conversations or talk. Instead, talk presupposes objects. A mere change in structure is, therefore, more likely to 'backfire' on the change effort.

## STRUCTURE AND PROCESS

In managing change, it is always useful to remind oneself of the difference between 'structure' and 'process,' and that both have an impact on the effectiveness with which change is initiated. We know from basic principles that structure is defined in terms of three central dimensions: levels of formalization, specialization, and centralization. We also know that 'structural change' involves altering the pattern (configuration) with which job and role relationships are designated. We often use organizational charts to depict such design relationships.

Structure is not the only issue, however, as process is also important. The relational approach between these entities takes second place. Every entity is treated as an object, with no presupposed relations or process that connects and gives meaning to these relations. A relational approach involves altering attitudes and/or behaviors through talk, conversations, and narratives.

---

### QUANTUM MECHANICS: CAN ORGANIZATIONS BE MANAGED BASED ON OBJECTS AND ENTITIES?

There is a problem in the way we go about managing organizations, that stems from treating organizations as consisting of entities, such as structure, strategy, and systems of paperwork. Such entities and the fit between them are considered pivotal in almost all consultation efforts. People are assigned to manage and lead these entities. Objects on their own, however, do very little but lead to stagnation and monologues. Relations presuppose objects but objects do not presuppose relations.

Clearly, structures do not presuppose conversations. They are presumed as entities made functional through rules and procedures.

---

In practical terms, the Cartesian mode widens the gap between self and 'other.' In other words, it is driven by independence of thought and action. Considerations such as collaboration, responsiveness, negotiation of change, and how organizational members are enabled to identify with the organization are only paid lip service. By separating the object, be it strategy, structure, or systems, from the subject, there is the risk of entrapment in a straitjacket of thinking largely unsuited to the nature and magnitude of modern change.

Much of the drive towards the relevance of dialogue in managing change is inspired by the *word* and the fact that every utterance we make, both external and inner, takes place in a social context. Bakhtin (1984, 287) noted that people have no internal sovereign territory in the sense that they are always looking inside themselves and "into the eyes of another or with eyes of another."

In reflecting on how change is often managed, whether from within the organization, or across organizational borders, a vital part of the reading is, at present, obscured because there is not enough mention of joint learning. Bakhtin's (1984, 287) notion of learning has its own unique social dimension: "I am conscious of myself and become myself only while revealing myself for another, through another, and with the help of another." Bakhtin, therefore, did not see consciousness as some kind of single, undifferentiated whole but rather, as shifting and changing consciousness based on the exchange of utterances. Even though we talk about learning and collaboration, we remain over-reliant on our monologic 'I,' in the sense that we are always ready to assert ownership of what the monologic 'I' says. A monologic 'I' plays an important role in distancing ourselves from the other, and so it is not surprising that our organizations need a more involved notion of polyphony to achieve change and changing as an act of becoming. It is through the other that moments are shared, allowing for successive realizations to emerge. Bateson (1972, 304) noted that "the self will no longer function as a nodal argument in the punctuation of experience." His point is that without the other and the consciousness of the other, learning and collaboration will remain constrained. Lack of polyphony is often due to the monologic 'I' being at work in an exchange of utterances that requires 'many' working together in an exchange that is truly consensual, rather than one that is good enough to let things go, or a sort of pseudo-consensus (Jabri, Adrian, and Boje 2008).

For Bakhtin, every thought and every experience, every conversation of organization members, is internally dialogic in the sense that it is accomplished through utterance, and more importantly it is filled with struggle and open to inspiration from outside. "To live means to participate in dialogue: to ask questions, to heed, to respond, to agree, and so forth" (1993, 293).

## REFERENCES

Bakhtin, Mikhail Mikhailovitch. 1981. *The Dialogic Imagination*, edited by Michael Holquist, translated by Caryl Emerson and Michael Holquist. Austin, Texas: University of Texas Press.

———. 1984. *Problems of Dostoyevsky's Poetics*, edited and translated by Caryl Emerson. Minneapolis: University of Minnesota Press.

———. 1986. *Speech Genres and Other Essays*, edited by Caryl Emerson and Michael Holquist, translated by Vern McGee. Austin: University of Texas Press.

———. 1993. *Toward a Philosophy of the Act*, edited by Michael Holquist and Vadim Liapunov, translated by Vadim Liapunov. Austin: University of Texas Press.

Bateson, Gregory. 1972. *Steps to an Ecology of Mind: Collected Essays in Anthropology, Psychiatry, Evolution and Epistemology*. Chicago: The University of Chicago Press.

Bergson, Henri. 1946. *The Creative Mind*. New York: Carol.

Clark, Katerina and Michael Holquist. 1984. *Mikhail Bakhtin*. Cambridge, MA: Harvard University Press.

Cunliffe, Ann L. 2004. "On becoming a critically reflexive practitioner." *Journal of Management Education* 28 (4): 407–26.

Descartes, René. 1969. *The Philosophical Works of Descartes*, translated by E. S. Haldane and G. R. T. Ross. Cambridge: Cambridge University Press.

Dostoevsky, Fyodor. 1990. *The Brothers Karamazov: A Novel with Four Parts with Epilogue*, translated and annotated by Richard Pevear and Larissa Volokhonsky. New York: Farrar, Straus and Giroux.

Dufva, Hannele. 2004. "Language, Thinking and Embodiment: Bakhtin, Whorf and Merleau-Ponty." In *Thinking Culture Dialogically*, edited by Finn Bostad, Craig Brandist, Lars S. Evensen and Hege C. Faber, 133–46. London: Macmillan Publishers.

Elving, Wim. 2005. "The role of communication in organisational change." *Corporate Communications* 10 (2): 129–38.

Gadamer, Hans Georg. 1979. *Truth and Method*. New York: Seabury.

Gergen, Kenneth. 2008. *An Invitation to Social Construction*, 2nd ed. London: Sage.

Jabri, Muayyad. 1997. "Modes of classroom delivery of organizational theory: Implications for management education." *Journal of Management Education* 21 (4): 509–21.

———. 2005. "Narrative identity achieved through utterances: The implications of Bakhtin for managing change and learning." *Philosophy of Management* 5 (3): 83–90.

Jabri, Muayyad, Allyson Adrian and David Boje. 2008. "Reconsidering the role of conversations in change communication: a contribution based on Bakhtin." *Journal of Organizational Change Management* 21: 667–85.

Kakabadse, Nada, Andrew Kakabadse, Linda Lee-Davies and Nick Johnson. 2011. "Deliberative inquiry: integrated ways of working in Children's Services." *Systemic Practice and Action Research* 24 (1): 67–84.

Merleau-Ponty, Maurice. 1964. *Signs*, translated by Richard C. McCleary. Evanston, IL: Northwestern University Press. (Original work published in French in 1960 under the title *Signes*).

Newman, Neal. 2007. "Enron and the special purpose entities-use and abuse?-The real problem-the real focus." *Law and Business Review of America* 13 (1): 97–137.

Nielsen, Greg. 2002. *The norms of answerability: Social theory between Bakhtin and Habermas*. Albany, NY: State University of New York Press.

Pevear, Richard. 1990. "Introduction." In *Dostoevsky, Fyodor. The Brothers Karamazov: A Novel with Four Parts with Epilogue*, translated and annotated by Richard Pevear and Larissa Volokhonsky, xi–xviii. New York: Farrar, Straus and Giroux.

Pondy, L. R. and Ian Mitroff. 1979. "Beyond Open System Models of Organization." In *Research in Organizational Behavior*, Vol. 1, edited by Barry M. Staw, 3–39. Greenwich, CT: JAI Press.

Rescher, N. 1996. *Process Metaphysics*. New York: State University of New York Press.

Seikkula, Jaakko and Mary E. Olson. 2003. "The open dialogue approach to acute psychosis: Its poetics and micropolitics." *Family Process* 42 (3): 403–18.

Taylor, James R. and Elizabeth J. Van Every. 2000. *The Emergent Organization: Communication as Its Site and Surface*. Hillsdale, NJ: Lawrence Erlbaum.

Voloshinov, V. N. 1986. *Marxism and the Philosophy of Language*. Translated by Ladislav Matejka and I. R. Titunik. Cambridge, MA: Harvard University Press.

Whitehead, Alfred North. 1956. *Modes of Thought*. Cambridge: Cambridge University Press.

# 2   The Role of Utterances in Communicating Change

*To **be*** means to *communicate*.

Mikhail Bakhtin (1984, 278;
emphasis is mine; italics in original)

The world scene today is dominated by a drive for social representation and a growing recognition of the fact that the task of changing, in itself, belongs to no one and that change needs to be driven by the products of thought. This chapter explores the relationship between the work of the Russian philosopher Mikhail Bakhtin and the social construction of change. I start by providing an overview of the threads that connect language with the social construction of change, and draw on the role of dialogue and utterances in communicating change. I emphasize that a dialogic model of change requires a recursive and fully responsive interaction between two people, rather than an active speaker and a passive listener.

My emphasis on recursive talk is similar to that of the Russian novelist Dostoevsky (1821–1881), whose characters engage in conversation explaining what they have to say, and drawing attention to their talk. Dostoevsky's artistic style lies in showing, through conversation, that everyone has her or his own motives, which can be understood by others through dialogue, without anyone's voice being merged with any other. The author himself does not present or impose his own views of the world.

## BAKHTIN'S POLYPHONIC THEORY

Bakhtin developed his polyphonic theory from the work of Dostoevsky. He characterized Dostoevsky's writing as polyphonic, with many voices being expressed simultaneously, but freely and independently of each other. Bakhtin (1984, 121) noted that "the main artistic element in the structure of [Dostoevsky's] heroes" was based on characters being able to express and put across their viewpoints in a manner that gives them complete authorship of the novel. This novelistic style enabled the characters to stand out and express themselves freely, without having to merge their views into one single discourse.

In short, Dostoevsky's characters were given full freedom to put across their own ways of seeing the world around them and make their own utterances. They were able to make their experiences known as they were fully aware of their desires, feelings, and aspirations. They were always ready and willing to put these utterances forward without merging them with the utterances of others.

Basically, the author's ambition was to show not how he himself saw his characters but how the characters saw themselves in relation to others. He was concerned with the way in which they argued their case, and particularly how people are given the opportunity to define their roles in the light of their lived experiences, and their felt meanings and perceptions, rather than how the organization prescribes the roles. Gardiner (1999, 67) noted, "Dostoevsky's novels contain a plurality of unmerged consciousnesses" and "for Bakhtin, Dostoevsky's utilization of polyphony as a pivotal artistic device is the centrepiece of a dialogical principle."

Bakhtin used the work of Dostoevsky as a case in point. There was a reason for this choice of novelist. Throughout his writing, Dostoevsky displayed a profound understanding of human nature. More specifically, he wrote about the border that connects, rather than separates, one discourse (one subject) with another even though each and every discourse is unique in its own right and has its own reason. Bakhtin explored Dostoevsky's reasoning through the notion of "border sensibility" (1984, 284); he noted that "discourse lives, as it were, on the boundary between its own context and another, alien context" (1984, 284).

> **SUMMARY DEFINITION**
>
> Polyphony is simultaneity of many voices. It is about managing change as collections of voices: some in harmony; others in conflict. Polyphony elegantly explains how people are given the opportunity to put their case and their views on how change is managed, with excitement and exuberance, as they bring their lived experiences and felt meanings into their presentation.

As we read Dostoevsky, we become engaged in how the characters do their own authoring. For example, Alyosha in *The Brothers Karamazov* displays insights into the depths of the human self through his own utterances as he reasons with his brothers (Dostoevsky 1990). Much of this depth is also addressed through connections between his experiences and those of his brothers even though their experiences and aspirations are markedly different.

Why would polyphony benefit organizational change and be worth the effort? Is polyphony something that organizations owe to their members? We are not talking about organizations having a univocal culture of the sort that is created through the application of models based on sameness and evenness. Rather, with polyphony, we are talking about the desire for organizational life to be promoted as multivocal, and achieved through ongoing talk and conversations. Even though organizational culture might appear to be fragmented, there will always be a wealth of knowledge if we find new ways of listening.

Holquist (1983) suggested that Bakhtin always sought the minimum degree of homogenization and held the view that it was better to preserve heterogeneity. It takes great courage to recognize and accept difference, and to understand that wherever one goes there is huge variation among people and cultures. That is where we can recognize differences in outlook, and "discover that each voice, each person, is his or her centre of any organization" (Hazen 1994, 16).

That describes Bakhtin's analysis of Dostoevsky's writing. But there is a point that is often overlooked, namely that we cannot capture the importance of multivocality and the need to promote diversity without having to listen to people and the portrait of events that has been inscribed onto their souls and lives. Portraits are material objects bearing physical representations of people, including suffering. They are recalled in memory as concrete manifestations of elements that reveal the people in them. We gaze at these portraits, and see them as realities in their own right.

Looking at a portrait, we can see what lies beyond it. Bakhtin was an idealist and a materialist at the same time. What is important in Dostoevsky's work is how the characters draw their own portraits of themselves. Polyphony involves presenting each character as a separate reality and bringing all the portraits to the foreground together. The awareness and the subjectivity of each character is brought forward by that character and then contemplated as he or she speaks with others, relating, but without their utterances being merged. To extend the metaphor, each character's portrait has its own frame.

## FERDINAND DE SAUSSURE AND THE NOTION OF *LANGUE*

We can consider language as an arrangement or system of signs, whether spoken or written. We utter these signs as and when we want to convey our thoughts. According to Searle (1995, quoted in Sandberg 2001, 41), language is the most basic socially-constructed institution. It is a prime tool for seeing the thoughts of others and for formulating one's own thoughts. No portrait is complete without language.

The Swiss linguist and founder of modern linguistic analysis Ferdinand de Saussure (1857–1913), in his *Course in General Linguistics* (1983), suggested that the study of language (or *langue*, meaning language as a system of formal rules) should be separated from the concept of speech (*parole*, the actual use of language). Saussure argued that all meanings are created inside language. A sign is the basic unit of language, and so language consists of a grand and complete system of signs.

Signs are largely instituted. A basic assumption is that each sign is codified to convey a certain meaning. However, the problem with viewing language as a grand system of signs, having its own set of universal rules, is that it invests *langue* (grammar, syntax, structure) with powers to hold meaning.

To preclude a variety of interpretations, and to reduce the possibility of misinterpretation by someone making a statement, Ferdinand de Saussure rejected the inclusion of actual everyday speech or conversation. The obvious result of this rejection is that communication becomes centered on the codes used by the speaker (Shannon and Weaver 1949), based on language as a system of signs. Meaning is 'forced' to become fixed because language is used as a code for transmitting information.

## THE LIMITS OF SAUSSURE'S APPROACH

So far, we have tended to embrace Saussure's emphasis on *langue* in organizational life, in the sense that the change announcements we make, the systems we develop and the procedures we implement, as markers of the change effort, tend to rely on an impersonal code largely aimed at ratifying the change effort and with little emphasis on conversations. In time, such procedures become ratified as glorified '*objects of thinking*' to be followed. In short, we have materialized (reified) systems of rules and procedures. These are worked out in concert with an authoritative discourse (monologues), which bring out the worst in such rules.

There are two important limitations or consequences from Saussure's conception of language as a system of signs. These are:

- The adoption of signs as a code reduces the elasticity and suppleness deemed crucial for managing under conditions of continuous change. It calcifies our treatment of change by precluding discursive and recursive discourses from influencing the change effort.
- The adoption of signs as a code makes entities such as strategy and organizational structure appear definite, real, and factual, when, in fact, they should be treated as fluid and changing.

For Bakhtin, it was the 'stretch' of utterances, and not the abstract system of *langue* that explained the fundamental reality of relating to others through language mediation. Originally, Saussure (1983) divided language into *langue* and *parole* to exhibit language as something fixed and enable him to sketch out something that was essentially shifting and fluid. He recognized this in his influential idea that the semiotic linguistic sign is arbitrary. However, he later moved away from the full implications of this idea.

Bakhtin expressed his dismay with Saussure's structuralist approach to language; he thought it resulted in an approach that refused to take into account the shifting nature of language. He saw *langue* and *parole* as representing a false dichotomy. He therefore called for a synthesis between the two which prompted him to advance his views of language as a living thing dependent on an infinite and recursive chain of transmissions.

Saussure's ways of thinking about language led to a reduction in the interpersonal, and in the social elements needed to define change as the shifting of identities accomplished through speech (utterances). In accordance with his concept of language as a homogeneous system, Saussure's separation of *langue* from speech places a limit on identities. It precludes the ability to see oneself, and masks the potential for understanding change as shifting identities because it emphasizes language as the basis for generating fixed meanings, with a word as a code. In the absence of a fluid and shifting understanding of speech, fixed meanings are more likely to lead to an assumed sameness between the self and others, across more than one setting.

An important notion in the work of Bakhtin is dialogue, but it is an 'unusual' form of dialogue because it relies on making room for both parties to meet, so that each 'becomes' the other. This sees dialogue as being ingrained in people's being and consciousness through language. This is an important feature that distinguishes Bakhtin's approach to dialogue from the more prescriptive mode (Bohm 1996). Bakhtin believed that the 'stretch' of utterances, and not the abstract system of *langue*, explained the fundamental reality of dialogue through language.

Bakhtin's emphasis on speech enabled him to conceive of dialogue based on utterances that are 'unfinalizable,' rather than a process of transmission of fixed codes prescribed by Saussure's separation of *langue* from *parole*. Bakhtin believed that the line separating a system of signs is little more than a false dichotomy—resulting in an approach that refuses to take into account our inhabitation of change and how such inhabitation is reflected in meaning-making. Bakhtin called for a synthesis between *langue* and *parole*, which prompted him to advance his views of language as a living thing— dependent on an infinite and recursive chain of transmissions.

Here, it is useful to note that Saussure's way of thinking about language has some important consequences, in that it leads to an over-emphasis on *langue* and structure, in the sense that it puts more emphasis on what is formal and systemic, rather than on meaning-making that has the potential to be shared. It could, therefore, lead to a reduction in interpersonal exchange, and in the way we can define change as accomplished through speech (utterances). As noted earlier, Saussure's view of language as a homogeneous system has the net output of disguising the meaning we need most to understand change.

By adopting Bakhtin's notion of dialogue, it is possible to reverse the reductionist tendency inherent in the Saussurean approach. Dialogue can be conceived as being based on utterances that are 'unfinalizable,' rather than as being a process of transmission of codes that are fixed and prescribed by Saussure's separation of *langue* from *parole*. Through a Bakhtinian notion of language, identities are co-constructed through an ongoing exchange of utterances.

## BAKHTIN AND THE ROLE OF *PAROLE*

Bakhtin (1981) objected to Saussure's approach in structuring language as an independent system of signs dissociated from everyday speech. Bakhtin (1984, 183) understood language in terms of "its concrete living totality, and not language as the specific object of linguistics." Bakhtin provided a distinctive way of understanding change communication, because he offered a different way of seeing the role of conversations in thinking of and approaching change as an ongoing accomplishment achieved through speech. He rejected the assumption of language as a code by noting that "a code is only a technical means of transmitting information; it does not have cognitive, creative significance. A code is a deliberately established, killed context" (quoted in Morson and Emerson 1990, 101). Saussure's 'signs' emphasize a fixation on encoding, decoding, structure, and syntax. By contrast, Bakhtin's 'utterances' emphasize meaning-making achieved through responsive interaction. Our utterances provide more scope for interpretation because they allow for new discursive meanings as they are embodied and exchanged in speech.

Bakhtin (1984, 183) felt that an utterance was the "authentic sphere where language lives." He therefore questioned Saussure's emphasis on signs as he noted that, unlike our reliance on language as a code, "an utterance is a *real unit of speech communion*" (italics in original) because it reflects a real speech situation (Bakhtin 1986, 67). An utterance, therefore, reflects actual personal experience. Bakhtin (1986, 67) added that a study of utterance makes it possible to "understand more correctly the *nature of language units* (as a system): words and sentences" (italics in original).

As a new utterance is made, new shades and colors are brought to bear on the planning effort and its implementation. Utterances have a special relevance for change communication. They help us to liberate the language of change from the confines of signs and codes, and to make plans and planning efforts readier to embrace new meanings.

## SOCIAL CONSTRUCTION OF CHANGE ACHIEVED THROUGH *PAROLE*

Change constantly presents us with an inconstant fabric of experiences. We rely on our sensations, feelings, and bodies in an attempt to cope as we reflect on change. We reflect by thinking about the change itself as well as calling on the help of others. Our fabric of experiences is a co-construction achieved through the language we share with others.

Although language is fundamental to the way in which we create our reality of the situation around us, it is at the same time something that is socially constructed through people and their views (Sandberg 2001; Gergen 2008). In his work *An Invitation to Social Construction*, Gergen (2008) referred to the philosopher Wittgenstein (1978) to showcase the fundamental role language (speech) plays in the social construction of the things around us. In his seminal writing, *Philosophical Investigations*, Wittgenstein conceptualized language as a 'game' (Wittgenstein 1978, Section 7; quoted in Gergen 2008, 34). He noted that every language is a 'game' unto itself and can be judged only by its own rules. By reflecting on Wittgenstein's notion of language as a game of chess, we can see more about the role language plays in the social construction of events.

Importantly, Wittgenstein asked "What is a word?" and said that this was like asking "What is a piece in chess?" (Wittgenstein 1978, Section 7; quoted in Gergen 2008, 34). How are we to make sense of Wittgenstein's idea of language as a game of chess in which two players take turns in moving wooden pieces of various sizes and shapes across a checkered board?

Gergen (2008, 34–35) explained Wittgenstein's metaphor by noting that each piece in the chess set "acquires its *meaning* from the game as a whole" (emphasis added). It is all about the way in which they are given meaning in the context of the game. "[T]he small wooden chess pieces would mean nothing outside the game; however, once in the game [context], even the tiniest of pieces can topple 'kings' and 'queens'" (Gergen 2008, 34). Each and every chess piece would have its own role, or its own say, in speech. That role remains important at least as long as the rules that govern the game of chess stay the same.

Every chess piece is not objective and given. It is socially constructed in a way peculiar to the game of chess. Hence, it has little meaning in any other game. By analogy, an entity such as strategy or structure is not something objective and *pre-given*, whatever we might wish to think. Instead, such an entity is context-dependent, determined locally, and largely based on what we make of it, how we relate to it, and, hence, construct it through our own will.

Following Wittgenstein's (1978) work on the role of language in constructing the realities we inhabit, an increasing number of social scientists started to investigate how language was instrumental in constructing social realities. Cunliffe (2004, 409) explained that social construction started with the work of Goffman (1959) and Garfinkel (1967). In 1966, Berger and Luckmann wrote *The Social Construction of Reality*.

The central theme of Berger and Luckmann's work was that organization members working together form, over time, mental representations of each other's ways of thinking, and that these ways of thinking eventually become part of their knowledge base. People's conception of change, which is intersubjective, becomes embedded in tacit terms and is, therefore, said to be socially constructed. The interplay between the individual and collective levels is crucial in understanding how professional beliefs are produced and reproduced (Berger and Luckmann 1966, 21). Indeed, we cannot exist in everyday life without continually interacting and communicating with others (Berger and Luckmann 1966, 37).

To highlight the role language plays in constructing our desires and aspirations, Latour and Woolgar (1979) looked at the way scientists in the Jonas Salk Medical Laboratories talked to each other to determine ways in which their experiments, aimed at the discovery of new vaccines, should proceed. Upon analysis of their data, Latour and Woolgar (1979) found that a scientist's commitment to a specific way or method of measurement and testing was crucial in shaping the research direction of the group. They also found that research direction was largely determined by talk relating to grant funds and to the perceived importance of journal publication policies.

The studies of Berger and Luckmann (1966), Latour and Woolgar (1979), Shotter (1993, 1998), Weick (1995) and Gergen and Thatchenkery (1996) were all very important in promoting social construction within management and organization studies in general. However, it is only in the last two decades or so that social construction has started to show its direct impact on areas within the management of change (e.g., Hatch 1997). Much of this work continues to evolve through newer connections and extensions, including advances in how realities and identities are co-constructed in relational ways (Cunliffe and Jun 2005; Cunliffe and Coupland 2009).

Whose words are we using and by what rules are we playing? Bakhtin invited us to see that no rule or word can ever be neutral. He noted that there are:

> no 'neutral' words. Language has been completely taken over, shot through with intentions and accents . . . All words have the 'taste' of a profession, a genre, a tendency, a party, a particular work, a particular person, a generation, an age group, the day and the hour . . . all words and forms are populated by intentions.
>
> (Bakhtin 1981, 293)

In organizations, we therefore play by the rules we create and/or inherit. A situation where others are left with little choice but to follow the rules is one where monologue dominates. If within every language game, we have to function according to the rules, we still have to be able to question and reform these rules.

The question is how to allow the rules to change. Is it to our long-term advantage to change them? If so, how do we do it? If we are left with no choice but to change the rules, does that mean having to change the structure or the dominant culture of the place? If we were to change the structure and/or culture, what is the role of dialogue in achieving such change? And what precautions would we need to take to ensure that when the structure is changed, it will be done in ways that would not mask the authoritative intentions achieved through the rhetoric of participative modes embellished by calls for contribution and feedback?

## THE 'WORD' AND POWER

Foucault (1980) went further than both Wittgenstein and Bakhtin, by noting that the words we use are driven by intentions, which are related to power. What an organization sees as important is not determined so much by an objective pursuit of truth, as by the structures of power within that organization, and its surrounding context. He said that:

- We tend to use language to affirm and protect our own power base.
- We tend to use language to understand our context and the direction the organization is taking.
- We use language to understand political behavior. For example, we understand the behaviors of those who go with the flow, or against, and those who are always ready to 'jump on the wagon' and embrace what they see as beneficial for themselves.
- We tend to use language to understand activists who speak their mind about shortcomings.
- We listen to those who are afraid to speak their mind.

## LANGUAGE AND IDEOLOGICAL BECOMING

Bakhtin (1981, 293) noted that language is not an abstract system of normative forms, because there are no "neutral" words and forms. Almost everything lies on the border between oneself and the other, hence "the word in language is half someone else's." He viewed language as fundamentally dialogic:

> When a member of a speaking collective comes upon a word, it is not as a neutral word of language, not as a word free from the aspirations and evaluations of others, uninhabited by others' voices. No, he receives the word from another's voice and filled with that other's voice. The word enters his context from another context, permeated with interpretations of others. His own thought finds the word already inhabited.
>
> (Bakhtin 1984, 202)

When introducing his notion of 'the word we utter,' Bakhtin showed that we are all continuously engaged in relating to each other. There is always a state of '*heteroglossia*,' or different types of speech, as we relate to what the other is saying and also as we recognize meanings, subject to the extent to which the text is authoritative or persuasive.

In organizational life, we spend a fair bit of time in meetings and conversations, including email dialogue. Interestingly, as Bakhtin explained (1981), were we to eavesdrop on conversations in public, we would hear how often the words "they think that, " "we think that," "he says," "people say," "he said," and "she says" occur in our everyday conversations as we co-construct or even de-construct change.

All such conversations have a degree of 'otherness' built into them. It is not unusual for us to listen to other people telling us how the authoritative discourse is imposing itself on their ways of thinking and doing the job. Imagine the situation of a newly recruited project manager who has been asked to work on the existing model in line with the dominant discourse, or the prevailing way or strategy, and nothing else, and hence is unable to put a personal stamp on the work.

We also live the experience of wanting to take part in conversations. Through ongoing talk, we willingly spend a fair bit of our time commenting on other people's words, opinions, desires, and aspirations and wanting to contest subversion. We do so in the hope of getting things to change and frame a new subjectivity, or some new representation.

## THE NEED FOR THE 'OTHER'

For Bakhtin (1984), we need others as much as they need us, and talk is full of the intentions of others. In Bakhtin's view, an utterance is half someone else's. It becomes our own only when we bring on board our own intentions, desires, and aspirations. We selectively appropriate the words of others as they selectively appropriate ours.

So we do place some importance on what the other has to say about change. We talk about them as much as they talk about us. Why do we do that? Bakhtin believed that the answer lay in our attempt to understand the other as much as they understand us. We also want, or prefer, to remain in the safety zone, because we want to feel comfortable about what people say when they talk about us. Such talk undeniably assumes importance in our lives, especially in understanding and interpreting the words of others.

## IDEOLOGICAL BECOMING AND IDENTITY

Conversations give way to change and so people become who they are. Their ways of thinking and beliefs change as words come knocking on their doors. Meaning is carried on as we assimilate what the other has said in the light of what we have said and the way in which we discover more of his or her words. These conversations between people give way to the notion of ideological becoming, which Bakhtin (1981, 341) defined as "the process of selectively assimilating the words of others." It is also a process of moving from an authoritative discourse to an internally-persuasive one. Through the other, our words 'become' and their words knock on the door to us. Through the other, we become who we are.

It is the individual, with a personal narrative identity, who is most able to comment on the extent to which the setting tends towards polyphony. That is because there is a mutuality of dependence between ideological becoming and discourses of shifting identities. Identity, especially that achieved through narrative, is more about the ever-changing state, namely how we come to be who we are. Such a state is also influenced by the stories and narrations influencing the realities of others. Narrative identity remains subject to centripetal (authoritative) and centrifugal (persuasive) forces, and we selectively assimilate the words of others.

There is a mutual dependency, an entanglement, between ideological becoming and narrative identity of the person. Ideological becoming is largely dependent on the authoritative discourse that inhabits our lives. As Bakhtin noted:

> The tendency to assimilate others' discourse takes on an even deeper and more basic significance in an individual's ideological becoming, in the most fundamental sense. Another's discourse performs here no longer as information, directions, rules, models and so forth—but strives rather to determine the very bases of our ideological interrelations with the world, the very basis of our behaviour; it performs here as *authoritative discourse*, and an *internally persuasive discourse*.
>
> (Bakhtin 1981, 342; italics in original)

Like narrative identity, ideological becoming is subject to tensions between centripetal discourse (authoritative) and centrifugal forces (persuasive discourses aiming to flee the center). As Bakhtin noted:

> The authoritative word demands that we acknowledge it, that we make it our own; it binds us, quite independent of any power it might have to persuade us internally; we encounter it with its authority already fused to it.
>
> (Bakhtin 1981, 342)

The 'polyphony' and the ever-changing nature of identity is not a fantasy and that is because the subject is left with no choice: either taking on board what the authoritative discourse says or having to question its principle or the directive it is based upon. That process itself has a lot to do with how the quantum of narrative identity of the person is left to be in an ever-changing state, namely wanting to come to know *'who am I?,'* or *'who we are.'* This is illustrated in Figure 2.1, where ideological becoming of the person is viewed as entangled with narrative identities struggling to come to terms with change.

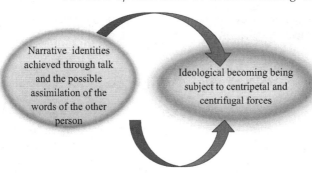

*Figure 2.1*   Entanglement of narrative identity with ideological becoming

The likelihood that polyphony will take root is greatly reduced when talk does not move freely, prohibiting ideological becoming from emerging. It can only take root when people are given the opportunity to freely assimilate the words of others and be able to comment on them. Such freedom is crucial for excess of meaning to grow and develop in ways that would affect identity.

## THE UTTERANCES WE SHARE

In this section, I have one specific aim, and that is to prepare to elaborate on polyphony. I therefore wish to build on the notion of utterance to introduce Bakhtin's (1993) idea of *co-being* as an event (*sobytie*). In particular, I wish to expand on consciousness as having its own social property, leading to the notion of polyphony. Bakhtin speaks of polyphony as the time when utterances get "fully realized" (Bakhtin 1984, 63), giving way to '*eventness,*' which he defined as genuine involvement between two or more people. Utterances are the foundation upon which Bakhtin's notion of polyphony is situated, together with the simultaneity of talk and the way in which consciousness comes to have its own social dimension, necessary to demonstrate the unmerging of voices, which is truly the basis for much of Bakhtin's thinking about polyphony. Such consciousnesses come from the "contact between the word and the concrete reality" (Bakhtin 1986, 87), as opportune (supreme) moments are arrested.

I start by capturing three opportune moments: *noticing* the feelings of the other; *feeling* the feelings of the other; and *arresting, or experiencing* the feelings of the other *to oneself.* I construe the flow of such moments as moments in consciousness. For example, we make sense of the organic unity between opportune moments emerging from a change in the work design of an overworked nurse. We see what the nurse experiences in feeling and caring for a patient as well as moving with dedication from one site to another and then going back and caring for the same patient, thus *feeling* the feelings of such moments to oneself.


## CONSCIOUSNESS IN PROCESS TERMS

Moments can play a crucial role in changing and energizing the way we see, feel, and act. We use them in communicating our opinions and thoughts. A moment is a product of the distance to a new point of awareness (in Greek: *kairos*). In capturing moments, we often do so in opportune time and by responding to what another is saying or experiencing. It is through the organic unity of moments that utterances and events emerge. As Holquist (in Bakhtin 1990, xli) reminded us, there is benefit in saying to oneself that "to be human is *to mean*," and that the "human being is the *production* of meaning."

Bakhtin (1986, 87) spoke of creating "meaning," but not in terms of arriving at a static agreement. Rather, he saw meaning as a reflexive process (Jabri, Adrian, and Boje 2008). Bakhtin (1986) described a co-creation of meaning through moments expressed in utterances foreshadowed by everyday mundane talk with oneself, as well as through responsive listening. An inner dialogue is not, therefore, an incidental feature, but a process component of almost any conversation. Through the words that are spoken, a connection between moments is established. Bakhtin described the importance of three key moments:

- Experiencing the 'I' (*awareness of oneself, namely one's own utterance*);
- An awareness of the other (I-for-the-other; *being drawn to the other*); and
- *Experiencing* the utterance (retrieving *the utterance of the other*).

All three moments are dialogic, because they are constituted through utterances that are exchanged in the context of the relationship between the witness and the sufferer. The three moments are really to do with how the two parties come to relate, and how they come to relate not only to each other but also to the moment of suffering as it is experienced by both of them, based on an exchange. In this way, the separate moments may be absorbed into each other.

When Bakhtin (1986, 87) spoke of consciousness having its own social property, he saw meaning-making as a simultaneity of voices or utterances. Meaning-making is, therefore, not an individual accomplishment, but requires the connection with what the other is saying or feeling. In a similar vein, Voloshinov (1986, 86) described utterances as a "bridge thrown between myself and another. If one end of the bridge depends on me, then the other depends on my addressee." All conversation is a never-ending process (unfinalizable) and all conversational episodes are dialogic.

Utterances proliferate in conjunction with each other and yet remain as one organic social unity. The proliferation remains in a ceaseless state of process movement (flux). Hence, for example, noticing the pain of another is also about arresting the feelings of the other to oneself. For any of these moments, it is difficult to identify a specific beginning and/or end. That is because by the time 'noticing' the utterance of the other occurs, there is also the likelihood of utterances being arrested on the part of the other person. Each and every moment provides an opportunity for relating to the consciousness of the other, and so the knowledge of how they all relate to each other is intuitively captured through the notion of an event, or co-being with the other.

This notion of proliferation of moments is also supported through the ideas described by Deleuze and Guattari (1987). A *kairotic* moment, or critical moment in time, is rhizomatous in the sense of its continuity and multiplicity, and its entanglement with other moments we experience. A rhizome is a part of a plant that sends out shoots and lateral buds as well as roots. It provides an image of arresting moments as opportunities for nurturing compassion. Such moments take root elsewhere and everywhere, having no beginning or end. In workplace scenarios, all moments are presented as intertwined, in the sense that noticing and *feeling* the feelings of the other are constitutive of each other. Such intertwinement is *kairotic* in the sense that it is the situated knowledge of moments we see or experience that constitute our co-being.

For Bakhtin (1993), meaning is a function of a growing relationality between people. Utterances cannot be final as they require people to remain conscious of becoming, while revealing themselves to another with the help of that other (Bakhtin 1986). Bakhtin observed, "just as the body is formed initially in the mother's womb (body), a person's consciousness awakens wrapped in another's consciousness" (1986, 138). He also said: "I live in a world of others' words. And my entire life is an orientation in this world, a reaction to others' words" (1986, 143). Whether an utterance is internal or out loud, we come to relate to the other as we go through each of the three moments. Bakhtin (1993, 52) suggested that there is always a time when the witness moves from '*I-for-myself*' and starts to take into account personal answerability through '*I-for-the-other*' and to consider what the suffering of the other would mean for oneself in '*other-for-myself.*'

Bakhtin (1981) suggested that any fact or utterance is colored by a complex interaction between two types of forces, centripetal (forces of meaning that unify utterances, tending towards the center and stability) and centrifugal (forces of meaning that disturb, tending to flee the center). A centripetal force emphasizes the status quo and sameness, effectively making the 'other' more familiar. In contrast, a centrifugal force is committed to 'being with' the other, even in the midst of differences in the way the reality of the situation might be conceived.

We continue to discover meanings, because they come from the "contact between the word and the concrete reality" (Bakhtin 1986, 87). As such,

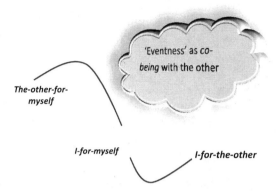

*Figure 2.2*   The *sobytie* of 'eventness' as *co-being*: experiencing 'I-for-myself' (*awareness of oneself*), 'I-for-the-other,' and 'the-other-for-myself' (*feeling the feelings of the other for myself*)

meanings come to be shaped and re-shaped through moments of experiencing 'I-for-myself,' 'I-for-the-other,' and 'the-other-for-myself.' Figure 2.2 shows how these moments of experience render consciousness as a property having its own social dimension in terms of an event as co-being.

Whether an utterance is internal or aloud, we relate to the other as we go through each of the three moments. The sequence is important, because one needs the 'I,' feeling for oneself, then 'I-for-the-other,' and the 'other-for-me.' Bakhtin (1993, 52) suggested that there is always a time when the character moves from 'I-for-myself' and starts to take into account personal answerability through 'I-for-the-other,' and to consider what the other is saying in 'other-for-myself.' 'I-for-the-other' takes the form of 'would-be action,' awaiting fulfilment into polyphony, or simultaneity. Polyphony can, therefore, mean simultaneity of talk in responsive terms since the movement between 'I-for-myself,' 'I-for-the-other,' and 'other-for-myself" is a never-ending cycle, embedded in everyday talk, storytelling change, or conversations about change and changing.

Utterances continue to return into the polyphonic process, influencing it, as long as consciousnesses inter-animate or crisscross each other. That is one reason why Bakhtin (1984, 63) saw polyphony as time-contingent on utterances becoming "fully realized," and it is in this way that 'eventness' plays a role in moving us through becoming aware of what the other is saying. Jabri (2005, 2012) explained that, according to Bakhtin (1986), an utterance does a fine job in aesthetically connecting people, but only if and when they draw on each other's words. When an utterance is made, the other is almost always there ready to respond, usually with more words. It is this relational aspect based on consciousnesses having their sociality, or social dimension, that enables us to cross between self and other, and which, therefore, gives dialogue its polyphonic character.

# DIALECTIC AND ANTINOMY

The characterizations of dialectic noted at the beginning of the chapter bring us to a discussion of antinomy. An antinomy may be seen as an oscillation between two contemplative voices, utterances, or points of view, each of which is valid. Both seem equally justified given a change situation. Each option for change, or strategy, is supported by a valid explanation or proof of some sort. Applied to change, an antinomy is about two or more poles, strategies, or ways of seeing change that appear to contradict each other. Both are held to be either true or false.

Unlike paradox, where one utterance contradicts the other, leading to a defiance of logic, an antinomy is about both utterances being equally true. Both are logically feasible. According to the *Oxford English Dictionary*, an antinomy is: (1) "a contradiction in a law or between two equally binding laws; (2) a contradictory law, statute, or principle; an authoritative contradiction."

The term 'antinomy' emerged within the critical philosophy developed by the German philosopher Immanuel Kant (1724–1804). It was labelled as 'critical' because Kant wanted to critique the limits of knowledge obtained through pure reason. Kant used the word 'antinomy' to suggest that even with reason, and the desire to go beyond experience, the possibility of resolving the contradiction between any two equally valid perspectives remains present.

Antinomies are basically opinions, or points of view, each of which contains a very valid and convincing reason. When such reasons collide, they often result in unresolvable differences in handling change situations. An antinomy lies with the person or in a group setting. It is the person who experiences the state of contradiction, in the course of arguing the case with others. Antinomies can be useful in exploring conflicting claims or assertions.

Antinomy, as an oscillation between two contemplative voices, utterances, or points of view, each of which is valid, helps to chart new boundary lines. These highlight productive tensions between dialectic and dialogue. With Bakhtin's notion that utterances cannot be finalized, we can assert that a statement made about an option for change can have more than one purpose. Given change situations where competing courses of action are supported by reason and/or proof, this raises important questions such as what an organization needs to do to resolve conflicting points of view, strategies, options, or plans which seem equally justified. In a paper on the role of antinomy in the exploration of mathematics, Asenjo noted that

> Our thought processes are often antinomic, which in turn reflects the parallel fact that reality itself is often antinomic.
>
> Asenjo 1996, 53)

Even when two desired situations are juxtaposed as contradictory, it would be possible, through utterances, to appreciate and contribute to the richness of lived experience, and, therefore, show the relevance and significance of dialogue. Antinomy also arises when competing courses for change have equal feasibility or merit, or when mutually exclusive courses of action are argued to have equal merit. Bulgakov elaborated on the role of antinomy, noting that:

> An antinomy testifies to the equal significance, equal strength, and at the same time, to the inseparability, unity and identity of contradictory assumptions.
>
> (Bulgakov [1999], quoted in Blank 2010, 15)

Blank made the point that:

> We must keep in mind that in antinomy, two ideas are juxtaposed as contradictory but are at the same time united into a single conceptual whole.
>
> (Blank 2010, 14–15)

When two ideas are juxtaposed, they cannot be separated from the situation or the context of their production. Ideas become the means, and it is through them that we are able to move beyond experience, to think of new 'plateaus' that are connected despite their differences. Deleuze and Guattari (1987, 21) talked about a 'plateau' as a number of thoughts, or concepts, connected to other thoughts or concepts by some underground stem "to form or extend a rhizome."

Here, Deleuze and Guattari were thinking in parallel with Bakhtin. Bakhtin talked about the exchange of utterances, yet without calling for the merger of voices. Through utterances, he focused on an exchange through plurality of voices. Here, convergence between Bakhtin and Deleuze and Guattari becomes evident. I think there is a general compatibility between Bakhtin and Deleuze, and that utterances produce creations. Deleuze and Guattari also reminded us of the need to contest our assumptions in the way we communicate. They noted:

> We do not lack communication. On the contrary, we have too much of it. We lack creation. We lack resistance to the present. The creation of concepts in itself calls for a future form, for a new earth and people that do not yet exist.
>
> (Deleuze and Guattari [1994, 108];
> quoted in Jabri, Adrian, and Boje 2008, 56)

An example will show how ideas are juxtaposed as contradictory in their wording. Consider the following set of statements depicting points of productive tensions where each of the two statements could be, and is held to be, true:

- Altruism characterizes organizational achievement;
- Competitive behavior leads organizations to outperform others.

- Consumers are empowered through the operations of markets;
- Consumers have little choice but to obey the operations of the market.
- R&D should be leading the marketing function;
- Marketing should be the prime mover.

Now consider a conversation between two opinionated individuals, where each opinion is held to be true:

> "She is playing the role of a senior person."
>
> "Oh no. The role is playing *her*."
>
> "She finds satisfaction in the role playing her."
>
> "Well, she gets paid extra for it."
>
> "Pay is not important."
>
> "Pay is important."
>
> "The people above her in the hierarchy are playing her."
>
> "Oh no. She thinks *she* is the one playing *them*."

Perhaps the worst enemy of antinomy is *pseudo-consensus*, where a resolution is forged as a superficial or 'pretend' agreement. This occurs when the top management team, or someone in authority, wants to resolve the antinomy through some coercive measure or by noting that '*rules are rules and would need to be followed*,' or with the support of an elite group, to get everyone else in the organization to agree. This resolves the antinomy politely and/or through sanction. Whatever the top management team might espouse, including changing conversational styles to achieve consensus, such a shift in focus converts an antinomy into a monologic practice.

We often encounter contradictions in rules and policies, and it is not unusual to see a contradiction erupt following a merger of two distinct groups or entities. Theoretically, antinomy appears to make sense at the deeper level, even when a contradiction is inherent in what is being said. Although any attempt to achieve consensus cannot rationally or logically resolve the contradiction, the fact remains that we have a multiplicity of voices, and when directed into polyphony, that can lead to a 'surplus of seeing.' In practice, it is always possible to interpolate solutions by involving people, while helping them to improvise in new ways.

Antinomies provide the motivation for involved analysis of strategy and the direction an organization could take. In the process of developing strategy, there are always affirmations and negations of options well before a final strategy is settled and formulated.

All organizations have their own written procedures and/or spoken rules (norms) constitutive of what should work. When conflict arises from the interpretation of a certain rule, it is obvious that some deduction and reasoning would need to be brought in to clarify the case under consideration. Nikulin noted that:

> Modern reason is preoccupied with its own self-transparency and self-accessibility, particularly with establishing the transparency (through a

precise order of steps, each of which clearly follows from the premises and previous steps) of the proofs it produces and spins out of itself.

(Nikulin 2010, 88)

For example, an organization that is about to update its human resource system will continue to import rules and procedures in search of transparency. Precise rules are laid down for the completion of forms. Adding new rules on top of the existing ones is one way through which apprehension is managed and reduced. The ongoing nature of dialogue might entice the addressee to think through the issues that are being raised in a dialogue as an invitation for continuing (unfinalizable) utterances.

## MODELS OF COMMUNICATING CHANGE

In change communication, there is an ongoing discussion of different communication models (Lewis and Seibold 1998; Taylor and Van Every 2000; Johansson and Heide 2008). According to Jabri (2012), the most widespread and well-known classification consists of three models or perspectives:

- The **transmission model,** in which communication is determined (decoded through Saussure's emphasis on *langue*) through the transmission of the message between a speaker and a listener. Both form and content of the message are determined by unidirectional flow, based on encoding followed by decoding.
- The **social construction model,** in which communication is informed by a focus on understanding and sense-making. Both form and content are determined through ongoing talk that produces and co-produces people's social reality: a view that is multidirectional.
- The **polyphonic model,** in which communication is guided by an ongoing (recursive) chain of utterances between two active participants, a change agent and a change recipient. The emphasis is on the relational, dynamic, and responsive interaction with other subject(s) to create something that never existed before, a view that is largely polyphonic or multi-voiced, where more than one organizational level is implicated.

The **transmission model** is driven by an instrumental, information-processing view of *communication*. It was originally developed by Shannon and Weaver (1949), based on Claude Shannon's mathematical theory of the signal transmission of codes that he designed for Bell Telephone in the late 1940s. Shannon and Weaver's model places all the emphasis on the transactional nature of the communication process.

According to this model, change is basically an information-processing conceptualization. It involves transmitting information to influence the path of change. Modern theories of communication emphasize monologic messages to persuade a listener or audience to do something the speaker desires: *what I really want is for you to agree with my predetermined action* (Jabri, Adrian, and Boje 2008).

In this model, communication is viewed as a tangible substance that flows upward, downward, and laterally within the organization (Kanter 1985; Kotter 1996). The emphasis here is on a unidirectional flow of communication. It is top-down and carried out in practice through an ongoing search for consensus and the presentation of unity (common ground) among organization members.

Central to the development of the transmission model is that a message travels in a unidirectional way, between sender and receiver, accompanied by a feedback loop. Basically, it involves the transmission of information through announcements and other modes and directives aimed at facilitating change. There are two roles: speaker (sender) and listener (recipient).

These roles shift back and forth, depending on the location of the people involved. When the recipient responds to the person sending the message, they become the sender, and the sender assumes the role of recipient. The content and meaning of messages play a secondary role, since meaning is assumed to reside in the message (channel). Decoding and encoding of the message are assumed to take place.

In the transmission model, the assumption is that implementation problems will disappear if and when organizational members are provided with information and so understand the change and their role in the process (Kotter 1996). Organizations are assumed to be rational systems that will respond to planned change efforts in a predictable fashion (Johansson and Heide 2008). Communication is thus reduced to a tool for announcing change efforts with an emphasis on what to announce, or say, when to make the announcement, who makes the announcement, and how to deliver it (Johansson and Heide 2008). The transmission model has been criticized for simplifying communication (Jabri, Adrian, and Boje 2008; Johansson and Heide 2008). Communication is taken at face value, as if it exists as a tool in isolation from the ongoing nature of change.

A later transformation in thinking and development of a new model was largely driven by **social construction** (Berger and Luckmann 1966; Latour and Woolgar 1979; Czarniawaska 1997; Gergen 2008) and the role of language as a transparent medium for communicating change (Alvesson and Kärreman 2000; Heracleous and Barrett, 2001; Jabri, Adrian, and Boje 2008). This model suggests that communicating change relies on speech, rituals, symbols, and the utterances we make as we construct change. Ford and Ford (1995, 542) noted that change as an organizational phenomenon "occurs and is driven by communication rather than the reverse." Change communication is, therefore, about social co-construction and multiple points of view. Ford and Ford (1995) believed that communication is, in fact, the medium within which change occurs.

For process scholars, both change and communication are always in a state of becoming (Tsoukas and Chia 2002). Weick (1979) called for more emphasis on dynamic *verbs* and less on static *nouns*. Pettigrew et al. (2001) showed that Weick, in almost all his work, argued that a more active and energizing treatment of organizing requires the sublimation of the more familiar word 'organization.'

To put it a different way, the notion of 'organizing' should become part-and-parcel of our own change vocabulary. Interestingly, Pettigrew et al. (2001, 700) showcased the impact of Weick's seminal work by noting that "[i]n 1979, in the second edition of Weick's book entitled *The Social Psychology of Organizing*, Weick followed up with an even more emphatic plea, which can be paraphrased as 'Stamp out nouns and stamp in verbs'."

In line with Weick and Quinn's (1999) call that the task verb 'changing' should be used more often, communication too should be energized through the verb 'communicating' rather than the noun 'communication.' The growing use of the gerund (task verbs that end in '-ing' being used as nouns) indicates the desire to move towards dynamic ways of understanding change and communication (Weick and Quinn 1999).

Tsoukas and Chia (2002) saw social construction as an emergent process in which organizational members communicate, improvise, and co-construct change to fulfill their roles. They emphasized the importance of inviting the 'other' to communicate their viewpoint in an effort to capture the social reality they wish to produce and co-produce, in time and space (Balogun and Johnson 2005; Johansson and Heide 2008).

The final model is **polyphonic**. As we have discussed, much of the drive towards the relevance of the dialogic model in managing change was inspired by process philosophers, including Alfred North Whitehead and Mikhail Bakhtin. Whitehead (1956, 48) saw "language as thought and . . . thought [as] language." Like Bakhtin, Whitehead's (1956) notion of language places emphasis on speech (*parole*) rather than structure (*langue*). Whitehead (1956, 55) saw language (speech) as "immersed in the immediacy of social intercourse" and therefore dialogic. Both Bakhtin and Whitehead focused on language in terms of interactions (recursive) rather than as analysis of self-standing actions (Jabri 2009).

In dialogue, the call is for change communication to become more reliant on recursive dialogue, with interactions having a responsive character. Change is achieved based on promoting recursive (responsive) utterances between two active participants, the change agent and the change recipient(s). Contesting and reaching out for the subtlety of the message, *alongside* use of recursive talk, has important implications for enhancing the process of changing and interpreting and communicating the change effort.

According to Shotter (1998), the ultimate goal of any discursive and/or recursive talk is to *co-construct* and achieve some shared meaning. Such shared meaning becomes a means of attaining a "workable level of certainty" (Hammond and Sanders 2002, 17) or, to Ellinor and Gerard (1998) and Yankelovich (2001), a way to use dialogue to align people with a shared point of view or perspective on the issue under consideration. Bakhtin's view (1986, 119–120) was that the ultimate goal of a discursive and/or recursive talk was achieving a dynamic (responsive) interaction with another subject (or subjects) to "creat[e] something that never existed before, something absolutely new and unrepeatable, and, moreover, [something that] always has some relation to value (the true, the good, the beautiful, and so forth)."

In their editorial introduction to Bakhtin's (1990, xli) essays on 'Art and Answerability,' Holquist and Liapunov reminded us there is benefit in saying to oneself that "to be human is to mean" and that the "human being is the production of meaning." This clearly implicates communicating as a dialogic process involving the relational exchange of utterances, rather than the mere transfer of communication as a tool for getting things done. "Language lives," said Bakhtin, "only in the dialogic interaction of those who make use of it" (1984, 183).

---

## SUMMARY

The differences between the three models can be summarized as:

- Under the transmission model, communication is an event involving the transfer of information between a speaker and a listener. Speaker and listener assume their turns in an atomistic and sequential mode.
- Under the social construction model, communication is an *accomplishment* achieved through ongoing talk and conversational episodes. Every round of interaction leads to a new construction.
- Under the dialogic model, there is a shift from conversations as accomplishments to the potential of conversations to inspire communication about change for those who want to understand, be understood, and feel hopeful, but without doubting their roles, or feeling vulnerable to criticism and attack.

---

## THE ROLE OF RESPONSIVE UTTERANCES

Bakhtin's notion of dialogue is concerned with how recursive talk simultaneously constructs and produces the relationship between individuals and their immediate setting. It requires "a plurality of consciousness, one that cannot in principle be fitted within the bounds of a single consciousness" (1984, 110). In other words, it is about people becoming conscious of their views changing, while revealing their views to and with the help of another.

Bakhtin's interest in responsive relations between people is a recurrent theme of his work. Harris (1997, 144) noted that "what we may learn from Bakhtin in this respect may be summarized with deliberate simplicity." Some of Harris's points included:

- You can help me know myself better. I can help you know yourself better.
- The truth lies not in any particular point of view, but in the dialogue between points of view.
- To listen to your point of view, I do not have to abandon mine. If I did, I would be subject to your limitations rather than my own, and I would have gained no 'surplus of seeing.'

## CONSENSUS: MONOLOGIC VERSUS DIALOGIC

Meetings are often conducted in a search for 'consensus' and the presentation of common ground among organization members. As most of us will know, meetings can be useful but can also be a waste of time. Consensus, in reality, is often a massive compromise: it covers up large differences between people. Participants in a meeting can often show agreement on an issue without reorienting the dominant understanding of events and/or attempting to demolish the domination of the authoritative text.

Consensus often means agreement in disguise, achieved by participating in the discussion of the issues but without resorting to genuine discourses (polemics) achieved through disputation, arguing passionately and raising important issues associated with controversial matters. It also means wanting to maintain the status quo within the team or organization in preference to 'rocking the boat.' That is when the communication becomes reliant on people covering themselves behind the usual bogus-consensus, and not expressing their real views. The manager or leader has often already made up his or her mind that 'everything is fine' and 'we are all in agreement,' allowing the group to discuss the issues without resorting to polemics.

Jabri, Adrian, and Boje (2008) described pseudo-consensus as a counterfeit agreement exhibiting itself when a change agent wants very politely or with the support of group members to get everyone else to agree. Whatever the change agent might espouse, including changing conversational styles to achieve consensus, such a shift in focus converts generating consensus into a monologic practice. Phrases used might include, for example:

- We want you to accept our offer for workplace separation, please.
- We expect everyone to see the need for the proposed budgetary cut.
- We think everyone should agree with the new parking fees.

Many members will prefer to stay on the side of those in power. This can result in those in authority telling those in disagreement that no one else seems to have an issue with the decision. Whenever consensus proves difficult to reach, a vote is proposed, which is another way of pushing for monologic consensus.

Consider the common situation in organizations. Change agents determine that a certain change is necessary. To facilitate implementation, these change agents deem it desirable that everyone in the organization should agree that this change is necessary. Although the idea of creating such a 'consensus' carries connotations of 'participation,' this approach to change is best characterized as a 'monologic consensus' (Jabri, Adrian, and Boje 2008). The history of change and its implementation suggests that consensus often shows a state of nominal commitment, even though the actual situation is one of lack of commitment. One reason for this is to avoid further arguments.

As I noted in Chapter 1, Jabri, Adrian, and Boje (2008, 673–74) made the point that consensus, in reality, often hides significant differences between people. There is no 'meeting of minds.' The consensus remains the proclaimed situation until it is tested in practice. This is usually when things fall apart, and change fails to happen. It is easier to express a consensus viewpoint and leave a meeting on good terms with everyone, rather than express unwelcome views. Here, we can begin to challenge the common view of change, a view that does not take into account that for any change to take root, we must invite the interpretations of others to clarify our own.

In a monologic consensus, the call to participate extends no further than the call to agree with a predetermined outcome. In these circumstances, the anticipation is that everyone will agree and so dissension is not a viable option. The call to consensus is essentially a monologue. The change agent might communicate in apparently consultative ways, including holding participative forums for discussion, paying visits to individual sections, and calling for focus groups, but they do not necessarily break out of the monologic frame. What appears to be dialogic communication can actually serve monologic ends (Jabri, Adrian, and Boje 2008).

This same situation arises inside organizations; managers, sometimes very politely and with the support of people who want to stay on the 'right' side, relate the view of those in authority. This can mean that there is little willingness to bring about innovation, using openness, freedom, and creativity. However, there can be neither change nor renewal without both *centrifugal* and *centripetal* forces.

## POLYPHONIC COMMUNICATION

Implicit in Bakhtin's (1981) conception of communication is a privileging of speech under the heteroglossia of two types of forces that are in constant interaction. These are centripetal (authoritative) forces—the centralizing forces of meaning that tend to communicate uniformity and status quo— and centrifugal (persuasive) forces, the decentralizing forces of meaning that seek freedom, tending to flee the center of uniformity. In organizational settings, such forces are particularly relevant, because they are always changing and challenging each other. For example, the top management team may be unwilling to be inclusive or lack the patience to hear of differences of opinions and outlooks, and so may insist on its own authoritative stance or direction (centripetal) as opposed to all other persuasive discourses present in the background conversations depicting the need for change (persuasive).

'Heteroglossia' comes from the Greek *hetero* (different) and *glōssa* (tongue, language). Heteroglossia is defined by *Merriam-Webster's Dictionary* as a diversity of voices, styles of discourse, or points of view. Bakhtin saw communication as heteroglossic and as being completely "unfinalizable" (1981); there is no such thing as "strictly speaking" (Morson and Emerson 1990, 36–37). That is because the operation of these two forces (centripetal and centrifugal) is constituted in a continuous state that is never-ending.

Consider the examples in the box below:

---

**CENTRIFUGAL AND CENTRIPETAL TALK: AN EXAMPLE**

Maura: In my view, we should keep this structure. The existing levels of formalization and the centralization of decisions should stay the same.

Sigmund: In my view, we should remove that structure. That structure really sucks.

Maura's view is centrifugal; Sigmund's centripetal. Each utterance is made in anticipation of an active response, creating a framing context for new utterances that did not previously exist. Each utterance enters the other. Each embodies the other, and, at the same time, allows for further utterances.

---

Each set of forces is given magnitude and direction through utterances and dialogue, rather than through the dialectics of sentences (atomistic and discrete), as in the transmission model of Shannon and Weaver (1949).

Bakhtin observed that:

> Every concrete utterance of a speaking subject serves as a point where the centrifugal as well as centripetal forces are brought to bear. The processes of centralization and decentralization, of unification and disunification, intersect in the utterance.
>
> (Bakhtin 1981, 272)

Other characteristics of utterances at the core of Bakhtin's thinking, and to which he referred frequently, include innovation, 'surprisingness,' the genuinely new, openness, freedom, and creativity (Morson and Emerson 1990). Every utterance is (at least) double-voiced: "This change is good;" "Yes, this change is good." Each utterance enters the other. Each embodies the other, and, at the same time, allows for further utterances and the possible emergence of surplus as utterances intersect (see Figure 2.3).

The same applies to two non-identical statements: "This change is bad;" "This change is good." Through utterances, context is formed and reformed

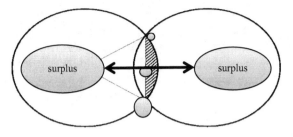

*Figure 2.3*   Utterances intersecting and yet unmerging

through multiple opposing positions, leading to a dialogical tension that transcends the organizing property of an authorial voice. These utterances, both centripetal and centrifugal, influence the way people come to 'co-inhabit' their own experiences in light of the 'inhabitation' of others. Bakhtin's (1986) view on how communication applies to change is more of a perspective on 'life' and our ways of thinking and action. We can only hear as we listen. Harris noted:

> Mikhail Bakhtin, then, has something to tell us: listen. Listen and you will hear a verbal carnival of such depth and diversity, of such extravagance and exuberance, that your ears will never be the same again . . . This question, the engine humming at the centre of Bakhtin's vision, generating alien words like heteroglossia and polyphony, is one that rhetoricians do not ask.
>
> (Harris 1988, 168)

Change that is initiated and managed with an emphasis on listening to others and with particular emphasis on creating conversational space for people wanting to engage in mundane talk is, therefore, not something that is absolute, as in a calcified (formal) plan of change. Rather, change achieved through dialogue obtains its vitality through the surplus of insights achieved by the genuine efforts of those who want to share in the dialogue between points of view. Unless change is driven by a surplus of seeing, it is difficult for communication to incorporate new encounters, voices, and otherness.

## CONCLUSION

Bakhtin's work on dialogue is a source of inspiration. His distinction between monologue and dialogue could be used in the service of a wide range of spheres within management, including managing change and creating cultures for learning. The emphasis on dialogue has led to important achievements in the area of change communication, such as his notion of utterances, used to explain excess of meaning obtained through responsive exchange, his views about the role of language in creating understanding between people, and those relating to the way we embody our experiences as we build and develop our relationship with the world (Bakhtin 1993).

The notion of dialogue has great potential in change communication as well as adding value to current drives towards hybridization and polyphony. Hazen noted that hearing differences of opinions and outlook is crucial for change and that:

> When we bind our understanding about organization processes and change to monolithic, closed visual models, it does not occur to us to listen for and to the voices of all who are working together . . . If we conceive of organization as many dialogues occurring simultaneously . . . [we] discover that each voice, each person, is his or her centre of any organization. And it is from each of these dynamic centres that change occurs.
>
> (Hazen 1994, 16)

However, it is quite possible for top management to embellish change in structures by making it appear as if the change has already been agreed upon after listening to differences of opinions and outlook. Top management teams can quite reliably hear such opinions and yet respond by 'papering over' the differences. This enables them to proceed with change, giving a rational explanation but treating people's opinions as of little importance or as inevitable resistance.

## REFERENCES

Alvesson, Mats and Dan Kärreman. 2000. "Varieties of discourse: on the study of organizations through discourse analysis." *Human Relations* 53 (9): 1125–49.

Asenjo, Florencio G. 1996. "Antinomicity and the axiom of choice: a chapter in antinomic mathematics." *Logic and Logical Philosophy* 4: 53–95.

Bakhtin, Mikhail Mikhailovitch. 1981. *The Dialogic Imagination*, edited by Michael Holquist, translated by Carey Emerson and Michael Holquist. Austin: University of Texas Press.

———. 1984. *Problems of Dostoyevsky's Poetics*, edited and translated by Carey Emerson. Minneapolis: University of Minnesota Press.

———. 1986. *Speech Genres and Other Essays*, edited by Carey Emerson and Michael Holquist, translated by Vern McGee. Austin: University of Texas Press.

———. 1990. *Art and Answerability: Early Philosophical Essays*, edited by Michael Holquist and Vadim Liapunov. Austin: University of Texas Press.

———. 1993. *Toward a Philosophy of the Act*, edited by Michael Holquist and Vadim Liapunov, translated by Vadim Liapunov. Austin: University of Texas Press.

Balogun, Julia and Gerry Johnson. 2005. "From intended strategies to unintended outcomes: the impact of change recipient sensemaking." *Organization Studies* 26: 1573–601.

Berger, Peter L. and Thomas Luckmann. 1966. *The Social Construction of Reality: A Treatise in the Sociology of Knowledge*. New York: Anchor/Doubleday.

Blank, Ksana. 2010. *Dostoevsky's Dialectics and the Problem of Sin*. Evanston, IL: Northwestern University Press.

Bohm, David. 1996. *On Dialogue*. London: Routledge.

Bulgakov, Sergei 1999. "Antinomiia ikony". In *Pervoobraz I obraz: Sochineniia*, translated by Ksana Blank. Moscow: Iskussvo.

Cunliffe, Ann L. 2004. "On becoming a critically reflexive practitioner." *Journal of Management Education* 28 (4): 407–26.

Cunliffe, Ann L. and Chris Coupland. 2009. "Making mundane experience sensible: a relational approach." First International Symposium on Process Organization Studies, Pissouri, Cyprus, 11–13 June.

Cunliffe, Ann L. and Jong S. Jun. 2005. "The need for reflexivity in public administration." *Administration and Society* 37 (2): 225–42.

Czarniawska, Barbara. 1997. *Narrating the Organization: Dramas of Institutional Identity*. Chicago: University of Chicago Press.

Deleuze, Gilles and Félix Guattari. 1994. *What Is Philosophy?* New York: Columbia University Press.

———. 1987. *A Thousand Plateaus: Capitalism and Schizophrenia*, translated by B. Massumi. Minneapolis: University of Minnesota Press.

Dostoevsky, Fyodor. 1990. *The Brothers Karamazov: A Novel with Four Parts with Epilogue*, translated and annotated by Richard Pevear and Larissa Volokhonsky. New York: Farrar, Straus and Giroux.

Dufva, Hannele. 2004. "Language, Thinking and Embodiment: Bakhtin, Whorf and Merleau-Ponty." In *Thinking Culture Dialogically*, edited by Finn Bostad, Craig Brandist, Lars S. Evensen and Hege C. Faber, 133–46. London: Macmillan Publishers.

Ellinor, Linda and Glenna Gerard. 1998. *Dialogue: Rediscovering the Transforming Power of Conversation*. New York: Wiley.

Ford, Jeffrey D. and Laurie W. Ford. 1995. "The role of conversations in producing intentional change in organizations." *Academy of Management Review* 20 (3): 541–70.

Foucault, Michel. 1980. *Power/Knowledge: Selected Interviews and Other Writings, 1972–1977*. New York: Pantheon Books.

Gardiner, Michael. 1999. "Bakhtin and the Metaphorics of Perception." In *Interpreting Visual Culture: Explorations in the Hermeneutics of the Visual*, edited by Ian Heywood and Barry Sandywell, 59–75. London: Routledge.

Garfinkel, Harold. 1967. *Studies in Ethnomethodology*. Upper Saddle River, NJ: Prentice-Hall.

Goffman, Erving. 1959. *The Presentation of Self in Everyday Life*. Garden City, NY: Doubleday.

Gergen, Kenneth. 2008. *An Invitation to Social Construction*, 2nd ed. London: Sage.

Gergen, Kenneth J. and Tojo J. Thatchenkery. 1996. "Developing dialogue for discerning differences." *Journal of Applied Behavioral Science* 32: 428–33.

Hammond, Scott C. and Matthew L. Sanders. 2002. "Dialogue as social self-organization: an introduction." *Emergence* 4 (4): 7–24.

Hatch, Mary Jo. 1997. "Irony and the social construction of contradiction in the humor of a management team." *Organization Science* 8 (3): 275–88.

Hazen, Mary Ann. 1994. "Multiplicity and change in persons and organizations." *Journal of Organizational Change Management* 7 (5): 72–81.

Harris, Max R. 1997. "The surplus of seeing: Bakhtin, the humanities, and public discourse." In *Standing with the Public: The Humanities and Democratic Practice*, edited by James F. Veninga and Noelle McAfee. Dayton, Ohio: Kettering Press, 136–68.

Harris, R. Allen. 1988. "Bakhtin, Phaedrus, and the geometry of rhetoric." *Rhetoric Review* 6 (2): 168–76.

Heracleous, Loizos and Michael Barrett. 2001. "Organizational change as discourse: communicative actions and deep structures in the context of information technology implementation." *Academy of Management Journal* 44 (4): 755–88.

Holquist, Michael. 1983. "Answering as authoring: Mikhail Bakhtin's trans-linguistics." *Critical Inquiry* 10 (2): 307–19.

Jabri, Muayyad. 2005. "Narrative identity achieved through utterances: The implications of Bakhtin for managing change and learning." *Philosophy of Management* 5 (3): 83–90.

———. 2009. "Bakhtin meets Whitehead: a process view of leadership." First International Symposium on Process Organization Studies, Pissouri, Cyprus, 11–13 June.

———. 2012. *Managing Organizational Change: Process, Social Construction and Dialogue*. Basingstoke: Palgrave Macmillan.

Jabri, Muayyad, Allyson Adrian and David Boje. 2008. "Reconsidering the role of conversations in change communication: a contribution based on Bakhtin." *Journal of Organizational Change Management* 21: 667–85.

Johansson, Catrin and Mats Heide. 2008. "Speaking of change: three communication approaches in studies of organizational change." *Corporate Communications* 13 (3): 288–305.

Kanter, Rosabeth M. 1985. *The Change Masters: Innovation and Entrepreneurship in the American Corporation*. New York: Simon & Schuster.

Kotter, John P. 1996. *Leading Change*. Boston: Harvard Business School Press.

Latour, Bruno and Steve Woolgar. 1979. *Laboratory Life*. Beverly Hills, CA: Sage.

Lewis, Laurie. K. and David Seibold. 1998. "Reconceptualizing organizational change implementation as a communication problem: a review of literature and research agenda." in *Communication Yearbook*, Vol. 21, edited by M. E. Roloff and G. Paulson, 93–151. Newbury Park, CA: Sage.

Morson, Gary S. and Caryl Emerson. 1990. *Mikhail Bakhtin: Creation of a Prosaics*. Stanford: Stanford University Press.

Nikulin, Dmitri. 2010. *Dialectic and Dialogue*. Stanford: Stanford University Press.

Pettigrew, Andrew M., Richard W. Woodman and Kim S. Cameron. 2001. "Studying organizational change and development: challenges for future research." *Academy of Management Journal* 44 (4): 697–713.

Sandberg, Jorgen. 2001. "The constructions of social constructionism." In *Invisible Management: The Social Construction of Leadership*, edited by Sven-Erik Sjostrand, Jorgen Sandberg and Mats Tyrstrup, 28–48. London: Thomson Learning.

Saussure, Ferdinand de. 1983. *Course in General Linguistics*, translated by Roy Harris. London: Duckworth.

Searle, John R. 1995. *The Construction of Social Reality*. New York: Free Press.

Shannon, Claude E. and Warren Weaver. 1949. *The Mathematical Theory of Communication*. Urbana: University of Illinois Press.

Shotter, John. 1993. *Conversational Realities: Constructing Life Through Language*. London: Sage.

———. 1998. "The dialogical nature of our inner lives." *Philosophical Explorations* 1 (3): 185–200.

Taylor, James R. and Elizabeth J. Van Every. 2000. *The Emergent Organization: Communication as Its Site and Surface*. Hillsdale, NJ: Lawrence Erlbaum.

Tsoukas, Haridimos and Robert Chia. 2002. "On organizational becoming: rethinking organizational change." *Organization Science* 13: 567–82.

Voloshinov, V. N. 1986. *Marxism and the philosophy of language*, translated by Ladislav Matejka and I. R. Titunik. Cambridge, MA: Harvard University Press.

Weick, Karl E. 1979. *The Social Psychology of Organizing*, 2nd ed. Reading, MA: Addison-Wesley.

————. 1995. *Sensemaking in Organizations*. Thousand Oaks: Sage.
Weick, Karl E. and Robert E. Quinn. 1999. "Organizational change and development." *Annual Review of Psychology* 50 (1): 361–86.
Whitehead, Alfred North. 1956. *Modes of Thought*. Cambridge: Cambridge University Press.
Wittgenstein, I. 1978. *Philosophical Investigations*. London: Macmillan.
Yankelovich, Daniel. 2001. *The Magic of Dialogue: Transforming Conflict into Cooperation*. New York: Simon & Schuster.

# 3 The Role of Dialogue in Managing Change

*The obsessive question at the heart of Bakhtin's thought is always "Who is talking?"*

Michael Holquist (1983, 307).

This chapter explores some of the important themes needed to understand the notion of dialogue. Bakhtin explored dialogue through his recourse to the Socratic method. He believed that this was the foundation, or source through which dialogue obtains its inspiration in action. There is always anticipation targeting the other person so that both partners are looked upon and treated as equals needed to arrive at a new insight.

Dialogue for Bakhtin, therefore, was inspired by Socrates in that it is based on responsive talk between two or more people reaching out to and needing each other. It is about being with ourselves, as well as with others, as we communicate.

Zappen (2011) described dialogue as a uniquely Socratic genre which was sidetracked by Aristotle. Aristotle moved away from conversations and their spontaneity to a much more rationalized treatment, based on reasoning, which was largely top-down or univocal, effectively where the reasoning is addressed to some external entity, rather than another person and as if that real other is not there. Since then the emphasis on objective modes of reasoning has developed and been instrumental in communication where participants feel detached from each other.

## DIALOGUE AND THE SOCRATIC MODE

Dialogue was first promoted by Socrates (c. 469 BC to 399 BC). He left no written text of his own; the general supposition is that Socrates did not write, or possibly that he might have believed thought much more important than writing. Ehrenberg (1973) described Socrates as the least known among the philosophers of the period. Most of what we know about his method is through the writing of his student Plato (c. 428 BC to 348 BC) (see Figure 3.1). Plato founded the 'Academy,' and it is generally accepted that his scheme of thinking and ideas have played a central role in shaping what we now think of as Western thought and institutions.

Perhaps Socrates's most important contribution was his way of speaking and listening to people as a way of exploring ideas rather than a means of imposing his ideas upon others. Robinson (1953) described *elenchus* (from the Greek term for 'critical examination') as the process of examining a statement and then putting an utterance calling for further utterances, in the hope that they will determine some new meaning. It involves breaking down an issue into utterances whereby people interact with each other against a continually-evolving background of self-formation. Each person responds, adding to previous utterances to create an excess of new insights, or an interpretation that is novel and more meaningful than its predecessor. In the illustration below, derived from Jowett's (1986, 61) famous translation

*Figure 3.1*    Socrates and Plato, showing Plato standing behind his master

*Source:* Based on a thirteenth-century work by Mathew Paris (1217–1259). Reproduced with permission of The Bodleian Libraries, The University of Oxford.

of *The Republic*, we note how Plato reports on his master and how *elenchus* is exhibited through an exchange of utterances. All such utterances are saturated with developing meaning and aimed at revealing the truth, namely how people should specialize in their own field of workmanship. The example below shows an ongoing talk, one of the mundane and daily conversations that Socrates had in the streets of Athens. It is not very different from our own, and yet deep enough.

We can see how new insights are generated and also how the other (Adeimantus) appears to be treated as if he is being led by Socrates' utterances. Such talk, however, aims to persuade Adeimantus to share in discovery. The question one should ask is whether Adeimantus is truly and justly doing his independent share of such discovery?

| | |
|---|---|
| SOCRATES: | And will you have a work better done when the work[er] has many occupations, or when he has only one? |
| ADEIMANTUS: | When he has only one. |
| SOCRATES: | Further, there can be no doubt that a work is spoilt when not done at the right time? |
| ADEIMANTUS: | No doubt. |
| SOCRATES: | For business is not disposed to wait until the doer of the business is at leisure; but the doer must follow up what he is doing, and make the business his first object. |
| ADEIMANTUS: | He must. |
| SOCRATES: | And if so, we must infer that all things are produced more plentifully and easily and of a better quality when one man does one thing which is natural to him and does it at the right time, and leaves other things. |
| ADEIMANTUS: | Undoubtedly. |

*Source:* Jowett (1986, 61)

Many scholars maintain that it was Socrates who inspired Plato and his writings. Plato used various terms to describe Socrates's notion of dialogue, including inquiring, interrogating, and refuting the point of view of the other. However, he used none of them consistently to capture the double-voiced nature of the *elenchus* and its centrality as a process culminating in an on-going anticipation of responses from one another.

It was Bakhtin's reading of the *elenchus* that drew attention to its double-voiced nature, and indirectly to the way Plato came to present or even misappropriate Socrates. Bakhtin, in effect, questioned Plato's interpretation of the Socratic *elenchus* and the way in which Plato presented his master as if confronting others, rather than helping the other to think. It was also Bakhtin's reading of Socrates that drew attention to the way in which Plato might have misconstrued how Socrates defined dialogue. Bakhtin's idea is that dialogue can be achieved through contestation of utterances, but only when this is responsive. The doubt that develops is important for creating understanding. While doubt might produce loose ends or even unanswered questions, that does not mean that elenchus is dialectic or confrontational.

Simon Blackburn, in his 2006 book *Plato's Republic: A Biography*, went further. He described Plato as 'betraying' his master:

> An equally shocking thing about it in some people's eyes is that in writing *Republic* Plato utterly betrayed his teacher Socrates. Socrates is the first and greatest liberal hero and martyr to freedom in thought and speech. For writers like John Stuart Mill and George Grote—practical, liberal, utilitarian thinkers—this was the real Socrates. . . But in *Republic* he is presented as an out-and-out dogmatist, rather than the open-minded, patient, questioning spirit his admirers love. He is shown as the spokesman for a repressive, authoritarian, static, hierarchical society in which everything up to and including sexual relations and birth control is regulated by the political classes, who deliberately use lies for the purpose. He presents a social system in which the liberal Socrates would have been executed a great deal more promptly than he was by the Athenian democracy. In *Republic* the liberal Socrates has become the spokesman for a dictatorship. In presenting this figure Plato even betrayed his own calling, being once a poet, who now calls for the poets to be banned.
> (Blackburn 2006, 16–17)

We will never know for sure whether Plato misconstrued his teacher intentionally or unintentionally. His construction certainly stopped short of elevating the way we communicate to a level where refutation is something to be desired on a social level. Bakhtin, however, believed that Socrates used it to get others involved in thinking about new ideas.

The Platonic view has, therefore, given way to one where the Socratic method is thought to focus on getting to the bottom of what the other is thinking or saying. Not all scholars, however, believe that it is based on a simple and straightforward refutation of the other. Ehrenberg (1973) warned against ignoring those who believe that Socrates was perhaps misrepresented in his choice of method and that 'refutation' was basically a method for getting people to see the benefit of exploring more than one point of view. Rather than using direct refutation, this aim was in fact achieved by stimulating doubt. This method targets the 'excess of meaning' that we obtain as we probe what the other is thinking and saying. We derive insights from generating questions. This implies that the Socratic method's main purpose is to create new insights achieved through talk, which may involve stimulating doubt (*aporia*) and resolving these doubts through conversations.

Bakhtin (1981, 24) believed that the centrality of the *elenchus* is achieved through Socrates and his image "wearing the popular mask of a bewildered fool . . . with the image of a wise man of the most elevated sort . . . this combination produces the ambivalent image of wise ignorance." Bakhtin came to realize that the root mistake in the way we treat dialogue is allowing exchange and responsive utterances to be foreshadowed by monologic tendencies. Here, the person assumes the heroic stance of a leader who knows more and is wiser than those following, rather than the Socratic view that "I am wiser than everyone, because I know that I know nothing" (Bakhtin 1981, 24). For Socrates, knowing oneself to be uninformed was far more conducive to learning and problem resolution than holding clear views that might be incorrect. Accepting a lack of knowledge encourages the discarding of false conceptions and hence enhances readiness for learning.

At its purest, the Socratic method encourages self-doubt. This is in no way selfish. Stimulating doubt is not about concealing one's own knowledge, but encouraging people to share and come up with their own utterances. Bakhtin viewed this as the basis for generating double-voicedness. In this way, self-doubt is an intentional act to encourage others to partake and perhaps to dream. However, once again, this is something Plato never discussed about Socrates' approach.

Likewise, little has been said to reflect the role of the speaker and listener. Bakhtin (1984) noted that the double-voiced nature of Socrates's *elenchus* has an important role in bringing the world we inhabit closer to what the other is saying, as it goes beyond the superficial boundaries of 'me' and 'you.' The fundamental aim of *elenchus*, therefore, is to see what the other is saying, and take on board their words. Bakhtin asked us to reflect on the importance of the double-voiced nature and how enormous is the weight of what "everyone says" (1984, 338).

The strategy that is built in to *elenchus* consists of two complementary ways of thought. It often starts with questioning the statement made by the other person, but then moves into a phase where specific aspects are brought to the fore, asking questions to invoke doubt. This leads to the idea of creating real reservations, uncertainty or doubt, *aporia*, about where to begin or what to do next, with the aim of creating a 'second loop' (Argyris 1993) aimed at revising or learning from the situation.

---

### SUMMARY: BAKHTIN'S VIEW OF *ELENCHUS*

Bakhtin emphasized that Socratic dialogues are a communication genre consisting of transcriptions of recorded conversations always driven by some theme, story, or narrative. These Socratic dialogues were never aimed at some pointless refutation, namely winning and defeating the other.

In other words, they were never aimed at reaching some quick and desired outcome. Instead, Bakhtin viewed Socratic dialogues as having a true and meaningful communicative emphasis (understanding) where emergent conversations and the very being of the other person is brought into oneself and fully experienced only in "deepest communion" as people come to relate (Bakhtin 1984, 278) and where voices from a variety of perspectives are brought to bear on what is being discussed.

Interestingly, Zappen (2011) described Socrates's *elenchus* as having comparisons and analogies representing not so much a strict logical system of thought as a multiplicity of perspectives on the world. Bakhtin noted that:

> [In *elenchus*] we have laughter, Socratic irony, the entire system of Socratic degradations combined with a serious, lofty and for the first time truly free investigation of the world, of man and of human thought. Socratic laughter (reduced to irony) and Socratic degradations (an entire system of metaphors and comparisons borrowed from the lower spheres of life—from tradespeople, from everyday life, etc.) bring the world closer and familiarize it in order to investigate it fearlessly and freely.
>
> (Bakhtin 1981, in Epic 25)

Bakhtin argued that dialogue is largely driven by true consensus, that is, the meaningful agreement of all parties involved. This is achieved only after everyone has shared and put his or her views forward, even when such views appear to contradict or spoil the chances for some conclusion to be reached. There is no manipulation, and no artificial system of rules designed to achieve some conclusion based on pseudo-consensus.

## THE SOCRATIC NOTION OF DIALOGUE

As a process of inquiry, the Socratic notion of the dialogic remains attractive in many circles and organizations are no exception. For some it has its own potential contribution in terms of fostering thinking, listening, searching for evidence, nurturing ideas, and sharing with others how to go about the breaking down of talk into themes and subthemes, making issues and concerns more amenable to reflection and responsive talk. Even during his trial in 399 BC, Socrates was quoted by Plato as asking the citizens of Athens to examine their lives in an elenchic mode achieved by putting reflective questions and answers to oneself, on the grounds that the path pursued needs to be meaningful to oneself.

Because Socrates never wrote anything, almost all that we know about him is through the work of Plato and Aristotle. Zappen (1996) noted that no one in the history of philosophy has been more misappropriated than Socrates for, as Bakhtin commented (1984), the dialogue that was reported by Plato was presented as monologic and its *form* was largely distorted. Zappen (1996) rightly concluded that Socratic dialogue exhibits many voices, including the many voices of Socrates himself and those of the other parties to the dialogue. Plato was Socrates's student and he wrote most about dialogue. Socrates's notion of the dialogic nature of the method was also appropriated by Aristotle, one of Plato's students. For Zappen and many others, the Socratic notion of dialogue and its exploration as a dialogic mode has been traditionally read as merely monologic. The origination of Platonic/

Aristotelian philosophy, and the way in which Aristotle's notion of scientific truth was embraced, did little but expound ready-made ideas. To a large extent, the *form* that Socratic conversations took has been left unattended in communication and management studies even though many of the methods we already use in managing change have been largely influenced by the approach used in developing the Socratic method.

Aristotle's writings appear to undermine the 'scientific' status of the method. As noted by Zappen, any strict retrospective re-enactment or reconstruction of Socrates is not, and probably never will be, possible. To attain some optimal state in terms of what one could hope for involves drawing attention to the highly creative mode with which the deliberative inquiries were conducted and the collaborative atmosphere of many voices characteristic of Socrates's method of dialogue.

## BAKHTIN'S NOTION OF THE SOCRATIC METHOD

The notion of the Socratic dialogue, as viewed by Bakhtin, is reliant on the word and the impulse it has when it comes to conversation with oneself or the other. As we continue to elaborate on polyphony, let us have a look at what Bakhtin said on the *impulse* of the word:

> Discourse lives, as it were, beyond itself, in the living impulse toward the object; if we detach ourselves completely from this impulse all we have left is the naked corpse of the word, from which we can learn nothing at all about the social situation or the fate of a given word in life.
>
> *To study the word as such, ignoring the impulse that reaches out beyond it, is just as senseless as to study psychological experience outside the context of that real life toward which it was directed and by which it is determined.* (All italic in the original)
>
> (Bakhtin 1981, 292)

So if we were talking about change, what I said was influenced by what you said. Your word will have its inclination to convey, as will mine. After all, this is how we communicate; namely, through Socrates's notion that we all contribute to forming each other's sense of truth, where we become more prepared and ready to embrace a dialogic sense of truth.

My word is exported (uttered) by myself to you; your word is imported (uttered by you to me). Both words meet in space and that is where meaning is constituted. If I was to say this change could proceed '*this way*' and you say to me that change should proceed '*that way*,' then 'change' itself is the object but it is my word besides your word that makes the conversation.

The inclination to convey something to you, therefore, is in the *word*. Polyphony exhibits many words, and each word has its own 'impulse' (Bakhtin 1981). A word could also signify differences in the composition of the workforce as well as differences in identities brought by members from various backgrounds. Each word has its own inclination to influence every other one, and all words come to influence each other. Bakhtin (1981, 279) noted that "the word is born in a dialogue as a living rejoinder within it." To paraphrase Bakhtin, the word is shaped and re-shaped in time and pending the object of the conversation. The shaping and re-shaping is accomplished through utterances in speech. Each word has its own impulse. It will always attract a response and so will always have its own rejoinder as a comeback:

A: This change is good.
B: This change is good.

In other words, a word will have a rejoinder born inside it. The word lives and obtains a new life as it is joined in and through another word. A word is therefore always on the move. When uttered, it can go forward, but it will also have its own comeback and comeback is shaped by the utterance of the other, forming the idea and concept of change. A concept of change is formed only when utterances are exchanged. The exchange is never final for there is no end to a change in the word. Each new word exerts its own influence once it arrives. Words, as with languages, do not exclude each other. In fact, they inter-animate in many different ways, so my conception of change might augment yours and your conception of change might augment or supplement mine. We might start with the idea of a new job design in a new team, but end up with a new job design for the whole section. Each new word might supplement a new design. Bakhtin noted:

> at any given moment of its historical existence, language is heteroglot from top to bottom: it represents the co-existence of socio-ideological contradictions between the present and the past, between differing epochs of the past, between different socio-ideological groups in the present, between tendencies, schools, circles and so forth, all given a bodily form.
> (Bakhtin 1981, 291)

A word opens new possibilities, or it might bring the conversation to a close. However, the effect of a new word can promote renewal and enrichment (Bakhtin 1984).

Bakhtin's interpretation of the Socratic dialogue is, therefore, reliant on the word and its impulse when it comes to conversation. There is an internal movement of the word and its rejoinder(s) that gives the conversation its dialogic character. It is within that movement that the form, as a structure, is determined at least for a while until another round is complete. The conversation is an "inter-text" (Todorov 1984, 54). It is reliant on an addressor and an addressee, rather than a sender and a receiver. It is determined through the word as if it lives.

## MONOLOGIC TENDENCIES

High levels of formalization are associated with monologic tendencies. Bakhtin made the point that there is never one direction or uniform (consensual) point of view, whatever anyone may argue. Instead, there are many competing forces that co-exist and push and pull in their own distinct way. Bakhtin (1981, 428) noted that "all utterances are heteroglot in that they are functions of a matrix of forces practically impossible to recoup."

In organizations, the drive for efficiency places an emphasis on monologue. This is often supported by a desire to formulate rules and procedures on the basis that governance requires policies to be documented and then enacted. There has been a significant tendency to consolidate the change effort through the recital of narratives depicting organizations that have succeeded in achieving their goals or turning around organizational fortunes through the efforts of one person; Lou Gerstner at IBM would be one such. There are dangers here, because such narratives may camouflage monologic tendencies. Newly-formed organizations and those undergoing change are formed on the basis of arguments derived from accounting and sales figures.

In consequence, tendencies toward high levels of formalization have their own cascading effects. Units at the lower-middle levels of the organizational hierarchy are prompted to formulate their own rules and procedures and align them with what is required from the top. Little leeway is allowed for individual units to formulate or build their own dialogic climates, so that monologic realism increasingly becomes the principle driving organizational life.

Part of the problem is that the push for rules and systems has often given way to ineptitude in procedures. This, in turn, has given way to increasingly bureaucratic controls, leading to insensitive treatment of people, often resulting from blind adherence or misinterpretation of controls.

We find organizations and their leadership living a never-ending search for rules and the consolidation of procedures. We also, however, meet situations where such rules and procedures are constantly changing and separating people from their organizations. This is shown by presenting one voice that is clear in the face of the situation and yet rarely on the lookout for what others have to say. This is the problem with creating categorical boundary lines between resolving the situation through the 'rules of the game' (for example, job descriptions, policies, and restrictions on budget) and doing so by talk aimed at stimulating doubts and then resolving them through dialogue. My criticism of leadership as monologic and finite has important consequences. Instead, I suggest a path for understanding change through Bakhtin's interpretation of Socrates. This suggests how the idea of 'double voices' might help to manage change.

Dialogue hinges on an emphatic understanding of the other, and at the same time listening to the other in a way that gives them the courage to disclose their own word. The fear of rules and regulations is replaced with a conviction that one's own views, passions, and experiences will be appreciated, taken on board as useful, rather than ignored by treating them as unimportant or less factual. The dialogical other is encouraged to express his or her thoughts, rather than be treated as an object. Difference is accepted. For such an expression to take shape and form, narrative must assume a special place. In many organizations, however, multi-voicedness (polyphony) is increasingly being replaced by dialectical systems, in the belief that charts, official feedback systems, and performance appraisal systems can be orchestrated to provide plausible explanations.

Dialogue is also about taking onboard the multi-toned narration of diverse views and capturing them through focus groups. Varied perspectives and approaches are needed to sustain changing identities but dialogue is deemed crucial. Personal and multi-layered access is encouraged, on the basis that feedback should not be opportunistic or flattering. It should not come only from those surrounding the leader, because they often tell leaders what they want to hear, thereby consolidating and cementing a leader's expectations. This, in turn, prompts leaders to continue to use dialectic and information-based objective systems of knowledge.

Bakhtin's dialogue is an unusual form because it relies on making room for the addressor and the addressee to meet, allowing each to 'become' the other. He saw dialogue as being ingrained in people's awareness of themselves and their consciousness of others. Bakhtin (1984) felt that 'to be' and to feel one's own existential realm meant to be for another and through the other, for oneself. This important feature has to do with one's own being in terms of who the person is and what becomes of that person before and after having communicated with someone else. This distinguishes Bakhtin's way of thinking from dialogue as a prescription for achieving better communication, using skills or techniques to be acquired and used as and when the need arises.

> *To be* **means to** *communicate*. (Bakhtin 1984, 278; italics in original, bold is mine)
> To be means to be for another, and through the other, for oneself. A person has no internal sovereign territory, he is wholly and always on the boundary; looking inside himself, he *looks into the eyes of another or with the eyes of another*.
> (Bakhtin 1984, 278; italics in original)

Bakhtin's polyphony and dialogue are closely intertwined. Much of their affinity is due to the dialogic nature of truth as well as of human thinking (people wanting to know). In other words, people think and want to look at an action or a set of conceptions or a way of thinking with a view to finding the truth, even though the truth may have been masked by an official version. Bakhtin explained this as:

> The dialogic means of seeking truth is counterposed to *official* monologism, which pretends to *possess a ready-made truth*, and it is also counterposed to the naive self-confidence of those people who think that they know something, that is, who think that they possess certain truths.
>
> (Bakhtin 1984, 110; italic in original)

People may give up seeking the truth; they may abdicate and accept the fact that there is an 'agreed line,' or authoritative discourse, around them; they may even give up and abandon the desire to change the status quo. To guide the change effort, someone, or some event, would need to be there to light the wick of a lantern to guide the way. The light could spread. It might even get diffused with rays from other lanterns, or it might be extinguished or made to flicker by the power of the 'company line.'

The diverse reality we inhabit and how diverse identities are made visible or invisible is not simply born nor is it found inside the head of one person. Bakhtin (1984, 110) believed that diversity, and for that matter, receptivity of the other is "born between people." Diversity emerges as a collective process. It is inspired by a dialogic conception as we come to talk, rather than being based on a subject-centered (monological) conception of the other. It is achieved through building on talk and utterances made under conditions which generate the additional understanding needed to create a new surplus of diversity: an overflow of vision and visibility needed to see the other.

## DIALOGIC SPACE ACHIEVED THROUGH UTTERANCES

Utterances develop from within a socially-specific framing (or dialogic space). Within a framing context, in which each person holds a unique place, utterances are simultaneously constituted and interpreted. They thus implicate one another as each is formed and reformed through an ongoing process of linking and transposing the meaning of one into another. An utterance responds to previous utterances; in a sense, utterances come to be inhabited by others. It is important to recognize that the context within which all utterances are framed and reframed remains subject to further changes as more utterances follow, and as frames become 'populated' by different positions. A frame continues to change in the course of speaking, as meaning is carried over from one utterance to another. As I noted in Chapter 2, Bakhtin stressed that no word can be neutral:

> There are no 'neutral' words and forms. All words have the 'taste' of a profession, a genre, a tendency, a party, a particular work, a particular

person, a generation, an age group, the day and the hour . . . all words and forms are populated by intentions.

(Bakhtin 1981, 293)

All intentions are subjective. This gives utterance a colorful real meaning that allows identities to be implicated in speech, rather than by the mere application of a narrative closure. Language thus emerges not as an abstract system of forms (*langue*), but rather as a "concrete heteroglot" (Bakhtin 1981, 293): a heterogeneous reflection of a world infused with contradictory intentions.

## SHIFTING IDENTITIES

Bakhtin's work was fully grounded in a dialogic ontology in which the self is not substantive (unitary) but relational. The self is dialogical, meaning that individuals come to a consciousness of themselves through dialogue with others. Bakhtin commented, "I live in a world of others' words" (1986, 143).

The view that the self is relational brings a crucial insight to change, as shifting identities are accomplished through utterances. This insight flows from the formation of identity based on utterances that are made in anticipation of the other's active response. Bakhtin (1984) described a subversive theory of the 'carnival' (Boje 2001). This emphasizes the profound and ever-changing nature of identity (language) in a festival atmosphere of shifting meaning anchored in social interaction. This is an epistemology in which both the external and internal being of an individual is inextricably related to others.

Bakhtin suggested that identity is always involved in dialogue:

I am conscious of myself and become myself only while revealing myself for another, through another, and with the help of another.

(Bakhtin 1984, 287)

In his view, every internal experience ends up on the boundary where it encounters another experience. Identity is always shifting and always "looking into the eye" of another. This is because an utterance is infused with the speaker's sense of self, the influence of others that they have heard in the past, and the *heteroglossia* of their particular change situation.

Bakhtin (1981, 428) defined heteroglossia as a "locus where centripetal and centrifugal forces collide." The competing forces for and against strategies, structures, and systems determine the way change is constructed. All such constructions and co-constructions are achieved through utterances and the shifting context within which utterances are made. For Bakhtin, change is a *process* that is situated within the framing context. The process through which such constructions take place is seen as infinite. Bakhtin noted:

> [When] everything means, is understood, as a part of a greater whole—there is constant interaction between meanings, all of which have the potential of conditioning others. Which will affect the other, how it will do so and in what degree is what is actually settled at the moment of utterance.
>
> (Bakhtin 1981, 426)

As I discussed in Chapter 2, rather than seeing change as a phenomenon outside the self, it is conceived in terms of heteroglossia because of the variety in utterances, and the fluidity and dispersion that result from the collision of centripetal and centrifugal forces in language. For example:

Centripetal: "The merger will help us all."
Centrifugal: "I don't think it will. I just don't see how."

Each utterance can stand with others and each one can change the course of the conversation. Meaning is thus accomplished through utterances that are constituted within centripetal forces (forces that unify utterances, tending toward the center) and centrifugal forces (forces that disturb, tending to flee the center). From Bakhtin's general principle of heteroglossia, it is possible to deduce, and allow for, all possible particulars within a conversation. It allows a participant to see change as a project that is relational (Baxter and Montgomery 1996; McNamee and Gergen 1999). Change thus becomes, fundamentally, an act of co-authoring, in which desires and aspirations are transposed.

The central element is the notion of the 'word.' That word could be a very familiar word or it could be a new one that is unfamiliar, strange, unknown, and even foreign to us. Paraphrasing Bakhtin (1981), we have our own set of words and ideas that are organized into a system of our own. That system belongs to us, and is the core we use to understand others. It is very familiar to us and so when a new word arrives, the core may reach out to it, or it may not. The new word waits on the boundary to be accepted or rejected. It lives, as it were, on the boundary between its own context and another, alien, one.


## RELATIONAL SELFHOOD

The notion of polyphony is exemplified through Dostoevsky's style of novelistic writing, in which he gave his heroes the opportunity to present themselves and their subjectivities in a way that gave them complete authorship of the novel. Dostoevsky's writing relied on a plural of unmerged representations which were left intact, in the sense that they were not subordinate to an authoritative voice. Dostoevsky's style of polyphonic writing was underpinned by a conviction that the author's role is to facilitate: that it is the characters, rather than the author, who should be explaining themselves. The characters do their own interpretation of the context, each exploring themselves by themselves. There is, therefore, no hero or heroine. Every character wrestles with their own values, aspirations, problems of belief or unbelief, and identities. Some of these questions, including beliefs, are not straightforward, and so Dostoevsky leaves them to the character to explore.

In Dostoevsky's work, as explained in Chapter 1, all the characters have their own image of themselves, in the sense that they sustain their own voices. The authority of the utterance is fully given to the character. From an organizational angle, polyphony has its own variety, as people present their reasons and wrestle with their own desires, values, and aspirations. Everyone comes to explore their own situation and cope with ever-changing structures and designs. There are many voices, including their own.

The characters in the story provide their own description of themselves. They talk and so we come to know more about them as they present their rationale. All the characters have their own say, and authority is handed over to them. Each character expands on the reasons for personal choices. They argue their views of the world around them as they present their reasoning for their actions. The rest of this chapter will examine the concepts deemed necessary for understanding polyphony.

## 'I-THOU' AND BAKHTIN

It is possible to identify two main lines of thinking about dialogue: (i) the prescriptive approach, and (ii) the process approach. The *prescriptive* approach to dialogue, which concentrates on the methodology and epistemology of dialogue, includes the work of Buber (1970) and his notion of the 'I-Thou' relationship. Buber's work emphasized the need for dialogue to be conceived as a fully conscious effort sustained by the depth of a spiritual relationship, where an appreciation of the other is ultimately what drives us to appreciate the presence of the other in relation to our own existence. One of the great things about Buber is his emphasis on the way we all relate to each other (inter-subjectivity). However, he stops short of saying much about relationality in the sense of utterance. Considered in this light, Bakhtin's work represents another attempt to work out the relationality between self and the other.

Hirschkop (1999) noted that Bakhtin's work is more about the "excess of meaning" we are able to obtain as we converse with the other. It therefore moves beyond the 'I-Thou' and the spirituality of its Buberian connotation to a more corporeal sphere where *'what you say to me becomes truly mine'* and '*what I say to you becomes truly yours.*' This applies even when we disagree. This way, Buber's 'I-Thou' obtains some new and profound depth that has some important implications. Such implications have important consequences for the way new and more novel excess of meaning is brought to bear on how change is shaped and co-shaped through conversations. This also applies to the extent to which we are able to appreciate and move on with our conversations in ways that build on knowledge and experiences of both self and other. The 'I-Thou,' therefore, emerges as more involving between 'you' and 'me' and may even affect my own identity and that of the other (Jabri 2004). In other words, Bakhtin provides a way of building on learning, capabilities, and compassion for the many voices, or multi-voicedness, the term Bakhtin used for polyphony.

More importantly, the more corporeal approach to dialogue, which Bakhtin exemplifies, affirms not only the ontological aspect of how we relate to each other but also the more mundane and fully-conscious aspect of dialogue present in speech. Bakhtin's notion of dialogue (1984, 110) requires "a plurality of consciousness." As I noted in Chapter 2, Bakhtin (1986) likened the links between consciousnesses to the way in which "the body is formed initially in the mother's womb." Such an interest in the ontology of identity is a recurrent theme of Bakhtin's work.

## HETEROGLOSSIA AS A FACET OF POLYPHONY

Bakhtin's notion of dialogue is consistently concerned with how language simultaneously constructs and reflects the heteroglossia of relationships between individuals and their immediate setting. Bakhtin discarded the dualism of transmissions between an active speaker and a passive listener in favor of utterances made in anticipation of the other's active response. Rather than seeing meaning-making in change management as being based on ready-made subject-centered codes, Bakhtin's approach sees it as irreducibly dependent on a complex unity of differences in utterances, or heteroglossia, through which meaning develops.

As I noted earlier, Bakhtin's conception of heteroglossia contains an implicit understanding that speech is driven by two sets of forces. Centripetal forces unify utterances, tending towards the center, and centrifugal forces disturb, tending to flee the center. Bakhtin, therefore, saw utterances as being completely infinite.

For Bakhtin (1984, 21): "The essence of polyphony lies precisely in the fact that the voices remain independent and, as such, are combined in a unity of higher order than in homophony." But how independent are these voices and in what context can such independence of unmerged voices lead to polyphony? Bakhtin believed that they are truly independent when they reflect and reinforce the thoughts of the beholder. He went on (1984, 75): "These voices are not self-enclosed or deaf to one another. They hear each other constantly, call back and forth to each other, and are reflected in one another."

Bakhtin (1984, 6) noted that there are no "voiceless slaves but free people," meaning that everyone has their own voice. There is a diversity of unmerged points of view. Speaking of Dostoevsky, Bakhtin noted (1984, 6) that a "plurality of independent and unmerged voices and consciousness" provided the basis for producing a genuine "polyphony that is dialogic *through and through*" (Bakhtin 1984, 40).

## TYPES OF DISCOURSE

Bakhtin (1981) noted that when several discourses interact, we struggle to assimilate two contrasting types: 'authoritative discourse' and 'internally persuasive discourse.' The term 'authoritative discourse' refers to the dominant ways of thinking and acting within a tradition or culture. Bakhtin defined authoritative discourse as:

> The authoritative word is located in a distanced zone, organically connected with a past that is felt to be hierarchically higher. It is, so to speak, the word of the fathers.
>
> Its authority was already *acknowledged* in the past. It is a *prior* discourse. It is therefore not a question of choosing it among other possible discourses that are its equal . . . for example, the authority of religious dogma, or of acknowledged scientific truth or of a currently fashionable book.
>
> (Bakhtin 1981, 342–3)

The distanced location of authoritative discourse and its emphasis on domination has an important role in maintaining the 'centripetal' emphasis on coherence and hierarchy in line with particular interests and goals (Jabri 2005). The authoritative word demands that we acknowledge it and make it our own. Our choice is rather limited, because it has the benefit of binding us and "might have to persuade us internally; we encounter it with its authority already fused to it" (Bakhtin 1981, 342).

Such authoritative discourse can be understood as that of organizational culture reflecting a normative order that emphasizes high levels of formalization. It includes acknowledged organizational values and adherence to norms and procedures. It is embedded in the existing designs, structures, organizational processes, and styles of leadership and decision-making. In effect, it asserts that individual and social obligations are to be observed and that there is consistency and sameness of the self with social others. It therefore precludes consideration of diversity and plurality.

Not all organizational culture and processes conform to this approach. Another approach is embedded in the sort of discourse that is "backed by no authority at all, and is frequently not even acknowledged by society" Bakhtin (1981, 242). Such discourse is internally persuasive as it consists of the thoughts and persuasions of individuals. It is thus emergent and 'centrifugal' in nature. Internally persuasive discourse is also experimental in nature, because it reflects both the person's own desires and aspiration and also those of others. It therefore involves the adaptation of the word in language to one's own intentions. Internally persuasive discourse requires other selves, not only 'I-for-myself,' but also 'I-and-the-other' (Jabri 2005). It has its own novelty in the sense that it prompts individuals to move on to other and more representative spheres and ways of thinking. In defining internal persuasive discourse, Bakhtin wrote:

> Its creativity and productiveness consist precisely in the fact that such a word awakens new and independent words, that it organizes masses of our words from within, and does not remain in an isolated and static condition.
>
> (Bakhtin 1981, 345)

Internally persuasive discourse thus relates to what others want to be said and to hear (Jabri 2009a, b). It is able to capture the sense-making of one actor as it relates to that of another. Jabri, Adrian, and Boje (2008) described internally persuasive discourse as rooted in *parole*, rather than *langue*, hence having neither a first nor last meaning.

Because of this, people negotiate between the authoritative discourse and the themes of their own tangible situations. This typology of discourse is, therefore, helpful in highlighting the importance of persuasive discourse and its negotiation with authoritative discourse in facilitating a crossover from sameness to diversity and from univocal to multivocal (polyphonic) representations. Changes in identity become possible when such negotiation occurs. When other people have their own living discourses, identity begins to disseminate among multiple actors at more than one level (Taylor et al. 1996). The two types of discourse are, by definition, related to multi-voicedness and the importance of diversity in organizational settings. Bakhtin's distinction provides a gesture of openness in transgressing the limits of sameness (authoritative discourse). No organization can be understood only on its own authoritative ground. Any analysis would need to allow for the presence of the second type of discourse.

## CENTRIPETAL AND CENTRIFUGAL FORCES

Bakhtin believed that utterances are always infinite. They are subject to heteroglossia, which he defined as the interplay of *centripetal* and *centrifugal* forces of meaning. Bakhtin (1981, 272–3) referred to these forces as "the unifying, centralizing, centripetal forces of verbal ideological life [and the opposing] . . . centrifugal, stratifying forces."

Centripetal utterances are about authoritative talk. These utterances have an important role in the maintenance of social coherence with particular interests and goals brought on board by different individuals or groups. They are embedded in the existing modes of thinking of organization members who are willing to use them as discourses for disciplining, regulating, and controlling the extant mode with which diversity is considered or interpreted. Centripetal clauses are thus about talk and writing that aims to get people to reason and act based on sameness and evenness of the self with every other self. By contrast, centrifugal clauses occur in initiatives or narrations that act for diversity and in reaction to centripetal clauses. They 'disturb' the harmony of centripetal narratives by questioning rules and levels of formalization.

A centripetal force tends towards uniformity and singularity of meaning. It functions as a mechanism through which collective group interests are played out in the social practices of individuals (Van Dijk 1997). It emphasizes the status quo, sameness, and evenness between actors, effectively reducing the 'other' to the '*selfsame*' and the familiar (Jabri, Adrian, and Boje 2008). In contrast, a centrifugal force is committed to 'being with' the other, even in the midst of tension and conflict. A discourse calling for a greater level of autonomy in a workplace setting is an example of one relying on a centrifugal force, pushing for actors to be allowed to manage their own initiatives.

Actors do not necessarily arrive at *the* 'meaning,' but continue to discover meaning as long as they interact with others. Meaning arises from the "contact between the word and the concrete reality" (Bakhtin 1986, 87), and reality is shaped and re-shaped through utterances from other actors at more than one level. A corollary of this is that an apparent "single-voiced discourse" (Bakhtin 1984, 189) is, in fact, a multi-voiced dialogue. For example, a teacher's single-voiced discourse about a heavy teaching load could also be construed as reflecting the discourse of a surrounding network of colleagues. At more than one level, discourse constructs identity and identity constructs discourse. The two thus come to 'inter-animate' one another.

In line with Bakhtin, I contend that the intersection of different forces in a social setting (centripetal and centrifugal) causes people to co-construct their becoming and their views of change as they make sense of change and the direction it should take. In change situations, such forces operate almost all the time. It is in the nature of change that such forces would lead to a coherent entity that is stable and enduring. Often, it emerges as a "concrete heteroglot" (Bakhtin 1981, 293), or a heterogeneous reflection of a world infused by intentions aimed at moving away from aspects of stability to one more thoroughly understood in terms of *becoming* rather than *being*, grounded in change and renewal.

When constructed in its original *form*, the Socratic notion of dialogue has its own potential interest in managing change. It has guided many change efforts. Cooperrider and Whitney (2005), for example, championed Socratic dialogue as the way to migrate the emphasis from refuting and cross-examining to dialogue. According to Kakabadse et al. (2011), the approach has invoked inspiration and guidance for many contemporary scholars, not only those in philosophy and politics, but also from other areas, including the management of change. Importantly, Kakabadse et al. (2011) noted that Socratic dialogue underpins various forms of action research, action learning, and appreciative inquiry. They gave an example of helping to embrace the challenge of enhancing the provision of children's services within a London borough in the UK, in which they presented a comparative scrutiny of dialogue-based inquiry approaches. They detailed a comprehensive account of the Socratic, deliberative dialogue mode of action inquiry and highlighted the suitability of adopting Socratic philosophy to examine the organizational integration requirements within the children's services department of the borough. Their work provides a fine example of dialogic-based inquiry approaches. In their findings, Kakabadse et al. (2011) noted that Socratic deliberative inquiry was found to help participants to embrace the method and to enhance the confidence and skills of all those involved.

Why the Socratic method should be useful for elaborating on dialectic and dialogue will become fully evident only later in the course of this book, but can be briefly mentioned here. The Socratic method will be seen to rely on logic and epistemology as a method of reasoning, much more than anthropology and ontology as inherent to the human condition. As noted earlier on, that ontology is truly relational (inter-subjective), rather than unitary and substantive. Hence, each person comes to consciousness through dialogue with some other. Through others, we come to feel what it is like 'to be,' conscious of the difference in perspective or approach of the other. That is when we give meaning to how we are integrally connected to the other person, in the sense that we are able to get to grips with the diverse identity of the other.

Nikulin (2010) noted that dialectic does not need the specifically human component, nor presuppose the uniqueness of a person or a personal other or require narration and narratives, whereas dialogue is impossible without these. Most importantly, dialectic relies on a linear perspective of the other, whereas dialogic relies on an inverse perspective. This linear-reverse contrast will in turn be seen to ground the most apparent difference between the two, although one that will prove much more complex than it first appears.

Change is accomplished through an exchange of utterances in communication, rather than reliance on syllogism. The field of change communication is, therefore, uniquely positioned and arises from the composite methods with which contributions from reasoning and dialogue are used to announce the forthcoming change effort and to build its case. In reviewing the literature on change, Ford and Ford (1995, 542) noted that change as an organizational phenomenon "occurs and is driven by communication rather than the reverse," and that communication is the very medium within which change occurs. Research on change management has emphasized the role of communication in leading to mutual understanding at the level of everyday conversations (Ford and Ford 1995; Weick and Quinn 1999; Jabri, Adrian, and Boje 2008). Kakabadse et al. (2011) noted that dialogue is critical to the effective adoption of change methodologies and so the onus is on organizational leaders to search constantly for the best communication practices within and across shifting organizational boundaries. Dialogue is critical because communication plays a central role in enhancing readiness for change, building the case for change, shaping interventions and in announcing new change initiatives.

## BAKHTIN'S NOTION OF HETEROGLOSSIA

Bakhtin (1981) posited the concept of 'heteroglossia' as a specific form of talk achieved through everyday language use. According to Bakhtin (1981, 430), talk is a discourse "peculiar to a specific stratum" within a given social system or profession at a given time. Through conversations, words interanimate and intersect each other in a variety of ways, forming "new socially typifying languages" (Bakhtin 1981, 291).

Bakhtin (1981, 411) was, therefore, insistent that "a language is revealed in all its distinctiveness only when it is brought into relationship with other languages," but this involves tensions. According to Bakhtin (1981), talk is bounded by tensions between centripetal and centrifugal accounts of life. Bakhtin (1981, 272–3), wrote of "the unifying, centralizing, centripetal forces of verbal ideological life," to which are opposed "the centrifugal, stratifying forces" of everyday life. When centripetal and centrifugal forces are juxtaposed, a Bakhtinian conception of heteroglossia can prove useful for explaining manifestations of change, because of the dialogue it could generate.

## IDEOLOGICAL BECOMING

Ideological becoming, according to Bakhtin (1981, 346), is "an intense struggle within us for hegemony among various available verbal and ideological points of view, approaches, directions and values." He went on:

> One's own discourse and one's own voice, although born of another or dynamically stimulated by another, will sooner or later begin to liberate themselves from the authority of the other's discourse.
>
> (Bakhtin (1981, 348)

This liberation is the beginning of ideological becoming, which Bakhtin (1981, 341) talked about as the "retelling in one's own words" but through the other. All the words we encounter play a role in shaping the way we think, in creating readiness, and in mounting resistance. Ideological becoming, then, is the act of putting across our own way of thinking and our sense-making to others. For example, resistance in organizational settings often begins to arise through background conversations as changes are launched.

## IDEOLOGICAL BECOMING AS A STRUGGLE BETWEEN THE INDIVIDUAL AND THE SOCIAL

As an individual property, self-consciousness involves returning into oneself to see whether or not the change is warranted. It is also about "return[ing] to our own place" (Bakhtin 1990, 260) outside the change effort, in an attempt to form and consummate the reason for change. At this point, it is an individual effort more than anything else. It is also about personal readiness and the embodiment, or disembodiment, of the change effort.

Consciousness as a social phenomenon is something quite different, in the sense that it is only achieved when dialogized, and turned outward in conversation with others. It is truly and genuinely collaborative, and has its own momentum. It is not about returning to the social rather than oneself, as it is truly social in construction. It stands as a collective, having been co-constructed through the other, making it truly collaborative. However, consciousness as a social phenomenon can backfire when the other is not ready. Then, a defection is warranted and we prefer to eject or even defect from relating to the other, reducing the relational emphasis.

Can we truly achieve consciousness as a social phenomenon? The problem is that even though we talk about constantly exchanging meanings, we remain tied to a dominant selfhood, or a strong 'I' taking charge. Our ability to see consciousness as a shared social phenomenon is constrained by our view of it as an individual property. Bakhtin demonstrated awareness of this throughout his writings. Are we truly genuine in practicing the social in our dialogue?

There are always forces that push and pull the individual away from truly relating to the social. An awareness of working with each other and each of us wanting to defend our territorial rights spurs the desire to meet the other and to cross the boundary that separates. However, we then tend to keep consciousness as an individual property and protect our rights from others, which introduces into our consciousness an inclination to avoid 'playing the social game,' even though we know that it is necessary.

Such inclination often outstrips consciousness as a social meeting for another and through the other. It prevents us striving to relate to the other as a social property of our talk and conversations and in a genuine way. Without investing in our own consciousness (individual property), the desire for collaboration fades away. Because we have been tied up with a dominant 'I,' an arresting moment only reveals the powers of social consciousness.

Change is a genuine effort (self-consciousness) aimed at altering the status quo. It is also, and at the same time, a socially co-constructed effort shared with others on the basis of the commonality of the socially-embodied experiences of change. This is why it is important to ensure that the individual is given the opportunity to become self-aware of the change effort, but also why the collective effort needs to be mobilized for change to take root.

## EMBODYING UTTERANCES

There is an important issue concerned with the embodiment of the change effort. Consciousness and embodiment are closely entangled. They resonate with each other. Each of us brings our own views into contact with a range of other views. Internal dialogue is viable and in change, people often assume that a leader can have the 'leaderfulness' to be intellectually or dialectically self-sufficient. A leader who leads by ignoring or demolishing what the other is saying receives praise for making the argument compelling. For Bakhtin, however, that is not sufficient, because he sees the importance of the leader's internal dialogue resonating with what the other is saying in conversation as an interpersonal exchange. Here, consciousness emerges as social property. That was one important reason why Bakhtin explicitly emphasized the importance of embodiment in the interpersonal sense, namely one that is not singular (see Figure 3.2).

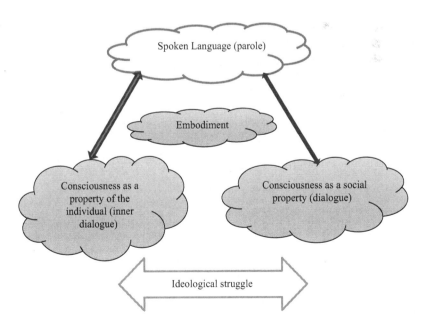

*Figure 3.2*   Bakhtin's treatment of consciousness, as an individual property and a shared social phenomenon

Bakhtin argued for consciousness as a social property but was also aware of the power of the dominant 'I' in deflating the social. For him, embodiment was about the body beginning to live for oneself, unified by cognitive, ethical, axiological, and aesthetic categories. However, he went further, noting that it is not only the embodiment of oneself but also of the other. He wrote:

> Only the other is *embodied* for me axiologically and aesthetically. In this respect, the body is not something self-sufficient: it needs the *other*, needs his recognition and his form-giving activity. Only the inner body (the body experienced as heavy) is *given* to a human being himself, the other's outer body [the phenomenal body] is not given but *set as a task*: I must actively produce it.
>
> (Bakhtin 1990, 51)

Note the meaning Bakhtin attached to his distinction between the body in the 'physical' sense and that of the phenomenal body, and how the latter always needs the relational other, embodying the 'other in me.' That is about our ability to relate to that other phenomenal body, providing us with the insight that their body is not that different from ours and that ours is not that different from theirs.

## DIALOGUE AND DIALECTIC

The concept of dialogue cannot simply mean 'pure dialogue' or to be 'without any dialectics.' Dialogue should not be seen as the one and only way of being dialogic. Rather, the principle of dialogue coincides with that of dialectics. As a concept, genuine dialogue implies a readiness to bring on board reason and dialectics as and when necessary. An open-ended dialogue is inclusive of authenticity and diversity. Bakhtin's thinking is in fact much more comprehensive than we have been led to think. Could it be that it should include aspects of dialectics? Bakhtin noted:

> The single adequate form for *verbally expressing* authentic human life is the *open-ended dialogue*. Life by its very nature is dialogic.
>
> (Bakhtin 1984, 293)

The dialogic process, therefore, cannot remain the same and is never a perpetuation of itself. It cannot be preserved in a fixed, unchanged formula absent of interruptions and conflicts likely to arise as we relate to the other and otherness. Sooner or later, it inherits the need for dialectics. This includes reasoning to itself through change and exchange with the other and otherness. Dialogue, therefore, needs to be co-established through dialogue and dialectics. Plastic bounds begin to dissolve to further its reach. It is also true that under certain conditions, dialogue is best with the 'tools' of dialectics, and might well call for elements such as objective measures, charts, forecasts, and tabulations.

Dialogue also inherits the need for polyphony. Pearce made an important distinction between the two dialogues and polyphony. She noted:

> 'Polyphony' is associated with the macrocosmic structure of the text (literally, its 'many voices') and 'dialogue' to reciprocating mechanisms *within* the smaller units of exchange, down to the individual word. (Italic in original)

(Pearce 1994, 46)

Clark and Holquist (1984, 242) saw the two terms as interchangeable, in the sense that 'polyphony' can be construed as the same as 'dialogic.' They noted that "the phenomenon that Bakhtin calls 'polyphony' is simply another name for dialogism."

## SOCIAL CONSCIOUSNESS AS A PROPERTY OF DIALOGUE

Dialogue involves reflecting and being aware of oneself as well as of other 'selves.' This point about consciousness being a social property needs some exploration. An important aspect of Bakhtin's thinking was his idea of dialogue migrating across boundaries. Pollard provided a thesis that fundamentally saw consciousness (internal dialogue) as social. She painted Bakhtin's work as largely anchored in social consciousness. Pollard's interpretation of Bakhtin is convincing, though largely misunderstood. On the basis that boundaries separate the individual from the social, Pollard (2008, 36–37) concluded by noting that "consciousness is therefore not a property of the individual but a shared social phenomenon." She did not defend her interpretation that the social offsets the individual.

The most obvious take on Pollard is that she was ignoring the ontology of the person wanting to relate to the other and otherness. I therefore disagree with her for a very simple reason: that lived human experience is not a one-dimensional interpretation of the social. The individual and the social are both lived at once and cannot be separated. Pollard's suggestion that Bakhtin productively saw consciousness as merely social is difficult to accept, although justified on the grounds that dialogue is a shared social phenomenon that is constantly in flux due to changing contexts. For Bakhtin, however, consciousness stemmed first and foremost from being on the boundary, and reflecting on oneself. Here there is a reasonable inclination for self-questioning and reflection based on what the other is saying. Bakhtin's idea that "the self is the gift of the other" (quoted in Kershner 1989, X) suggests that selfhood is influenced by what the other gives. This means that the way that we relate is not only social. This deep awareness of

## Everybody should be quiet near a little stream and listen

*Figure 3.3*    Everybody should be quiet near a little stream and listen
*Source: Open House for Butterflies* by Ruth Krauss, illustrated by Maurice Sendak

the self as related to the other makes us willing to inhabit what the other is feeling and thinking—their desires, dreams, and aspiration, or even the job they are about to lose. This could prove insightful when considered in the light of changes. It may even be that the sound of music or of running water can be considered as utterances that alter the self (see Figure 3.3).

Bakhtin's explanation of consciousness is, therefore, far from exhaustive. It ignores the prospect of linking how we feel to how we physically become aware of the other. Even though Bakhtin conceived of consciousness as a seamless interrelationship of both intra-actions with self (internal, as I-for-myself) and interactions between people (social activity, as in I-for-the-other and the other-for-me), his account stops short of drawing on the body as the locus of being. It does not fully consider the notion of embodiment. Such a view is not a full interpretation of "look[ing] into the eyes of another" (Bakhtin 1984, 287) because it unacceptably stops short of a more explicit account of the inter-corporeal.

In implicating change and changing, I suggest that Bakhtin's explanation of consciousness can be rendered more complete by adding Merleau-Ponty's existential thinking, where the phenomenal body is brought to bear on how we think and act. Merleau-Ponty noted:

> It is my body which gives significance not only to the natural object, but also to cultural objects like words . . . the word 'warm', for example, induces a kind of experience of warmth . . . [t]he word 'hard' produces a sort of stiffening of the back and the neck.
>
> (Merleau-Ponty 1962, 235 and 273)

I argue, therefore, that Merleau-Ponty's treatment offers a more comprehensive account, where embodiment is clearly of consciousness. If the very existence of dialogue can be defined in terms of consciousness, which Bakhtin's explanation implies, then where is consciousness located in relation to embodiment? A re-examination of consciousness invokes, and in fact allows for, embodiment. Such a view provides a better interpretation of "looking into the eyes of the other" because it invokes embodiment and brings it into consciousness.

The identification of consciousness with embodiment is important, because it signifies a progression towards the idea of a relational being. It confirms consciousness and how we feel about change as a genuine representation of embodiment shared with others. Pollard (2008, 87–88) insightfully noted that "to describe consciousness purely in dialogic terms does not account for human desires." A more complete account of consciousness could and should include human desires as well as prehensions (feelings). This would reveal how consciousness is inter-corporeal when supplemented by our own desires to understand the world around us and the challenges we face as we inhabit ever-changing situations. By recognizing consciousness side-by-side with embodiment, the commonality of stress and strain are understood and acted upon. This understanding reveals that change and the willingness to embrace it should be linked to embodiment, ensuring that the individual can become self-aware of the change effort.

## POLYPHONY: A SENSE OF TRUTH

Polyphony is constituted by an important criterion: a dialogic sense of truth, closely linked to the willingness to express that sense of truth through utterances. Bakhtin explained that this dialogic sense of truth means that we often run into distinct beliefs, ways of thinking or organizing that are "separate thoughts, assertions, propositions that can by themselves be true or untrue, depending on their relationship to the subject and independent of the carrier to whom they belong" (Bakhtin 1984, 93).

As I noted earlier on, the notion of polyphony means simultaneity of talk unmerged into any unified perspective, in the sense that no one person's talk is subordinated to any other and so each voice has its own embodied meaning. In his book *Problems of Dostoevsky's Poetics* and his essay *Discourse in the Novel*, Bakhtin talked about certainty and truth as entwined criteria constitutive of polyphony, and needed to develop an argument against the mind–body duality inherited from Cartesian modes based on separating one's own subjectivity from that of the other. He differentiated between two features of thought, or truth: monologic and dialogic.

As I discussed in previous chapters, the monologic is built on separate mindsets or positions of thought, and tends to build an authority on its own, based on a system of thought. Such systems are taken as unified and universal. They get taken independently and grasped as true. The dialogic, in contrast, "requires a plurality of consciousness . . . . [which] in principle cannot be fitted within the bounds of a single consciousness." By plurality of consciousnesses, Bakhtin means all the mundane and everyday talk during a meaningful conversation, when at least two voices come together.

The monologic applies to literature but when extended it could also apply to management thought and epistemologies, as in Weberian theories or explanations on the importance of formalization in extending or building bureaucratic organizations, or in the importance of large data sets in building management knowledge. It, therefore, has implications for managerial practice. It will have its own adherents and yet will remain monologic. A monologic thought could form its own subset with another that is consonant with it. We can, therefore, see managerialism as an ideology relating to new liberalism, even though its sphere of influence remains organizational functioning.

As noted earlier, a monologic sense of truth is based around the notion of "separate thought:" something that is independent of the person speaking (Bakhtin 1984, 93). The actual content of the thought itself, as in managerialism, is distinct. It is not something that the speaker has control over. Under managerialism, there is an obsession with standardized performance outcomes and spreadsheets, rooted in a rationalist epistemology. Bakhtin described such base of knowledge as "no-man's thought" (1984, 93), meaning that it stands outside the organization (e.g., Total Quality Management and its applications, or a system of digitized staff performance) in some reified way. The organization does little but bring it into the setting with some possible adaptations. It could easily be administered or spoken of through one person and even if it is managed by more than one person, can still be verbalized or articulated by one representative on behalf of the team. What is important here is the implication of such systems in extending the subtle reach of managerialism and its ideology. It is not the content of its ideological system per se as much as ways to sustain system controls based on the single consciousness of one person or the team. In terms of the aesthetics of change, they are neither about uplifting the post-human mode of management, in the sense of promoting the aesthetics of the human side, nor the embodiment of the change effort. Rather, they are about wanting to decenter the human factor by re-configuring organizational processes, including those of HR functions, in a way that promotes a monologic sense of truth.

Even if another consciousness, such as an external consultant or change agent, is co-opted into the system, that new consciousness may do little but agree or extend what is being said, often becoming fully merged. This is consciousness of consensus. It seeks feedback, interpretations, and extensions, only to take them on board on a very selective basis.

In monologic contexts, thoughts are seen as absolute. A monologic truth is more likely to receive attention and get circulated as an important email. It might even enjoy a warm reception because it has the intention to preserve order, unification, development of systems, and where fragmentation and diversity is masked by uniformity of rules and procedures. But that can only occur in contexts where consensus is dominant.

When a CEO invites people to attend a staff forum to discuss working together to make a healthy and safe workplace culture, such an invitation will have a genuine sense of truth only if the CEO is willing to listen to what people have to say. If the invitation to attend and the actual proceedings involve little but defining a 'safe workplace,' as imagined by the single consciousness of the CEO, such an idea will cease to be a theme. It will only be combined with the 'hero's' image. If the CEO already has ideas about a new top-down system of rules, procedures, and sanctions, then any move from the predetermined position is much less likely.

A monologic truth is dialectic because it has a structure that allows it to be comprehended by a single consciousness. Bakhtin is uncompromising in his rejection of a narrowly conceived view of the self separate from others. Such a view of the polyphonic self accords necessarily with Bakhtin's rejection of the mind separate from the body. For him, 'self' is social and is essentially human, because it is materially embodied through utterances. More importantly, because it is social it becomes "overpopulated with the intentions of others" (Bakhtin 1981, 294). Booth explained:

> We encounter these selves as what [Bakhtin] calls 'languages', the voices spoken by others. Languages are of course made not only of words; they are whole systems of meaning, each language constituting an interrelated set of beliefs or norms. 'Language' is often thus for [Bakhtin] roughly synonymous with 'ideology'. Each person is constituted as a hierarchy of languages, each language being a kind of ideology-brought-into-speech.
>
> (Booth 1986, 151)

Bakhtin explained that, peculiar to polyphony, we have an embodiment of a dialogic sense of truth because it is based on collective consciousness. He, therefore, saw it as a viable alternative to the disembodied notion of the monologic sense of truth. According to Bakhtin (1984), there are at least three conditions or benchmarks for a monologic sense of truth applied to organizational settings. These include that it:

- Insists on some "separate thought," in that a thought or way of thinking will have its own turf bounded by a certain preference to some explicit way of thinking.
- Seeks unity and uniformity within its own system and yet at the same time repels any other system having counter-thoughts.
- Rejects any outside input and sustains itself from within its own sphere of capability based on its own 'surplus'.

A correlate of the above is that a monologic sense of truth always awaits more standardization as it celebrates the achievement of systems. It is, therefore, functional in terms of providing a framework outlining the way in which an organization is governed in a social-scientific sense. It explains connections between components of governance that seek order, patterns, and unification, and so it is argued to be functional. It has its own form and structure that allows it be understood and repeated by a single accreditation, or singular consciousness.

Another correlate concerns the way in which truth is justified on the grounds of transparency, inclusiveness, and equity. The idea is that these should be construed as criteria for arriving at a single truth, and yet when it comes to applying that truth, we find that these grand statements fall short. This is because systems preclude the possibility of multiple consciousnesses entering the decision-making process. To challenge the view that all truth must be systematic, unitary, and monologic, Bakhtin moved away from considering that the world can be seen through a single voice or consciousness, by searching for a counter-narrative largely driven by a new interpretation that allows one to see the possibility of polyphony. Importantly, Bakhtin noted that:

> It is quite possible to imagine and postulate a unified truth that requires a plurality of consciousnesses, one that cannot in principle be fitted into the bounds of a single consciousness, one that is, so to speak, by its very nature *full of event potential* and is born at a point of contact among various consciousnesses.
>
> (Bakhtin 1984, 81; italic in original)

In an environment of managerialism, organization members contribute to forming each other's efforts in reinforcing the system. Even though they speak to each other and exchange information, their exchange is often confined to the protocols governing system adherence. Any utterance aimed at invigorating an exchange is sidetracked and so utterance, in the way it has been defined so far, is devalued. Genuine interaction of consciousness is almost immobilized through responses such as "these are the rules," "the onus is on you to follow," and "we will take this into account next time the procedures are being reviewed." When genuine interaction is not a feature of system maintenance, genuine dialogue becomes impossible. Managerial fads are an example of a dialectic act conceived and promoted as single consciousness. Examples of monologic truths that were ready to lend themselves to multiple consciousnesses include the persistent occurrence of Total Quality Management, and the significant changes in the way it made itself open to other systems.

## CONCLUSION

Dialogue will reshape, indeed is already re-shaping, the way we think of change and change communication. No issue will be more at stake than an in-depth treatment of polyphony. Diversity and plurality 'disturb' organizational studies debates in two key ways. First, how does an organization and its top management deal with issues of self and social representations as change is introduced? Second, how are different conceptions of dialogue treated, to the point of their exclusion of dialectics and reasoning?

Without the Bakhtinian notion of dialogue, the trouble will, of course, remain, with dialogue used loosely and little elaboration of either how excess of meaning is achieved or the role of heteroglossia, through which dialogue is accomplished. An unwarranted use of the term is evident in the more popular notion of dialogue (e.g., Senge 1990), and in the way it references the achievement of superficial levels of consensus driven by a hidden authoritative discourse, where individuals are manipulated.

The notion of polyphony has great potential for organizations and has garnered much interest. What is important is not how the organization sees its members, but how they see and explain themselves. The implication is how the rules and norms appear to organization members and how they see or define their roles and importance. Polyphony has great potential to add value to current drives in organizations toward the process of combining different voices, gender, race, and other differences such as religious, linguistic, regional, and professional groupings. Importantly, diversity is also about multi-voicedness. The emphasis on polyphony is therefore timely, given the burgeoning interest in designing organizations where diversity is valued.

## REFERENCES

Argyris, Chris. 1993. *Knowledge for Action*. San Francisco: Jossey-Bass.

Bakhtin, Mikhail Mikhailovitch. 1981. *The Dialogic Imagination*, edited by Michael Holquist, translated by Carey Emerson and Michael Holquist. Austin: University of Texas Press.

———. 1984. *Problems of Dostoyevsky's Poetics*, edited and translated by Carey Emerson. Minneapolis: University of Minnesota Press.

———. 1986. *Speech genres and other essays*, edited by Carey Emerson and Michael Holquist, translated by Vern McGee). Austin: University of Texas Press.

———. 1990. *Art and Answerability: Early Philosophical Essays*, edited by Michael Holquist and Vadim Liapunov. Austin: University of Texas Press.

Baxter, Leslie A. and Barbara M. Montgomery. 1996. *Relating: Dialogues and Dialectics*. New York: Guilford Press.

Blackburn, Simon. 2006. *Plato's Republic: A Biography*. Allen and Unwin.

Boje, David. 2001. *Narrative Methods for Organizational and Communication Research*. London: Sage.

Booth, Wayne. 1986. "Freedom of Interpretation: Bakhtin and the Challenge of Feminist Criticism." In *Bakhtin: Essays and Dialogues on His Work*, edited by Gary Saul Morson, 145–76. Chicago: University of Chicago press.

Buber, Martin. 1970. *I and Thou*, translated by W. Kaufmann. New York: Scribners.

Clark, Katerina and Michael Holquist. 1984. *Mikhail Bakhtin*. Cambridge, MA: Harvard University Press.

Cooperrider, David L. and Diana Whitney. 2005. "A Positive Revolution in Change: Appreciative Inquiry." In *Appreciative Inquiry: Rethinking Human Organization Toward a Positive Theory of Change*, edited by David L. Cooperrider, Peter F. Sorensen, Diana Whitney and Therese F. Yaeger, 3–26. Champaign, IL: Stipes.

Ehrenberg, Victor. 1973. *From Solon to Socrates: Greek history and Civilization during the 6th and 5th Centuries B.C.* London: Routledge.

Ford, Jeffrey D. and Laurie W. Ford. 1995. "The role of conversations in producing intentional change in organizations." *Academy of Management Review* 20 (3): 541–70.

Hirschkop, Ken. 1999. *Mikhail Bakhtin: An Aesthetic for Democracy.* Oxford: Oxford University Press.

Holquist, Michael. 1983. "Answering as authoring: Mikhail Bakhtin's trans-linguistics." *Critical Inquiry* 10 (2): 307–19.

Jabri, Muayyad. 2004. Change as shifting identities: A dialogic perspective. Journal of Organizational Change Management, 17, 566–77.

———. 2005. "Narrative identity achieved through utterances: the implications of Bakhtin for managing change and learning." *Philosophy of Management* 5 (3): 83–90.

———. 2009a. "Promoting exchange between East and West management cultures: the role of dialogue." *Journal of Management and Organization* 15: 514–23.

———. 2009b. "Bakhtin meets Whitehead: a process view of leadership." First International Symposium on Process Organization Studies, Pissouri, Cyprus, 11–13 June.

Jabri, Muayyad, Allyson Adrian and David Boje. 2008. "Reconsidering the role of conversations in change communication: a contribution based on Bakhtin." *Journal of Organizational Change Management* 21: 667–85.

Jowett, Benjamin. 1986. *The Republic: Plato.* New York: Prometheus Books.

Kakabadse, Nada, Andrew Kakabadse, Linda Lee-Davies and Nick Johnson. 2011. "Deliberative inquiry: integrated ways of working in Children's Services." *Systemic Practice and Action Research* 24 (1): 67–84.

Kershner, R.B. 1989. *Joyce, Bakhtin, and Popular Literature.* Chapel Hill: University of North Carolina.

McNamee, Sheila and Kenneth Gergen. 1999. *Relational Responsibility: Resources for Sustainable Dialogue.* London: Sage.

Merleau-Ponty, Maurice. 1962. *Phenomenology of Perception.* London: Routledge and Kegan Paul.

Nikulin, Dmitri. 2010. *Dialectic and Dialogue.* Stanford: Stanford University Press.

Pearce, Lynne. 1994. *Reading Dialogics.* London: Edward Arnold.

Pollard, Rachel. 2008. *Dialogue and Desire: Mikhail Bakhtin and the Linguistic Turn in Psychotherapy.* London: Karnac.

Robinson, Richard. 1953. *Plato's Earlier Dialectic*, 2nd ed. Oxford: Clarendon Press. Reprinted in *The Philosophy of Socrates* edited by Gregory Vlastos. Anchor, 1971. Edited in hypertext by Andrew Chrucky, June 2, 2005.

Senge, Peter. 1990. *The Fifth Discipline: The Art and Practice of the Learning Organization.* New York: Doubleday.

Taylor, James R., Francis Cooren, Nicoce Giroux and Daniel Robichaud. 1996. "The communicational basis of organization: between the conversation and the text." *Communication Theory* 6: 1–39.

Todorov, Tzvetan. 1984. *Mikhail Bakhtin: The Dialogical Principle*, translated by Wlad Godzich. Manchester: Manchester University Press.

Van Dijk, Teun A. 1997. "Discourse as Interaction in Society." In *Discourse Studies: A Multidisciplinary Introduction. Vol. 2: Discourse as Social Interaction*, edited by Teun A. Van Dijk, 1–37. London: Sage.

Weick, Karl E. and Robert E. Quinn. 1999. "Organizational change and development." *Annual Review of Psychology* 50 (1): 361–86.

Zappen, James P. 1996. "Bakhtin's Socrates." *Rhetoric Review* 15 (1): 66–83.

———. 2011. *The Rebirth of Dialogue.* New York: State University of New York Press.

# 4 The Role of Dialectic in Managing Change

> Where is the wisdom we have lost in knowledge?
> Where is the knowledge we have lost in information?
>
> T. S. Eliot (1934, 161)

Dialectics emerged from the work of Georg Wilhelm Friedrich Hegel (1770–1831), who believed that what is rational has to be real (Hegel 1977). In other words, he suggested that only what is verified or supported rationally is real and so what is real is also rational, reasonable, and substantiated. To know reality, one has to work through opposites providing rational explanations to form some sort of firm and rigid synthesis. The idea is to shape reality in a composite that is firm and inelastic and yet has synthetic unity between opposites. Applied to change, one could argue that downsizing would need to be evidenced (thesis) against outsourcing (antithesis), with both being supported in an effort to reach a synthesis. The synthesis will drive action. All information and costs would need to be detailed and this would need to be constituted as a reality concerned with downsizing.

Dialectics, therefore, has implications for the adoption of ideologies (e.g., managerialism) determining how change is managed in time and the thinking that goes with it. Dialectics has its own inherent logic. The whole truth exists between alternative explanations, not in terms of stages but in terms of the whole. Everything is subject to purposeful rules and comes to an end once these rules are enacted. A 'synthesis' has its own path of development in that the aim of every opposition is to reach a closure, or a milestone in decision-making, in ways that are intact and convincing, making the system appear functional.

In reflecting on dialogue and dialectic, we are confronted with a problem. Do we treat them as opposites or are they interrelated? Scholars, including Nikulin (2006), suggested that dialectic emerged from the spirit of dialogue, and vice versa. The choice between these ways of thinking, in a crucial sense, hinges upon whether one sees them as interacting or located in very different spheres and whether one should 'succumb' to dialectic modes of managing change or override these modes by giving preference to dialogue.

In dialectic, therefore, change is driven by rational explanations supported by a view of the world that human action can be reliably measured and that regularities can be discovered and reduced to their causes. We can explain the design of one team formation over another by positing a thesis for and a thesis against. We can then proceed to identify an explanation through which the solution is sought. A problem or an issue facing the team has to be shown to exist. Its manifestations would need to be shown and once this is done, we can seek explanations for a specified end point or solution.

## DEFINING DIALECTIC IN MANAGING CHANGE

To date, change management has to a large extent relied on strength of foresight from managing change as being based on the logic of discovery and inferences through precise identification of symptoms (e.g, declining sales) of the presenting issues. Understanding the relations between symptoms will have important implications for how causes are identified, readiness is created, and modes of interventions are formulated. In diagnosing change, for example, emphasis is often placed on alignment of entities, use of problem-centric diagnosis, and the formulation of rules and policies, all aimed at enhancing articulation of action plans and the achievement of objectives. Indeed, a dialectic mode has its own affinity to the knowledge of symptoms and causes based on a mode of thinking that is largely problem-driven. A problem-centric mode also leads to easily definable and measurable actions. Data can be gathered and measured and then appropriate interventions put in place based on the feedback and survey analyses. We can see the use of dialectic in the downsizing of operations where premises are argued for or against, as part and parcel of justification. It is easy for people to point out what does not work. However, when we ask people how they would like the situation, they have trouble articulating a vision, and so opt to point out what is wrong now.

A dialectic model, which is of course based on logic of explanations, has been popular in a world seeking to achieve certainty and predictability. Whether it is to reason or to put the case for one course of action over another, dialectics has made this discussion, as well as diagnosis, intervention, and evaluation, possible. Dialectics lends itself to ways of thinking and beliefs that aim to enhance efficiency, as well as control. It is widely accepted in meetings when it comes to arguing the 'case' and can be legitimated through rules and procedures working with the opposition rather than exclusion.

It is logical that if something does not work, you fix it (i.e., change it). Why would we change something if there is no problem? Then again, if we look from a 'continuous improvement' perspective, we will always be looking for ways to change and improve results. A major limitation is in the interpretation of the problem. One manager may see a totally different set of problems from another. The problem needs to be clearly analyzed, defined, and agreed before the change is embarked upon.

Success can be clearly articulated through measurements when an action is complete. The assumption is to identify and isolate one set of causes over another. We come to accept that symptoms can have multiple causes, which are not always evident from the outset. This means that the change has no distinct end. Identifying symptoms (e.g., declining sales) helps us to identify and possibly reverse the situation. However, such simplicity ignores the fact that symptoms are often in a state of flux, can have multiple causes, and the overlap between causes is often complex. All this detracts from dialogue and creates a culture where the emphasis is placed on locating the cause and allocating blame.

There are reasons for considering dialectic and its role in managing change. It can prove helpful to 'unsettle' the dominant emphasis on dialectic by allowing for more conversational space between people or by asking the 'unaskable,' such as 'What assumptions are you really making?' In their seminal article on modes of intervention, Blake and Mouton (1976) found that it is sometimes useful to ask people to confront their ways of thinking and reasoning, as well as the deep assumptions they are making. As symptoms and causes are discussed, attention should also be paid to the assumptions being made. Through dialogue, we are enabled to understand others' deep assumptions (described as the 'master program'). By doing so, a change agent is better able to see situations from more than one angle and so engage in learning and co-learning.

An emphasis on dialectic alone may sometimes prove unwarranted even under conditions where managerial logic is fully dominant. We need some sort of malleability, a notion that lies between fluidity and fixity, and to accept the capacity of the dialectic for deformation (Malabou 2005) or even for destroying systems and procedures. Dialectic can sometimes compel others to concede, even if they remain utterly unconvinced by the argument. The point here is not about us wanting dialogue to come to the rescue, but for dialectic to showcase malleability by surfacing the reasons for disbelief and even rewarding those who are keen to initiate change in rules and procedures.

## DIALECTIC IN ACTION

Dialectic is about the capacity to grasp relations and to reason and articulate them. Its underlying impulse is to make monologic decisions and put them forward as reasons or results driving action. The call for method started with Aristotle, but dialectic was later used by Kant in his scholarly investigation of reason. Gradually, however, the notion of dialectic was extended by Hegel (1977) to include reason.

*Figure 4.1*   Formation of structures and designs based on reification

Organizations and individuals tend to search for dialectic. There are no limits as to how norms (unwritten rules) give way to written rules and how written rules are set to achieve change. Rules can become very unyielding, and the more rules are created the more are needed (see Figure 4.1).

Dialectic has provided, and continues to provide, the dominant mode by which managerial logic is argued or problems are identified and diagnosed. Its use in communicating the reasons for change is so characteristic that it is difficult to see change happening without reliance on reason supported by evidence. Such reasons often include the need for changes in structures and systems and the benefits likely to accrue if the desired state is accomplished quickly and efficiently. Whether transitional or transformational change is considered, members of the organization are often expected to embrace change on the basis that the desired state needs to be achieved.

Sciabarra (1998, 286) saw dialectic primarily as a "methodological orientation" and as a "disposition" for offering a formal structure for analysis. He suggested that the emphasis is placed on arguing the case, identifying symptoms, and differentiating them from the causes of the presenting problem. Applied to change, reason invites the development of systems and rules. These are extended to key performance indicators, goal-setting routines, and performance reviews. Reason also calls for structures to be configured for systems and procedures to be maintained.

## DIALECTIC: AN EMPHASIS ON THE LOGIC OF SYMPTOMS AND CAUSES

In the problem-centric model, a change situation is framed as a problem (the glass is half-empty). A problem-centric mode of diagnosis is largely based on logical empiricism and its variant, positivism. Logical positivism is rooted in a philosophy of science based on the belief that knowledge is only valid when supported by assertions showing the cause of the problem and supported by measurement. Applied to diagnosis, the fundamental premise of logical empiricism involves two interrelated steps:

1. Searching for and logically verifying symptoms through data-gathering, measurement, and experimentation; and
2. Attributing symptoms to some defined reason or cause, and providing evidence that the symptom–cause relationship is factually meaningful.

According to Cronshaw and McCulloch (2008, 89), diagnosis is "highly desirable if not essential" for informed organizational development and change. A diagnostic (problem-centric) model is presumed to be most effective when it is aimed at a specific objective, and performed in a competent and sensitive manner, based on data. It is guided by the premise that there is one reality and that this can be discovered using objective problem-solving methods supported by data. According to Bushe and Marshak (2009, 350), valid data are assumed to "reflect or mirror an underlying objective reality." The process of data-gathering is, therefore, central to the diagnostic effort leading to outcomes such as downsizing, forced redundancies, restructuring, outsourcing, or mergers. In reality, such outcomes are treated as either 'trophies' or grotesque, much as Bakhtin describes in *Rabelais and His World* as "a study of the semantics of the body, the different meanings of the body's limbs, apertures, and functions" (Clark and Holquist 1984, 299). It is thus like the organization having a 'body' that celebrates through defecating (e.g., downsizing) and copulating (e.g., mergers) in what is argued to be an effective and reasoned way for managing change.

Dialectic is about putting forward an argument that provides an explanation, designed to inform decision-making. It is often used in discussions and debates in organizational settings including meetings, reports, and emails, newsletters, and marketing and corporate communication. It involves an act of 'dialecting' or drawing inferences (interpretations) affecting the work setting. It falls close to the definition of an act to provide factual or substantive support for a statement made or a premise based on some authoritative statement and supporting information. It relies on the use and application of what appears to be a logical method involving a statement, or a thesis, an inference, and then a relevant conclusion made in support of the statement (see Figure 4.2).

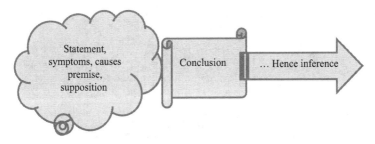

*Figure 4.2*   Process of an act of dialectic

The example below is based on an excerpt from a conversation which criticized the sole use of Total Quality Management (TQM) accomplished without a Just-in-Time (JIT) system for ordering of inventory.

> *Thesis:* We are using TQM anyway. What is the point of having another system?
> *Conditional inference:* . . . Therefore . . .
> *Conclusion:* I think such a proposition is a waste of time and money.

The second person responds with a counterargument (antithesis). Again, the antithesis consists of a *premise and a conditional inference. Both are immediately followed by a relevant conclusion(s).*

> *Antithesis:* TQM hasn't been working.
> *Conditional inference:* . . . Hence . . .
> *Conclusion 1:* We need JIT to supplement it.
> *Conclusion 2:* We need to ensure that optimal levels of stock are maintained.

Discussions and ongoing talk, therefore, start with inferences. Such inferences could be about almost anything. In an organizational setting, they often take the form of reasoning about issues such as levels of formalization, social and material aspects of the work context, span of control, coordination or leadership matrix design, pay and effort, enlargement and enrichment of jobs, and mergers versus acquisitions. They also explore areas of concern such as participation or the launch of an empowerment scheme, enhancing efficiency or effectiveness, and differentiation versus integration.

Inferences lead to more forms of talk based on alternating thesis and antithesis, followed by an attempt to remove the contradiction in a sort of synthesis. This is illustrated in Figure 4.3.

Our previous example illustrates the beginning of an argument understood as the disagreement. This contains an antinomy where the claim and

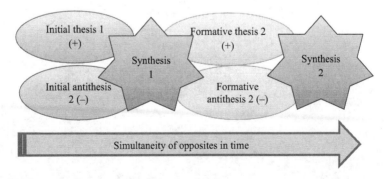

*Figure 4.3*   The process of synthesis in dialectic

counterclaim appear to contradict each other, but both are made to appear reasonably correct. Such an antinomy often occurs in discussion, where almost every statement appears valid and legitimate on its own.

Person 1: TQM has been working well.
Person 2: TQM has *not* been working well.

Person 1 wants to assert the 'truth' of the proposition that TQM has been working well. Person 2 responds with a verbal emphasis denoting that "TQM has *not* been working well." There is a strong potential difference brewing in the conversation, culminating in the need for a rule or evidence of some sort.

**SUMMARY**

Dialectic is driven by reason supported by inferences. It provides the basis for organizations to respond to change in the hope of attaining better management of systems and processes.

As Figure 4.3 shows, a synthesis might also give way to another round of alternating thesis and antithesis. In time, progression becomes necessary, leading to another round. Branching often occurs, as the implication of one decision starts to foreshadow the need for other decisions or interventions. For example, a synthesis may have been achieved by the development of a performance management system. This might invoke successive dialectic, involving the need for decisions about the development of alternative ways to complement the performance system, such as mentoring, training, and revision of lines of promotion.

## MANIFESTATIONS OF DIALECTIC

Synthesis is used primarily as a quasi-equilibrium point in the Hegelian sense, where it can always give way to another thesis and antithesis. In other words, change is accomplished by managing dialectic to achieve synthesis (equilibrium). Other important manifestations characteristic of dialectic include:

- Logical arguments are based on aggregates and supported by tabulations, statistics (for example, absences, turnover, and lateness), and use of evidence. Ranking and/or ratings of options are used for managing probable objections.
- Every change situation needs to be approached with possible 'conflict' in mind. Options to resolve conflict are understood in dialectic terms.

- Forces promoting change are dialectically identified and logically positioned with respect to counterforces resisting change.
- Interventions are meant to be direct and immediate, and are best achieved through the development of written rules and procedures, rather than norms and other informal ways.
- The material character (promotional lines, pay differentials, etc.) giving rise to conflict is analyzed.
- It is assumed that the system is reified and can be managed from a point or location external to stakeholders.
- It is assumed that the interaction of any two or more subsystems can be fully managed from a point external to the processes and actors.
- Perceptions determine behavioral tendencies. Such behavioral tendencies are measurable and can be aggregated in a climate audit or engagement survey and then used as feedback with objective validity.
- There is an emphasis on examining how parts fit together and function, and whether they should be amended or replaced.
- The concept of 'process' is replaced with 'product,' an emphasis on outcome, action, and achievement of goals.

## THE AFFINITY BETWEEN DIALECTIC AND THE PROBLEM-CENTRIC MODE

It may be useful to give a brief explanation of Katz and Kahn's (1966) open systems theory to showcase its close affinity with the problem-centric mode of diagnosis. Katz and Kahn developed open systems theory in an attempt to construct a fundamental model of organizations as functioning entities. Their theory has three important features:

- An organization is embedded in and is a creature of its environment, to the extent that it relies on profitable exchanges with its environment for survival.
- The organization is viewed as an open system of regularly interacting or interrelating subsystems. It has the ability to adapt to environmental changes.
- Subsystems (such as R&D or marketing) are viewed as critically important for the structuring of the organization. Differentiated subsystems have their own distinct areas of specialization. Such subsystems are central drivers for system effectiveness.

Diagnosis using an open systems perspective emphasizes the importance of proper analysis of environmental needs and the design of information systems, embracing market intelligence and control systems. The onus is on management to close gaps in performance, amend discrepancies between existing and desired states, and resolve performance issues stemming from a lack of coordination and integration of subsystems. The task of the change agent, therefore, involves making sense of the issues preventing the system from becoming better organized by clearing blockages in feedback and openness.

Diagnosis using an open systems perspective, therefore, involves detecting signs or symptoms of chaos or disorganization, as a measure of the problems and disruptions that exist in the organization. It also looks for ways to manage disorganized processes across all functions. It entails resolving problems and concerns whenever a gap emerges, as subsystems bring in energy and information, and export output back to the environment.

The reliance of the organization on profitable exchanges with its environment draws attention to the need to diagnose all outputs that the organization exports into the environment and to evaluate how these outputs are performing–for example, in terms of sales figures or through feedback from customers and other stakeholders.

Problems preventing the organization from fostering an environment of openness and feedback are diagnosed and dealt with. In the process of enhancing system capability, there is an emphasis on preventing disruptions that could hinder the creation of such an environment.

For example, the entities of strategy, structure, and technology are aligned in the design of an organization. The design should be sensitive to changes in each of these entities. Such sensitivity needs to be achieved on the basis of repeated cycles of ongoing adjustments in the degree of fit or misfit between each pair of entities. Such adjustments are organization-specific.

Problem-centric diagnosis is, therefore, viewed as vital for gaining a clear understanding of intended output characteristics, including quality and timeliness, and of the inputs required to achieve this. It should always aim to maintain the steady state and detect signs or symptoms of problems and disruptions.


## BAKHTIN'S STANCE ON DIALECTIC

Gardiner explained that dialectics is generally associated with a way of thinking that is essentially managerialist, in the sense that it relies on a mode, or even a code of thinking that claims to have a privileged insight into almost any type of change and is based on an approach that "assumes arrogantly that the essential structure of society [organization], and the overarching sequence of historical development, can be described and analysed with what Marx himself called the precision of the natural sciences" (Gardiner 2000, 119).

The ever-increasing emphasis on managerial logic has taken hold of organizations. In her work *The Future of Humanities*, Malabou (2015) identified a very important and very serious threat that appears to constitute a calamity facing organizations, as more and more organizations continue to pursue a path where measurement and precision of rules are used to manage change and are consciously embedded in managerialism based on exacerbating pursuit of a monologic sense of truth. There are externally constituted forces that push towards a frontier where organizations are managed as if they are constituted and articulated by the dictates of science and measurement. Malabou noted that

> the most accurate concept of the frontier is currently being elaborated and articulated by science, and no longer by the disciplines that constitute the Humanities any longer. Science is gradually becoming a discourse on frontiers, on limits, and has thus begun to deprive the Humanities of their proper content or task: the reflection upon frontiers and limits.
>
> (Malabou 2015, 1)

In configuring the frontier, there are thus both internal forces exacerbating managerialism, and also externally-constituted calamities. These enable and encourage organizations to continue with what they have been doing, strengthening the frontier through reliance on more dialectics and more rules, reviews, and ideologies largely driven by a monologic sense of truth where the human side of organizations is subordinated to science. It is not surprising that once the frontier of dialectics is consolidated, then polyphony in its dialogic sense of truth is internally compromised.

What was important for Gardiner (2000) and others who have written on Bakhtin is that structures and processes, whether social or organizational, are constituted as a social reality embedded in a dialogic process. Shotter (2008, 510) put this elegantly by noting that " even in my speaking of an object, of, say, a 'business plan', a 'spreadsheet', a 'person', . . . I am never speaking neutrally, indifferently, with no particular attitude," and so there are other alternative ways of conceptualizing social reality. Bakhtin's method is one such approach, where utterance is the most important entity in the way that reality is expressed.

Managerialism consists of pre-constituted entities opposing each other. Dialectics is used to resolve contradictions achieved through notions such as alignment of one entity with another based on some inherent logic. The dialectic celebrates the imposition of rules to ensure a state of fit, allowing for closure and conformity in line with the logic of a vision or strategic plan, where people are induced to celebrate at least two achievements:

- Celebrating equality and equity and yet ignoring differences, so polyphony is compromised by calling for more rules to reward those supportive of the system.
- Celebrating transparency by referencing practices that rigidly destroy voice. In dealing with noise generated by expunging difference, steps are taken to deputize decision-making, delegating and legitimating it

at lower levels within the organizational hierarchy, necessitating the generation of further rules to make it more achievable.

It takes a while to see why we should lament such apparent successes, much as it takes time to understand the pitfalls of managerialism. That is because understanding requires a close examination of rules and procedures and how these evolve over time to further the reach of stagnation, demise, and destruction. Under these conditions, it becomes hard for simultaneity of talk to replace monologic sense of truth, unless or until we introduce the notion of *plasticity*. This concept can be understood as "the capacity to receive form, and a capacity to produce form" (Malabou 2005, 9). She believed plasticity was highly disruptive and, therefore, enabled destruction of single-hearted monologic truth. Reflecting on her own experiences in respect of Hegelian dialectics and that Heidegger's reading of Hegel, Malabou (2010, 9; italic in original) elegantly noted "plasticity thus appeared to me from the outset as *a structure of transformation and destruction of presence and the present.*"

## CONTRASTING THE TWO MODES

The following table (see Table 4.1) highlights some of the important contrasts between dialogue and dialectic. The typology is only indicative of a very broad spectrum of differences and should not be construed as suggesting that the two are antithetical. In reality, there is continuity and this should not be viewed as Cartesian. In the next chapter, I explain more about the notion of plasticity and its role in furthering our understanding of how dialogue and dialectic complement each other in making the organization polyphonic. Both are needed for change to take root.

Nikulin (2010) noted that dialectic reasoning can become an expression of system anxiety. It is not unusual for organizations to continue revamping and downsizing just to reduce levels of anxiety. It is also not unusual for an organization to launch new rules of governance to enhance transparency just in case something might go wrong. The search for transparency is ongoing and much of this laying down of rules and systems is driven by managerialist arguments. External agencies increasingly require organizations to adopt procedures to ensure rules are as transparent as possible. The functionality of dialogue is suspended, as many of these rules are introduced with little representation. They are often formulated in response to troubleshooting and the occurrence of a one-off or a never-to-be-repeated incident.

Dialectic reasoning is inextricably tied to rules—to one set of policies and one historical context—and so can conceal the representation of people: these are the rules. But a further conclusion may not be so immediately evident: stringent rules allow us to discover the gap present in the reasoning, but we can see only as much as we allow the other to voice his or her concern and as much as we are willing to be with the other.

*Table 4.1*   Comparison between dialogue and dialectic

| Dialogue | Dialectic |
|---|---|
| Allows for the expression of oneself as well as the personal other | Allows for the expression of oneself |
| Dialogic, working with and through the utterances of the other | Monologic; its purpose is to win through one's strength of reasoning. |
| Understanding the rules based on talk and ongoing conversations | Finding shrewd and convincing reasons based on rules that have been laid down or that have not yet been shaped or legitimated |
| Excess of meaning (insight) | Constancy of meaning |
| Unfinalizable: never-ending rounds of utterances | Finalizable: finite number of steps of reasoning |
| Generates new *logos* | Reproduces conversations by reference to previous encounters |
| Speaking and listening with a view to building relational (responsive) understanding | Speaking with a view to responding |

Dialectic reasoning is also related to rhetoric (the art of oratory or public speaking). For Burch (2004), both rhetoric and dialectic have to do in general with discourse that examines arguments. Whereas rhetoric has to do with knowledge of the forms useful for public persuasion, dialectic has to do with knowledge and reasoning, through which logic is used to refute or uphold some truth. Burch (2004) noted that for Plato, the term dialectic generally meant a process of asking and answering questions about the essence of some matter as a way of searching for truth.

There is always a risk of idealizing dialectic as much as there is one of polarizing dialogue against dialectic. Dialectic plays a vital role not only in reasoning but also in allowing dialogue to glimpse the way reasoning is put forward. Dialogue also plays a vital role in helping dialectic to see what is beyond what is presented based on assumed logic. To support the use of both dialectic and dialogic in managing change, the next section expands on the notion of plasticity.

## THE NEW WAY AHEAD

According to *Merriam-Webster's Dictionary of English Usage*, 'context' is about 'weaving together' and is derived from the Latin *contextus* or connection of words having some coherence or logic. Sciabarra (1998, 289) found that the expression "to weave together" invoked the image of a tapestry being created as well as of change agents and change leaders working as weavers of the text to justify a change situation. Dialectic can be construed as a woven-together understanding of a change. It seems that such understanding is deemed critical and necessary to create meaning and start dialogue.

When Bakhtin (1986) spoke of creating meaning, he was not talking about a problem-based issue. Rather, he saw meaning-making as a continual process. All conversation is a never-ending process that cannot be finalized, and all conversational episodes among individuals are potentially dialogic (Shotter, 1998; Jabri, Adrian, and Boje, 2008). The example below shows this in action.

---

**BUILDING CONTEXT**

James: "I don't want to put the blame on anyone."
Kate: "Yes, but the main problem has been that Sales are not communicating with us about what is going on."
James: "Why is that? We need to know. I made it clear that the sales figures would specifically alter what we produce. Did you put this to them?"
Kate: "It's not an issue of blaming them, or me for that matter."
James: "I am not putting the blame on anyone."
Kate: "We need to talk to them about it. We need their help as much as they need ours. We need to bring them in."

---

Other examples of paired conversations used for building context include:

## Example 1

- A (dialectic): We need to look at the event and analyze its context before we respond to this query.
- B (dialogic): And this way, we can build on what we have achieved so far.

## Example 2

- A (dialectic): We need to consider this plan in much greater detail and in the context of the proposed strategic plan.
- B (dialogic): What are some of the new things we need?

## Example 3

- A (dialectic): These figures tell us that we need to downsize this section of the organization before merging it with the other sections.
- B (dialogic): But first we also need to talk to the people involved. We need to get them to see how things really are.

All three result in change being centered on the power of logic, where mono-logic reasoning is used for justification but dialogue is brought to bear on the solution at hand. With dialogue comes the feeling of appreciation and wanting to inquire further. The first is based on a concept of the organiza-tion as an objective entity, reified through rules and regulations. The second is based on appreciation and newness, where reality is viewed as a process achieved through dialogue. The newness emerges as an outcome of the dia-logue between characters. Bakhtin's conception of utterance endowed his work with facets characteristic of process. His treatment of becoming was relational (Jabri, Adrian, and Boje 2008). As we have noted before, he said:

> I live in a world of others' words. And my entire life is an orientation in this world, a reaction to others' words, beginning with my assimilation of them and ending with assimilation of the wealth of human culture.
>
> (Bakhtin 1986, 143)

Dialectic is operationalized through reason and cognitions. Yet the evidence for listening with affect and emotions is devalued. Taking on board the feel-ings of others is often ignored or side-tracked. In an interview with Edgar Schein, Quick and Gavin reported him saying:

> The reason why dialogue is an important concept in the whole theory of communication and listening is that it redresses the balance between observing the other and observing oneself.
>
> I think a lot of the listening theories that are floating around put way too much emphasis on intense observation and listening to the other, of watching their facial expression and their body language. In that process you get so preoccupied with the other that you pay very little attention to what is coming out of your own head and your own mouth.
>
> Dialogue gets you to say, "Wait a minute! Before you are even in a good position to figure out what this other person is doing, you have got to get acquainted with your own filters, your own assumptions, and your own biases." So by putting the focus on self-analysis and self-observation, I think it leads to much better ultimate listening. Listening to the other is secondary to listening to the self.
>
> (Quick and Gavin 2000, 32)

Every change effort needs the right amount of dialectic and dialogue. The problem this raises, of course, is how to achieve this. How does a change agent mix fluidity and rigidity when they do not appear to come together? We cannot, in fact, mix dialogue, which is fluid and cannot be finalized, with dialectic, which is rigid and finite, but instead we need to get them to interchange. They have to follow each other and take each other's place in some regular pattern. Malabou (2005) used the concept of plasticity as intermediate between fluidity and rigidity. Plastic is a material that can take several forms and has a capacity to accept deformation while resisting it.

## DIALECTIC IN TIME

Dialectic plays a role in emphasizing the importance of temporality and the notion of time. Time remains important and the urgency with which change needs to take place is often used to claim that change needs to be managed in a more direct, or centralized fashion. In managing such change, it is not unusual to see it implemented through imposition of rules and systems and/or the persuading of organization members through coercive refutations. Under conditions of urgency, there is always a tendency to use rational thought, and then claim that change needs to be rapidly implemented through a logically-structured timeframe, constituted and negotiated using processes of reasoning.

The reification of strategy through fixed time horizons and other periodic plans is emblematic of such conditions. All such plans (short, medium, and long-term) are treated as discrete and objective entities, based on a Newtonian 'static conception of time.' Here, every sub-plan is viewed as a discrete point, negating flow and becoming in time and space. The time factor and the fixation of strategy into timeframes have important implications not only for the analysis of systemic relations, but also for an understanding of their dynamic interconnections over time.

Sciabarra (1998) highlighted the importance of dynamism by noting that it was later made the centerpiece of many philosophies, including by Henri Bergson (1946) in his assault on treating time as discrete. Bergson, like Alfred North Whitehead (1956), did not see time as discrete moments, but as a continuous dynamic flow. They viewed every event as interpenetrating and permeating every other, such that they could not be disconnected from prior or subsequent moments. Both writers emphasized the point that we cannot reify and treat moments as separate from each other without damaging our understanding of the creative forces of change.

## DIALECTIC AND THE SYSTEMS VIEWPOINT

The core of change from the systems viewpoint is that it is propelled by systems and entities. To inspire change, the word 'system' is used as an undertaking that has important consequences in fostering processes. But systems do not talk. People talk on their behalf. If systems are rigid, then people will not be willing to waste their time and effort intervening at the system level.

Dialectic is capable of rational justification of systems and systems management, where each system is viewed as a reified entity. Rules and procedures are used to try to bring together various system components, such as strategy with structure, and to achieve some degree of fit between work and technology. Such reifications have serious consequences, however, because they tend to treat systems as external to those involved. The 'other' is viewed as a thing and thus cannot always be represented by a finite system. Besides, systems are hard to change, and procedures are even harder. This means that once procedures are put in place, then the chance for representation will be confined by the procedure and its underlying system. There is nothing wrong with that, but we would need to keep in mind that systems are driven by objectifying forces of change. When the culture is endowed with dialogue, the organization can attain new dimensions, where creativity and polyphony become characteristic of the setting and through which issues are resolved.

Dialectic is meant to lay down the bare structure for the system and to argue and consolidate the system's effectiveness. Through procedures built into the system, it enables us to escape the pitfalls of system malfunction and to ensure sameness and evenness across system recipients. Equity and the search for equality and transparency are deemed crucial in the implementation of systems. However, dialectic and the system it supports do not listen to individual cases, so sameness emerges as a characteristic of system implementation. Unlike dialectic and the use of reasoning, the ongoing nature of dialogue will always continue. Dialogue could, therefore, aid dialectic to modify the system and its procedures. Dialogue could persuade those in charge of the system to think through the quality and attributes inherent in it, as an invitation for continuing exchange of utterances to improve system performance.

Whatever type of change is advocated, dialectic remains important. All types of change resonate and rely on the use of logic and the analysis of a change situation into opposing and promoting forces, with a view of change based on the achievement of some desired end, goal, or purpose. That is where the design and purpose is given prominence through the transition to a new desired state achieved by altering forces of change, rather than by reference to the power of words.

## POLYPHONY IS BUILT ON ANTINOMY

Bakhtin was connected with the Brotherhood of St. Seraphim in the early 1920s and may, therefore, have met another writer, Florensky. In any case, Bakhtin must have read Florensky's published work on Dostoevsky, because Bakhtin's development of polyphony and multi-voicedness is clearly comparable to Florensky's musical terminology. Florensky was always keen to write about truth, and there are indications that his work on antinomy was designed to arrive at truth. Florensky wrote (1997, 109) "truth is truth precisely because it is not afraid of any objections" and he believed that was how antinomy should be approached or dealt with.

The subject of antinomy provides a major engagement between Bakhtin and Florensky. Both relied on Dostoevsky's writing as a source of inspiration, but each focused on the infinite in their own way. Bakhtin saw all conversations as never-ending, whilst Florensky saw discussion from what appears to be a Hegelian perspective, and refused to see the resolution as finalizable.

Florensky did not explicitly use the term 'unfinalized,' but the indication is that for truth to come to light, one person listening to the other is critical. Florensky and Bakhtin both believed that multi-voicedness presupposed a willingness to accept repudiation, negation, and even denial of one's utterance. The importance of the other being receptive is crucial in answering any doubt. That is because we are bounded by our own rationality. Being rational has its limits, which we can only surpass when our utterance is shared with others and is made subject to counter-utterances.

In discussing antinomy, Cassedy (2005) elaborated on Dostoevsky as an author who was good at taking two sets of ideas, presenting them as oppositional to each other, and then, in two places, submitting both sets to questioning and confirmation. Cassedy also asked a very useful question:

> What does it mean to take two sets of ideas and present them as an antinomy that, even in the its simplest forms, offers no plausible solution?
>
> (Cassedy 2005, 108)

This question is very useful for us, because it has its own relevance. What does it mean for an organization to instigate two sets of action plans and then expect its members to be able to cope with their resolution? And what does an organization need to do to discuss options or plans which seem equally justified, given a current change situation, and where each course of action is supported by a valid explanation or a proof of some sort? How is it possible for people to come up with their own suppositions, negations, doubts, and answers?

At this point, we can bring on board Bakhtin's notion of infinite, that there will never be an end to a contradiction. His supposition was that every utterance is conditional and based on both an option and its counter-option. For example, an utterance denoting the need for a new organizational design is invested with its counter-option, namely that there is no need for a new organizational design. If we cannot grasp an issue through a plastic reading of utterances, then there is a case for putting them across as contradictory.

If we were to subscribe to the prospect of contradiction, then there would be another counter-statement which may lead us back to our initial point or help us to explore and/or exhaust our analysis. Florensky (1997) noted that every utterance has to have its own antinomy, and that it can and should always be ready to encounter an objection to itself. There will always be another opposite utterance which might also be correct in its own way, being equally rational but having a contradictory outcome. After elaborating on the rules of logic and mathematics, Florensky (1997) concluded that antin-omy is a characteristic feature of our speech, and that Dostoevsky's world as well as ours is full of contradictions and antinomies. All our utterances are conditional. They are always subject to cancellation and refutation by another utterance having an equivalent degree of persuasiveness.

## ANTINOMIC AND NON-ANTINOMIC UTTERANCES

When it came to making judgements and taking decisions, Florensky (1997) distinguished between an antinomic and a non-antinomic utterance. He noted:

> Every non-antinomic judgement [dialectic-monologic] is merely accepted, or merely rejected, by rationality, for such a judgement does not surpass the boundary of rationality's egoistical isolation.
>
> (Florensky 1997, 109)

A non-antinomic utterance does not take on board another utterance. It is self-centered, ego-centric, and self-absorbed. In the Bakhtinian sense, a non-antinomic judgement is basically an utterance that is monologic, in the sense that it stems from a position of authority, so remains single-voiced. Building on Morson and Emerson (1990, 238–9), only the person making the judgement has access to his or her "ultimate semantic authority." He or she has already accumulated the power of the position, charisma, or charm to push for implementation.

By contrast, an antinomic utterance, which is dialogic, is polyphonic. The single-voicedness of the person in charge is replaced by polyphony and multi-voicedness. The person in charge ceases to exercise control. Florensky wrote that an antinomic statement was always ready to accept its own nega-tion in the sense that:

> [It] answers the doubt concerning its truthfulness by *accepting* this doubt into itself, and even in its limit. Therefore, truth is truth precisely because it is not afraid of its objections
>
> (Florensky 1997, 109; italic in original).

An antinomic utterance is, therefore, about the work of the people and their efforts to create reasonable and responsive utterances. People assume own-ership of the talk in an effort to clarify their own and others' viewpoint.

Applied to managing change, the prime purpose of a non-antinomic utter-ance is to put forward a *single-minded* solution for change. This will take root by creating readiness and enhancing receptivity, rather than proposing alternative formulations, advancing alternative constructions, and accepting doubts and concerns. When the desire is expressed for other viewpoints to be brought to bear, it is not unusual for the person or the group having the semantic authority to impose new rules to curb (reduce) the doubt, rather than investigate it. A polyphonic utterance allows for antinomy, contradiction, and opposition. By doing so, it gathers all life into itself, with all of life's diversity and all of its present and possible future contradictions.

Florensky's truth starts with Bakhtin's notion of utterance and yet is able to extend itself to encounter a counter-utterance. The purpose is not to consider Bakhtin's polyphony in isolation, but rather to develop it as a tool that explores polyphony by accepting the fact that for polyphony to take root, a certain acceptance of antinomic utterances would be needed through continued contradiction. This conjunctive approach, applied to the work of both Florensky and Bakhtin, is the most productive and valuable route for a polyphonic mode of analysis. It has the ability to cope with polyphony by accepting the need for contradiction.

Even pursuit of a so-called 'unified' strategy involves antinomy. There is always more than one truth, in the sense that any strategy is bound to include more than one option, mode of discovery, choice, and ideology, and the composite is more likely to contain antinomy even with a unified and fully agreed definition of rationality. Building on choice involves contradiction. Escalating the commitment for the choice of project A might involve having to discard the implementation of project B. Ranking and rating of projects involves an element of antinomy, even under conditions where costs and benefits are predicted and made convincing through quantifying the unquantifiable benefits or costs.

Every strategy is conditional in the sense that it includes an objection to itself in the form of another option, and sometimes a contradiction. An objection may go unnoticed initially but that does not mean it cannot have an impact later. An objection might be suppressed because of the tendency to escalate commitment to a failing course of action, or possibly the obligations of people to pursue pseudo-consensus, at least in the short term.

Florensky (1997, 108) noted that "life is infinitely fuller than rational definitions and therefore no formula can encompass all the fullness of life." Applied to options for change, there is no one formula that can replace creativity. Even a fully-fledged plan for change will inevitably be subject to concerns, objections, and even protests. Florensky suggested that:

> a rational formula can be above the attacks of life if *it gathers all of life into itself,* with all of life's diversity and all of its present and possible future contradictions.
>
> (Florensky 1997, 109; italics in original).

Antinomy is invaluable in promoting analysis of issues confronting organizations. Florensky (1997) believed that antinomies were inherent in our daily life and ways of thinking, not so much in the dichotomy of reason and faith, but in reason itself (Blank, 2010).

Bringing on board the diversity of life is also about including the people affected by change. It is about multi-voicedness of the organization's members and their desire to be heard. As Albert Camus (1955) wrote in *The Myth of Sisyphus*, a philosophical essay:

> What is the point of ceaseless and pointless toil working in an organisation and spending one's own best years of one's life in an organisation that forbids its own members from sharing? Integrity has no need of rules.

## MORE ON POLYPHONY

Polyphony is about taking on board objections and counter-positions, and seeing contradictions. It leads to foresight precisely because it has taken on board other representations and counter-positions.

Antinomies and contradictions lie at the core of decision-making. Decision-making relies on reducing uncertainty through methods such as SWOT, force-field, and scenario analysis to probe alternatives. In change management, it is not unusual for people to form focus groups to provide feedback and create readiness. These, however, remain confined within a monologic mode of analysis, as their prime purpose is to create readiness and enhance receptivity, rather than respecting and accepting doubts. They are, in fact, designed to downplay concerns.

Through polyphony, we discover the possibilities and impossibilities of choice and strategy. Antinomies draw attention to significant issues affecting organizational life, by providing motivation for deep analysis. They play an important role in exploring alternative options.

Many organizations strive for creativity but are often constrained by rules. An organization that invests in the status quo will strive to maintain and achieve that. During the process, it misses out on alternative options or ways of seeing the world. As the organization strives for creativity, it lays down rules for that creativity to be channeled or rewarded for achieving consistency. While these rules ground the organization, they end up constraining levels of creative achievement.

To get back to Dostoevsky, we have noted before that he delegated his authorial voice to the characters. Each character draws the contours of his or her own voice by insisting on an individual stance, and providing a personal reason. This reveals human nature by positing two contradictory statements. Diversity and the plurality of voices and positions were always at the canter of his writing, which prompted Bakhtin to think of polyphony and multi-voicedness.

As Morson and Emerson noted:

> In a monologic work, only the author, as the 'ultimate semantic authority', retains the power to express a truth directly . . . By contrast, in a polyphonic work . . . the author ceases to exercise monologic control.
>
> (Morson and Emerson 1990, 238)

Such control is replaced with the work of the people and their efforts to assume ownership of their talk and clarify each other's viewpoints.

That does not necessarily mean arriving at only one conclusion. It demands seeing each other as equal and comprehending what the other is saying, but without having to accept it. Bakhtin noted that accepting their views would require mindfulness and the realization or acceptance of another viewpoint. He suggested that this process of realization required individual consciousness to have its own meeting with consciousness as a social property. Each actor is skillful enough to show a personal point of view. In organizational terms, this means proficiency and skills, and being good at the task at hand. Much of this capability also comes from agreeing or disagreeing with each other so that a surplus of meaning is created.

Such association with what the other is saying means that the speaker is attempting to establish a logical link with what the other is saying, and giving the other the benefit of the doubt, as well as trust. There is doubt as well as suspicion, reluctance as well as keenness. Attempting to establish the link involves bringing the other. There is an inversion of perspective where, if you like, the distant image is brought forward. The background figure becomes larger than the foreground one in an effort to portray reality.

## CONCLUSION

In the introduction to this chapter, I claimed that in the majority of cases, dialogic has succumbed to dialectic, on the basis that the dialectical method provides the foundation of any 'scientific' research. My evidence lies in the fact that it has always been easier for organizations to create new rules and procedures rather than await the development of new unwritten norms. Developing new rules to ensure the smooth functioning of an operation has often been used as a panacea for managing difficult situations and resolving possible conflicts that may arise during change.

Whether we lean towards the dialogic or the dialectic has been predetermined, often due to the historical development of the two ideas. They complement each other, and both can be useful to further our understanding of issues surrounding the change effort. However, dialectic is not indeterminate, whereas dialogue is, because by its very nature, it cannot be finalized. To better understand the constructions of these two terms and their relevance for managing change, it is crucial to note that Aristotle's writings promoted the role of dialectic and overshadowed the dialogic conception which Socrates had been keen to present.

## REFERENCES

Bakhtin, Mikhail Mikhailovitch. 1986. *Speech Genres and Other Late Essays*, edited by Caryl Emerson and Michael Holquist, translated by Vern McGee. Austin: University of Texas Press.

Bergson, Henri. 1946. *The Creative Mind*. New York: Carol.
Blake, Robert Rogers and Jane S. Mouton. 1976. *Consultation*, 2nd ed. Reading, MA: Addison-Wesley.
Blank, Ksana. 2010. *Dostoevsky's Dialectics and the Problem of Sin*. Evanston, IL: Northwestern University Press.
Burch, Robert. 2004. "Dialectic." *ESC: English Studies in Canada* 30 (4): 16–20.
Bushe, Gervase R. and Robert J. Marshak. 2009. "Revisioning organization development: Diagnostic and dialogic premises and patterns of practice." *Journal of Applied Behavioral Science* 45 (3): 348–68.
Camus, Albert. 1955. *The Myth of Sisyphus*. London: Hamish Hamilton.
Cassedy, Steven. 2005. *Dostoevsky's Religion*. Stanford, CA: Stanford University Press.
Clark, Katerina and Michael Holquist. 1984. *Mikhail Bakhtin*. Cambridge: Harvard University Press.
Cronshaw, Steven F. and Ashley McCulloch. 2008. "Reinstating the Lewinian vision: from force field analysis to organization field assessment." *Organization Development Journal* 26 (4): 89–103.
Eliot, T. S. 1934. *The Rock*. London: Faber & Faber.
Florensky, Pavel. 1997. *The Pillar and Ground of the Truth: An essay in the Orthodox Theodicy in Twelve Letters*, translated by Boris Jakim. Upper Saddle River, NJ: Princeton University Press.
Gardiner, Michael. 2000. "A Very Understandable Horror of Dialectics: Bakhtin and Marxist Phenomenology." In *Materializing Bakhtin: The Bakhtin Circle and Social Theory*, edited by Craig Brandist and Galin Tikhanov, 119–41. New York: St. Martins Press, in association with St. Anthony's College, Oxford.
Hegel, Georg Wilhelm Friedrich. 1977. *Phenomenology of Spirit*, by A. V. Miller, with analysis of the text and foreword by J. N. Finlay. Oxford: Oxford University Press.
Jabri, Muayyad, Allyson Adrian and David Boje. 2008. "Reconsidering the role of conversations in change communication: a contribution based on Bakhtin." *Journal of Organizational Change Management* 21: 667–85.
Katz, Daniel and Robert L. Kahn. 1966. *The Social Psychology of Organizations*. New York: Wiley.
Malabou, Catherine. 2005. *The Future of Hegel: Plasticity, Temporality and Dialectic*, translated by Lisabeth During. London: Routledge.
———. 2010. *Plasticity at the Dusk of Writing: Dialectic, Destruction, Deconstruction*, translated by Carolyn Shread. New York: Columbia University Press.
———. 2015. The Future of Humanities. Transeuropeennes Revue international de pensee critique. Available at: http://www.transeuropeennes.eu/en/articles/voir_pdf/281 (Accessed on 01 August 2015)
Morson, Gary S. and Caryl Emerson. 1990. *Mikhail Bakhtin: Creation of a Prosaics*. Stanford: Stanford University Press.
Nikulin, Dmitri. 2006. *On Dialogue*. Oxford: Lexington Books.
———. 2010. *Dialectic and Dialogue*. Stanford: Stanford University Press.
Quick, James Campbell and Joanne Gavin. 2000. "The next frontier: Edgar Schein on organizational therapy/commentary on the Edgar Schein interview." *The Academy of Management Perspectives* 14 (1): 31–48.
Sciabarra, Chris Matthew. 1998. "Are we all dialecticians now? Reply to MacGregor and Friedman." *Critical Review* 12 (3): 283–99.
Shotter, John. 1998. "The dialogical nature of our inner lives." *Philosophical Explorations* 1 (3): 185–200.
Whitehead, Alfred North. 1956. *Modes of Thought*. Cambridge: Cambridge University Press.

# 5   Styles of Engagement: Dialogue with Dialectic

*Logic can often be reversed, but the effect does not precede the cause.*

Gregory Bateson (1980, 71)

In exploring the relationship between dialogue and dialectic, I start with a quick definition of the act of diagnosing, as it is often viewed in the literature on organizational development. I will elaborate on the main variations associated with diagnosis, particularly problem-centric (dialectic) and life-centric (dialogic). I then discuss the stand-off situation between problem-centric and life-centric modes and the issue of making a diagnosis as a collective undertaking. In elaborating on the stand-off, I draw on the notion of *plasticity* as explored by two very different writers, Bakhtin and Malabou.

First, I use plasticity in the Bakhtinian sense. Bakhtin's (1981) view was that plasticity denoted the ability to achieve and fulfill oneself through responsive utterances amenable to more than one revision or interpretation. He developed his idea of plasticity through studying Dostoevsky's novel-writing, which allowed characters the opportunity to showcase the malleability of their perceptions and ways of coping with the world around them. Having discussed Bakhtin's ideas, I then turn to the French philosopher Catherine Malabou. Like Bakhtin, Malabou (2010) suggested that plasticity is about the agent being open to all kinds of change based on the capacity to transgress personal limits and become the other. Malabou (2010) suggested that we should understand plasticity as the "spontaneous organization of fragments" (2010, 7) and "the capacity to receive form and a capacity to produce form" (2005, 9). This is to show that we can be more genuinely open to the future than we have ever been led to think. Importantly, Crockett in his foreword to *Plasticity at the Dusk of Writing* (Malabou 2010, xiii) noted that this is not an issue about accommodation and being flexible, as much as it is about some profoundly generative attempt to produce completely new forms through radical modification. Malabou attempted to support her philosophy by linking to recent advances in contemporary neuroscience and brain research, particularly for the idea that we can revise previous structures well beyond the fixity of forms relied upon by reason, thus moving away from the imposition of prevailing forms. In time, the search for plastic readings of dialectic led me to consider how transformation could occur by bringing the thinking of Bakhtin into a dialogical relationship with that of Malabou.

## DEFINING THE ACT OF DIAGNOSING CHANGE

Diagnosis is basically a human activity through which symptoms and causes are identified and delineated. Although the medical connotations of the word perhaps add to the activity's prestige, it remains a very normal human process that we handle almost daily. This is because we tend to narrate symptoms as we search for likely causes. As with medical diagnosis, symptoms have a cascading effect: one symptom may well be the result of another. For example, lack of collaboration in a team setting could be a result of lack of cohesion. This, in turn, may result from differences in levels of aspirations.

It is not unusual for a medical practitioner to start the diagnostic process by gathering data and conducting clinical tests. The results of these then require interpretation. This is followed by treatment, where some form of prescriptive action or intervention, such as a certain treatment or medication, can be administered or put into effect.

Although we are not seeking a mechanism for interpreting, say, the blood pressure of an organization, there is a correspondence between the use of the term 'diagnosis' in medicine and in organizations. Both involve the development of plausible explanations that rationalize what is happening and its cause. The next section begins by contrasting two of the most widely used modes for managing change.

## TWO BROAD MODES FOR MANAGING CHANGE

The epistemology of managing change has traditionally been guided by two broad modes. The first is based on the centrality of diagnosis in the medical sense, and the other on diagnosis that is more life-centric, and takes into account peculiarities that are characteristic of human organizing processes. Clearly, both necessitate the use of speech (utterances) reported as descriptive propositions designed to resolve an issue.

To a certain extent, both modes are evident in speech. For example, objective statements such as "chances are . . .", "based on the figures . . .", "evidence tells us that . . ." are often used to demonstrate causality, drawing on hard evidence. Here, emphasis is placed on diagnosis drawing on explanations and inferences, very much in the medical sense of the word. This form of diagnosis is dialectic. It is enacted in ways that separate knowing and being (Cunliffe 2004). Facts are made to appear compelling, especially by those in authority. A compelling ruling or procedure, however, does not necessarily take into account the emotions and utterances of those "on the other side of the fence" and their experiences of the situation.

Chapter 4 set out a pathway for diagnosis confined by the dialectic and its emphasis on logic, lucidity, and reasoning. This approach aims to describe symptoms, and attribute them to primary causes affecting organizational outcomes (problem-centric). The emphasis is placed on a Cartesian mode of thinking where issues and problems are assumed to exist somewhere 'out there' (Pondy and Mitroff 1979), and can be identified based on a conception of the 'certainty of the mind,' or *cogito ergo sum*, in this case "I think, therefore I believe, for certain, that this is where the problem lies."

Chapter 3, however, introduced the idea of utterances, as both external and inner speech, taking place in a social context. The point was made that diagnosis was more about the desire to build new connections with those who have been placed or made to locate on 'the other side of the fence.' If we were diagnosing an issue, whether a structure or, say, a problem with the flow of some process, then what I say is influenced by what you say and vice versa. Your utterance will have its tendency to convey, as will mine, and when our utterances 'meet,' meaning is conveyed and developed. In conversation, the 'living moment' is experienced.

The dialogic mode of diagnosing is life-centric, based on positive human organizing processes. It holds that change is not pre-given, but is socially constructed by people (Schwandt 2000; Gergen 2008). An understanding of change is, therefore, largely social, achieved through everyday shared consciousnesses and narrations, including mundane talk and conversations. Change is viewed as a shared intervention that unfolds over time as the participants agree on new ways of thinking. The social mode moves much closer to 'We talk and listen, therefore we are,' and new identities are formed and accomplished through utterances.

Dialectic highlights logic based on the simultaneity of opposites. Dialogue, however, emphasizes the social nature of subjectivity, namely relationality and being with the other. Dialogue emphasizes appreciation, positivity, and an openness of the person to individual cases. Dialectic emphasizes rules, persuasive (compelling) inquiries, and policy reviews designed to establish the cause of the presenting issues through reasoning. Each leads to different commitments on the part of change agents, in terms of choice of leadership, change agency practices, and styles. These differences affecting the practice of change agency have very important implications. One immediate implication is that the leadership shown by a change agent in choosing between problem-centric and life-centric modes may either function as a medium for diagnosing change based on blame (glass half-empty), or become the practice of freedom (identity) and appreciation (glass half-full). The leadership of a change agent aspiring for productive imagination could, therefore, evolve away from a Cartesian sense of selfhood and become immersed in dialogues and statements (utterances) shared by others.

The next section expands on these two variations of diagnosis. It covers first the problem-centric mode, which is based on a conscious effort to identify symptoms and causes, and then the life-centric mode. This is based on creating occasions for dialogue in an attempt to capitalize and build on what has already been achieved.


## PROBLEM-CENTRIC MODE

A problem-centric mode of diagnosis is one where the emphasis is on logical empiricism and its variant, positivism (Jabri 2012). Logical positivism is rooted in a philosophy of science based on the belief that we only know the cause of the presenting issue when it has been quantified and measured. According to Bushe and Marshak (2009, 350), valid data are assumed to "reflect or mirror an underlying objective reality."

Over the past fifty years, the problem-centric mode has become a convention in organizational development, and the standard mode used to diagnose change. Reason and dialectic are used to identify symptoms of the presenting issues and then to trace such symptoms to likely causes. Even these days, it is common for authors and practitioners to use the problem-centric mode of diagnosis and intervention, defined as one "producing an objective diagnosis against an ideal model to change behaviors" (Bushe and Marshak 2009, 352). In other words, despite the development of other ways of thinking about the management of change, including appreciative (life-centric) modes (Cooperrider, Whitney, and Stavros 2008; Bushe and Marshak 2009), search conferences (Emery 1999), and future search (Weisbord 1993), the strong image of reason and dialectic still pervades the way problems are identified and diagnosed.

Applied to diagnosis, the fundamental premise of logical empiricism would ideally use three interrelated steps. The first is the search for symptoms and their entanglements with each other. The second is attributing these symptoms to likely reason/s for the presenting issue. The third is designating and verifying causes of the presenting symptoms, and providing evidence that the designated symptom–cause relationship is factually meaningful. All these must ideally be supported by data-gathering, measurement, and experimentation.

Whether diagnosis is carried out through surveys, change audits, focus groups, or so-called engagement surveys, it implicitly or explicitly depends on how reason and cogency of explanations are made compelling. According to Cronshaw and McCulloch (2008), a problem-centric diagnostic model is presumed to be most effective when it is aimed at a specific objective, performed in a competent and sensitive manner, based on data, and guided by the premise that there is one reality and that such a reality can be discovered using objective problem-solving methods supported by data.


## LIFE-CENTRIC MODE

The fundamental premise of a life-centric mode involves two types of highly entangled commitments. The first aims to achieve growth and facilitation of ideas through social construction (Cooperrider and Srivastva 1987; Cooperrider and Whitney 2001; Gergen 2008). The second aims to create shared consciousnesses of the presenting issues based on moments of dia-logic interaction between people (Bakhtin 1986), where mutual exploration is encouraged.

Under a social constructionist view, social reality is not pre-determined, but socially co-constructed through ongoing talk (Schwandt 2000; Gergen 2008). Co-construction complements situations where appreciative inquiry and the pioneering work of Cooperrider and Srivastva (1987) are used. It frames all talk as an opportunity to affirm and energize the in-flow of exist-ing and new capabilities (energies) that already exist in the system, rather than searching for negative symptoms (signs of departure from the norm) in an attempt to remedy the situation.

The life-centric mode is about openness, curiosity, and creative question-ing. Its spirit involves an adventure into what lies in the future, and so it can be thought of as a medium for reaching to the other. It is, therefore, polyphonic in its emphasis on the need to listen to the other, inclusivity, and multi-voicedness.

The life-centric mode is also about appreciation of what has been accom-plished so far, but as a way to think about the future. It involves recognizing that there is value in the future. Appreciation requires change to be managed from a much more involved awareness of plastic dialectic.


## APPRECIATION


Appreciative Inquiry (AI) is closely linked with dialogue and social con-struction (Berger and Luckmann 1966; Cooperrider and Srivastva 1987). It is predicated on the idea that managing change should focus on asking positive questions (Ludema, Cooperrider, and Barratt 2001). It capitalizes on what is positive or already working. It sees 'changing' as a cause for optimism, seeking as it does to liberate change from conflicts and from the apportioning of blame. In this context, the word *appreciate* means to value those things of value. It is not so much a mode as a way of being and becoming.

Appreciative Inquiry is about the idea that every organization has some-thing that is working right, the things that give it life, make it effective and successful, and connect it to its stakeholders and communities (Cooperrider, Whitney, and Stavros 2008). It is from this very specific angle that plas-ticity can be pursued through an appreciative inquiry mode, in ways that give form to the future and enable the subjects to become as they open to themselves.

Appreciative Inquiry was created by David Cooperrider and Suresh Sriv-astva at Case Western Reserve University in 1987. It was developed as a new form of action research, but with a much greater emphasis on the idea that change should begin with appreciation based on moments shared between people (Cooperrider and Srivastva 1987). Such an appreciation is framed by the change agent and those around as an opportunity to build on what already exists in the system of things. The change agent or change team, through their leadership of the change effort, would attempt to diagnose and intervene, using these two as overlapping, rather than distinct, concepts. They collaboratively search for instances of vitality and openness where each person is enabled to relate to the other in ways that will fashion the future 'we think, therefore we are,' based on a non-Cartesian imagination of possibilities, giving form to the future.

---

Ap-pre'ci-ate, v., 1. valuing; the act of recognizing the best in people or the world around us; affirming past and present strengths, successes, and potentials; to perceive those things that give life (health, vitality, excellence) to living systems 2. to increase in value, e.g., the economy has appreciated in value.
Synonyms: VALUING, PRIZING, ESTEEMING, and HONORING.

In-quire' (kwir), v., 1. The act of exploration and discovery. 2. To ask questions; to be open to seeing new potentials and possibilities.
Synonyms: DISCOVERY, SEARCH, SYSTEMATIC EXPLORATION, STUDY.

*Source:* Cooperrider and Whitney (2005).

---

A number of scholars have tried to explain the emergent modes of appreciative inquiry that are distinct from the diagnostic mode (Cooperrider, Barrett, and Srivastva 1995). Appreciative inquiry has, however, often been criticized for neglecting much of the foundational work in the field of Organization Development (OD), such as process consultation (Schein 1988) and action research (Rapoport 1970).

Oswick (2009) proposed the need to reconfigure traditional organizational development approaches and their emphasis on problem-centrality, to embrace the philosophical underpinnings of appreciative and life-centric modes of analysis. That seems like a useful proposal, addressing an important gap that is likely to connect problem-centric with life-centric modes of analysis. But are we really there? Or are we still at a stage where such integration is more likely to lapse into problem-centric modes?

It may well be that the call to reconfigure the two is still a minor issue for those keen on traditional organizational development approaches. The problem is further exacerbated by the fact that many practitioners still treat appreciative modes differently, by attempting to promote their use under the rubric of the problem-centric mode. Resolving the impasse has been a rare focus. It has only been during recent debates published in the *Journal of Applied Behavioral Science* (Volume 45) that scholars have tentatively approached the topic.

This may explain why scholars still do not pay attention to the fact that the opposition of dialectic and dialogue can and should be questioned. In

Hegelian philosophy, dialectic before Derrida and Malabou was mainly understood as being based on negation, fulfilling its own monopoly on logic and argumentation. Prior to Malabou, negation was often assumed to take place within the secure borders of thesis versus antithesis. Self-knowledge and knowledge of how we have always approached change were taken for granted as sufficient. Malabou suggested that we need to be more conscious of how we think, and more willing to escape the impositions we have been accustomed to using—even when we have been made to think of the 'right' way to manage change.

Here we have two primary issues. One is the way we have been conditioned to think about how to diagnose and intervene in change. This has little to be said for it, because it could easily be bounded by what we have been told to do, by word of mouth, or by observing other consultants or organizations. Our reliance on word of mouth often replaces our genuine intent with a superficial one. In many change situations, it is easy to know superficially how to approach change based on some rationale, but quite hard to figure out what we should 'truly' believe or want. This suggests that we are not, in fact, arriving at self-knowledge. Instead, our self-knowledge is used unreflectively and hence taken for granted.

To know how we ought to respond to change requires self-knowledge, but this is bounded. According to Cassam (2014), a mere reliance on reason taken for granted cannot be cashed out and removed in rationalist terms. Instead, we have to pay more attention to what he called "substantial self-knowledge." This requires awareness of the limits of what we see, as being one of the conventions through which knowledge has been used in the past.

The presence of the gap that separates dialogue from dialectic is not surprising, since life-centric modes have developed quite distinct methodologies. These are based on an understanding of the premise behind the dialogic mode, namely that it is through utterances that a new logic could come to be shared, rather than one that precedes meetings and discussions where everyone comes with their own view. Discussions and meetings may characterize problem-centric modes, but that does not guarantee an in-depth understanding. It is easy to call for integration and predict its effect on paper, because it is less likely that dialogue will be involved. There will always be the temptation for managerial logic (managerialism) to gravitate towards problem-centric.

Any true integration should contribute to an understanding of dialectic in ways that will place creativity and plastic transformation at its core, and allow dialogue to emerge. Such a situation requires more than sitting back and calling for the two to be integrated. Malabou's notion of plasticity has something to offer and could influence the way we see dialectic. It could also influence how we proceed with change. There may be another decade of work ahead before possibilities of plasticity are truly understood as accomplishments that are fit for purpose and sensitive to the nature of this type of change in organizations.

## THE STAND-OFF (*IMPASSE*)

The literature on change has grappled with the alternative merits of problem-centric and dialogic modes (Bushe and Marshak 2009). An important reason why this stand-off continues to occur is the dominant emphasis on symptoms and problem-identification. This culture is very common today and seems likely to remain so in the future, because in one way or another, interest in problem identification is chronic. It is implicitly assumed, by virtue of the emphasis on the need to resolve the presenting issue. Some of the discursive possibilities that may help to resolve the impasse include:

- Do we tend to commit ourselves to forms of arguments without realizing the importance of moving beyond the logic of the situation, and investigating a range of effects?
- Might we need malleability to bring on board diverse utterances and neglected alternatives?

So far, little has been done to resolve the impasse, apart from recent calls to combine dialectic with dialogic, or to use problem-centric and life-centric modes of engagement in sequence or as phased components of wider organizational development initiatives (Oswick 2009). Such calls have been made on the grounds that dialectic and dialogic can and should co-exist in a mutually-dependent relationship. This means that it is possible to start with a problem-centric phase, and move to a life-centric one, using one to illuminate the other. Facilitation of change remains achievable by combining problem-centric with life-centric modes.

Problem-centric and life-centric modes are combined in the hope of achieving a synthesis, but may be more likely to produce a state of indetermination. It is quite possible that combining the two will either allow dialectic to take hold of dialogue and then to collide with it further down the track, or do little but reproduce the problem-centric mode. Despite the potential of the explicit recognition of the thoroughly relational (life-centric) nature of change (Bushe and Marshak 2009), most change efforts stay within a diagnostic (problem-centric) framework. This is because such transformations rarely occur and if they do, are often suppressed through managerial logic calling for problem-centrality. Dialogue is, therefore, seconded to the dominant narrative, largely based on managerial logic, in which negation remains the generative principle.

The challenge we face cannot be solved by simply combining the problem-centric with the life-centric. We need to be "struck" (Cunliffe 2004) through new moments in search for plastic—that is, the idea of a "plastic moment." We continue to need the utterances of one person to give access to the utterances of the other. We also need to meet in a space where dialectic is treated as malleable, for transformation to occur. That requires a sense of change that is not inherently dependent on dialectic. We need to develop and maintain the ability to receive, give, and annihilate extant structures (Malabou 2010).

It is useful to recall that Malabou's notion of plasticity is about mobility, as willingness to take care of our own 'being in the world'—a sort of desire for some "productive imagination" likely to accrue as we search for newer and more discursive possibilities. To put it more bluntly, we only overcome the binary through plasticity, particularly the willingness to treat dialectic as subject to suppleness, and not wanting to engage in the negation of each other. We attempt to overcome the opposition, not by combining the two modes or by synthesizing their opposing poles (Oswick 2009), but by using plasticity as an escape route. Our ultimate aim is to find change (transformation) again.

As noted earlier, the search for ways to overcome the binary led me to consider how transformation could occur by bringing the thinking of Bakhtin into a dialogical relationship with that of the French philosopher Catherine Malabou.

## PLASTICITY: BAKHTIN

Bakhtin explored plasticity by distinguishing it from anything that is fixed or constant. He suggested that you can always envisage another utterance, and so he rejected any finalization and closure because utterances and their exchange are "plasticity itself" (1981, 39). Bakhtin (1981, 39) described plasticity as a "genre that is ever questing, ever examining itself and subjecting its established forms to review." Plasticity was, he felt, what lay in the middle of the two utterances and opened the space for dialogue to occur. The success of change will depend on that middle ground, achieved through "ever-questioning, ever examining itself" (1981, 24) in search of another review.

Bakhtin also saw plasticity in terms of the person being a mobile subject, and open to themselves, which he described as "unconsummated—as subjects who are always becoming." This is not about reflections so much as rupture, a sudden realization of the desire to fulfill oneself much more than has so far been achieved. We are, Bakhtin said, "axiologically yet-to-be" (1986, 13). Like Malabou's, his notion of plasticity is ontological as he sees people suddenly wanting to change away from the dialectic of strict sentences once they realize their needs and aspirations to move on. They revise their views of the world around them in ways that give meaning as well as depth as they attempt to come to newer realizations through responsive exchanges with others. A CEO who suddenly comes to the realization that strategy should not be seen as some external or fixed entity will soon start making reference to the ongoing experiences of others and their narrations. The CEO's consummation of the new values and ontologies will start gaining an intrinsic need for fulfillment.

Bakhtin's description of plasticity as the desire for the "axiologically yet-to-be" is one of 'being,' and futuristically Heideggerian, as it awaits fulfillment that is unfinalizable. It has some likeness to what happens in organizations. His analysis fits well when thinking about utterances made at the grass roots level demanding reviews of systems at the organizational level. It may also call into question how dominant systems are entangled with core competencies as well as rigidities, often argued to constitute capabilities (Leonard-Barton 1992), when in fact they are core organizational constraints preventing the system from changing its organizational forms and structures.

An organization that is open to changing will also remain open to plastic readings of its own structures and policies. However, when policy review schedules are dialectically determined through a cogent system of logic, core rigidities, and justifications, the task of shaping, reshaping, and unshaping of organizational forms and structures becomes harder to achieve. That is when attempts are made to express concerns, through an authoritative discourse, when in reality the change agenda is controlled by hidden desires to maintain the status quo. Although amendments may be considered, or be called for, at intervals, the logic through which procedures become institutionalized prevents the meaningful sharing of such amendments. If, for instance, the voices of those who are being smothered by the dominant discourse allude to an injustice, the procedure is rarely suspended, because the dominant narrative, justified through solid reasons, is given preference. The dominant narrative and the procedure, therefore, become the source that constrains not only the managerial logic but also the logic of management, and others are discouraged from expression.

## PLASTICITY: MALABOU

The concept of plasticity also figures in the work of Catherine Malabou. Malabou's doctorate was supervised by Jacques Derrida. Her thesis on Hegel, published as *The Future of Hegel: Plasticity, Temporality, and Dialectic*, forced Derrida to re-evaluate his own reading and critique of Hegel. In her work on Hegelian philosophy, Malabou (2005) advanced the notion of plasticity to capture the potential for dialectic to be made more malleable and supple. She used the term with a profoundly new view, transforming dialectic into a concept that can help us grasp the whole. This means that, in one way or another, the future must be here and now if we were to approach change with much more openness to dialogue.

Malabou (2010) saw plasticity as the key to resolving the issue of 'otherness,' by asking questions that are truly pertinent to the theme of change and changing. These include: How can we reach toward the other? How can we respond to the other? How can we form the pathway? How can we work out a form of flight toward the other from within the closure of the world?

She noted that even using a Hegelian approach, we have not yet exhausted plasticity's range of meanings. She believed that these meanings were always changing:

> One might think, for example, of all the various forms of 'plastic' in our world: plastic wood, plastic money, plastic paint, and the dangerous plastic material of putty-like consistency that can be shaped by hand. . . plasticity appears diametrically opposed to form, describing the destruction and the very annihilation of all form
>
> (Malabou 2010, 67).

Why is the concept of plasticity able to help us overcome core rigidities? Malabou explained:

> The noun 'plasticity' is linked etymologically with two older words, the substantive 'plastic' and the adjective 'plastic'. All three words are derived from the Greek *plassein*, which means 'to model' or 'to mold'. 'Plastic' as an adjective has two meanings. On the one hand, it means 'to be susceptible to changes of form' or 'to be malleable'. Clay, in this sense, would be 'plastic'. On the other hand, it means 'having the power to bestow form,' as in the expression 'plastic surgeon' or 'plastic art' understood as 'the art of modeling' in the arts of sculpture or ceramics. Plasticity describes the nature of that which is plastic, being at once capable of receiving and of giving form.
>
> (Malabou 2010, 67)

Malabou started her work on plasticity by tracing the history of the development of the concept, starting with the philosophy of Hegel. Shapiro (2013, 73–74) noted that "Malabou applies her concept of plasticity to herself." She reflected on how her thinking was changing, and how she kept it open. She then progressed to the thought of Heidegger, for whom change and changing were more about crossing the thresholds of change achieved through his notion of *Dasein* (*being-in-the-world*).

For Heidegger, 'being-in-the-world,' or *Dasein*, as it is commonly known, was an important existential idea, describing what constitutes our becoming in time. In his work *Being and Time*, Heidegger referred to *Dasein* as the sort of change we encounter in our own experiences in time, and the sort of moves that occur in our subjectivities, desires, and aspirations. It also implies that we become aware of change and transformations as they occur. Malabou (2010) suggested that plasticity in Heidegger's work is *part* of the mobility and change we experience, and that mobility could become the source for negating the generative capacity that inhabits dialectic.

Malabou's analysis of plasticity is about successive moves on the basis that *Dasein* passes from one state of being in the world of our experiences to another. This is not about flexibility and adaptability. Malabou (2010, 69) clearly noted that "modification can be radical, violent; it can completely and utterly transform Dasein."

According to Ulmer (2015, 6) "plasticity provides a means of understanding how structural elements intra-act within dynamic processes of shaping, reshaping, and unshaping policy." The preference for problem-centric over life-centric mode enhances the sort of understanding noted by Ulmer. Such an understanding enhances the prospects for radically unshaping organizational settings and cultures. It remains an important way of thinking for polyphony to take root.

I use plasticity to describe how change leaders shape the direction of change and the possibilities of plastic readings aimed at giving, receiving, and destroying ways of thinking about change. What a plastic reading does, then, is illuminate those parts of the dialectic we rarely see, bringing back the lived experiences of people to illuminate the issues at hand.

A plastic reading provides a means to understand the limits of normative (managerialist) modes of thinking. A normative mode is one based on a "rationalist approach to formation of policies where issues are viewed as discrete concepts with clear causes, effects, and predictive capabilities" (Ulmer 2015, 9). It is based on the cognitions of those whose role is primarily to initiate revision and reviews of policies, but who do not fully understand the processes involved in shaping, reshaping, and unshaping policies and procedures. For Young (1999), they are the assumptions, norms, and traditions that are often taken for granted but which institutionalize traditional ontological, epistemological, and methodological elements.

Plasticity is also about responding to the representation posed by organization members by extolling the benefits of them sharing their feedback and experiences of such policies and procedures as subjects. Kirby (2011, 83) wrote, "one of the most pressing issues in political analysis today . . . is the question of critique—how to engage others more generously through interconnection." New shapes are given meaning through attention given to possibilities, allowing plastic readings to shape, reshape, and even destroy. Without a plastic reading, change will remain subject to a normative entitative approach, in which rules and policies are reflected from norms based on the lived experiences of those taking charge of policies.

## THE NATURE OF PLASTICITY

In her book *The Future of Hegel*, Malabou talked about plasticity as "all the excess of the future over the future" (Malabou 2010, 6). In her book *Plasticity at the Dusk of Writing*, Malabou summed up plasticity as something that has the capacity "to transform itself, to transgress its own limits, to displace itself, to become other (Malabou 2005, 24). The issue for plasticity then is not relying on what the present tells us, using some narrow modification or interpretation of seizing the present through dialectic and problem-identification, but seizing the future and bringing it *forward* to implicate the present, here and now.

In truth, this is more of the *double* sense of grasping, seizing, and understanding, which will soften how dialectic is adhered to in managing change. What a plastic reading does, therefore, is to illuminate the future and see it (without the future being here and now). This weakens the dominant managerial logic through which change is often practiced, with top-down modes being made to appear compelling due to urgency and the unpredictability of the situation. Plasticity is also about the stories we inhabit that modify our experiences and provide meaning to our emotional responses, wherever reason and logic are made to appear compelling. That is when the forces behind problem-centrality are altered to enable ability and creativity to be embraced.

Applied to change, plasticity is about our readiness to change the way we think of rules and structures in managing change, and whether or not rules are used in ways that promote or stifle novelty. This requires looking at the existing discourse with a view of unshaping and reshaping that is not simply a 'moment in time,' but is constantly open to changing and becoming. The leadership of change agents, in charge of the destiny of others, recognizes the benefit derived from reflecting on the need for the dialectic to be made malleable and supple, through adoption of life-centric modes where human processes, such as communication, are given the attention they deserve. We need dialectic but we also need a way of making it malleable. At the same time, we need to be aware of what dialogue can do. We do not need to arbitrate between the two, because both are supple and malleable to each other.

Malleability is, therefore, a necessary part of the process of changing. Malabou (2005) called for the need to "renounce the 'well-known' and familiar meaning of the future based on here and now and, as a consequence, the 'well-known' definition of time." She suggested that we need to move beyond the conventional meaning of the word 'future,' as a state that will eventually come. Malabou (2005) posited that the future can be thought of instead as "that which is now to come." The future lies in the seizing of its excess now, rather than waiting for that excess to occur. To seize "that which is now to come," we would need to forge an organic link between dialectic and dialogue.

For Malabou plasticity provides a surplus of meaning for us to add to what we already know. If we are able to anticipate when an organizational restructuring will and could occur, shouldn't we be more willing to include dialogue in the way we go about preparing for such an event? Shouldn't we be willing to rely on the excess that the other will bring as we come to co-construct that which is now to come? This allows us to render dialectic with a new *plastic* meaning, which can only refer to the beginning of dialogue.

In Malabou's (2005, 2010) view, there needs to be foresight, which may come from the necessity to secure change outcomes. It may also come from our own willingness to see the benefits of talking about the future. This

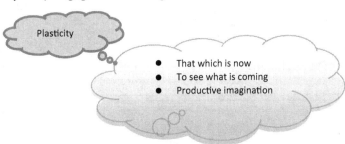

*Figure 5.1*    Plasticity according to Malabou

involves seeing what is coming through dialogue and the excess of meaning that the other is able to bring on board.

Malabou (2005) noted that plasticity involves focusing on the notion of "to see (what is) coming," rather than what has already come to be. The emphasis on what is coming is useful, even though there are aspects we cannot see. There is always some visibility, as well as invisibility. This also applies to organizations. "To see (what is) coming," therefore, means to see without seeing a future which is neither entirely present to the gaze nor totally hidden from it.

Rather than change being pursued as a matter of temporality, namely *time over time*, we are talking about the future being here and now, namely "that which is now to come," and so dialogue that engages in a "plurality of consciousness" (Bakhtin 1984, 81) is needed. This cannot in principle be fitted into the bounds of the consciousness of one person. Plasticity, unlike flexibility, is rich with creative powers. It can generate new practices in managing change, and provides a true promise of polyphony to empower organization members and enable them to share their views on change (see Figure 5.1).

Malabou's idea of plasticity was a mode of thinking and acting in ways that lie between fixed, order, and rigidity, on the one hand, and fluidity and change on the other.

## PLASTICITY IS ABOUT 'PRODUCTIVE IMAGINATION'

Catherine Malabou suggested that that we need to be more conscious of how we think. As she put it, "Our brain is plastic, and we do not know it" (Malabou 2008, 12). Drawing upon neuroscience, she used the term 'plasticity' to denote the capacity of neuronal systems to develop and regenerate newer systems through maintenance and repair (Malabou 2010).

In positive terms, Malabou's theory of change is based on the plasticity of neuronal systems and their capability for regenerative change, or readiness to embrace alternative modes of thinking and enacting agency. Her notion of plasticity has important implications for a discourse about diagnosing change as an appreciative inquiry project, in the sense that it could, at least in principle, make us rethink our preoccupation with problem-identification and the persistent impulse to assign blame.

Malabou's notion of plasticity involves recognizing the need for a "productive imagination" (Malabou 2010) achieved through a *conversion* in ways of thinking and action. A change agent remains knowledgeable about problem-centric modes and yet has no interest in using such modes. Plasticity is, therefore, about becoming committed to a way of thinking about change that is seen to be right. At that point, the change agent is no longer willing to go back, or dwell, on using the problem-centric. In an interview with Vahanian (2008), Malabou described plasticity as an achievement akin to the new state a sculptor is able to achieve while working on marble. Vahanian reported Malabou as saying "the marble once sculpted, the sculpted cannot be brought back to its original state . . . plasticity . . . means, at once, openness to all kinds of influences and resistances."

## FLIGHT ACHIEVED THROUGH PLASTICITY

Malabou treated plasticity as a concept that can help us grasp the whole, in the double sense of grasp as 'seizing' and 'understanding.' Plasticity is also about the flight from dialectic achieved through affects, or feelings. Crockett (2013, 72) noted that there is some resemblance between Malabou's notion of plasticity and Deleuze's work on concepts. Deleuze and Guattari (1987) suggested that it is through the feelings that they evoke, or affects, that we come to experience new concepts, and obtain newer meanings or extensions that were not previously experienced or thought. Plasticity is no exception. Through plasticity, we come to see variations that occur as we encounter the living moment on dialogue. Deleuze and Guattari described such variations as 'affects' or 'becomings' (Deleuze and Guattari 1987, 256). The intensity of the traces of the presenting issues, their colors, shades, and hues, start to collide or come into contact with newer shades and hues. Colman (2005, 11–12) wrote,

> "Affect is the change, or variation, that occurs when bodies collide, or come into contact. Affect expresses the modification of experiences as independent things of existence, when one produces or recognises the consequences of movement and time."

In other words, affect can become a source for changing and also for the malleability (plasticity) of our encounters as we go about interpreting change around us.

New realizations occur and the likelihood of fleeing (overcoming) dialectic becomes more relevant, despite the history of obsession with symptoms and causes. This is not because dialectic is associated with confrontation and fragmentation of organizational strengths, but because it truly fails to account for people and their subjectivities. It also fails to recognize the power of dialogue achieved through the utterance of one person giving access to the utterance of another.

## PLASTICITY IN ACTION

Plasticity has implications for change agency. It highlights how agents could apply concepts in an effort to keep their ways of thinking open to change. The notion of 'open-endedness' and being 'unconsummated' are essential to generating momentum as we move down the trajectory towards polyphony. Plasticity helps the organization to continue changing and to see what is coming, helping to build polyphony and heteroglossia.

In reflecting on dialogue and dialectic, we are confronted with a problem of choice. Do we treat them as opposites or are they entangled? The choice hinges upon whether we see them as inclusive or located in different spheres where dialogue is forced to capitulate to the dominant narrative. Unlike dialectic reasoning, which focuses on intensity and soundness of rules, the dialogic mode encourages people to bring forth their own experiences of those rules, with a view to creating responsive understanding and changing the rules if necessary.

Even though it may appear that we are positing a thesis (dialogic: feeling for change) and an antithesis (dialectic: managing and coping with change), the two are very much entangled in practice. It is sometimes helpful to 'unsettle' the dominant emphasis on dialectic and reason by allowing for more conversational space between people or by asking the 'unaskable,' such as 'What assumptions are you really making?' In their seminal article on modes of intervention, Blake and Mouton (1976) found that it is sometimes useful to ask people to confront their ways of thinking and reasoning, as well as their deep assumptions. As symptoms and causes are discussed, attention should also be paid to the underlying assumptions. Through dialogue, a change agent is enabled to understand others' deep assumptions (their 'master program'). By doing so, a change agent is better able to see situations from more than one angle, and so engage in learning and co-learning.

A sole emphasis on dialogue may sometimes prove unwarranted under conditions of urgency and where the time factor requires rapid implementation. It would, in fact, be difficult to imagine an organization that is purely dialogic. We need dialectic as well. However, a sole emphasis on dialectic may prove hypocritical: effectively, a subtle way of controlling, achieved through systems and procedures. Dialectic can sometimes compel others to concede, even though they remain utterly unconvinced by the argument. It is here that dialogue can come to the rescue, by surfacing the reasons for disbelief and using them to form focus groups to initiate change in rules and procedures.

One of the simplest things we recognize when it comes to the practice and reality of organizational life is that there will always be a need to relate dialogic and dialectic. At no stage does dialogue fade away to allow the omnipotence of dialectic. Blending driven by plasticity is necessary because no organization is either fully dialectic or purely dialogic.

Being reliant on reason, there is always the temptation to augment reason by drafting more rules to further its reach. Logically considered, justification of rules would require logic and dialectic. If our own dialectic is limited by the rules and reasons we have drafted, then we must open ourselves to the possibilities of dialogue through others. If our dialogue gives us an edge in seeing others, the other's dialogue gives us an excess of knowledge to step forward.

## EXAMPLES OF PLASTIC CHANGE

Chapter 3 pointed out that the Socratic notion of the dialogic is about accepting being with the other and the willingness to remain with the other, even when the other falls short of the expected capabilities or levels of skills and training. Many chief officers and other change agents come to see that life-centric modes achieved through plasticity can be a source of enchantment, helping them to see difference. In the following excerpts, I showcase a sample of utterances made by a group of experienced change agents as the notion of plasticity was introduced to them alongside appreciative inquiry. They are mostly indicative of an internally persuasive discourse that is largely affective and liberating.

As a regulation and compliance officer I am known for adhering to time schedules and by what the policy says. So far I feel I have been prioritizing problem-centric modes and I can see why it is basically a process of rulings lacking in responsiveness to change.

My organization has been undergoing a multi-phase restructure since October. There were times when this thing about the glass being half-full gave me the feeling of being split—gave me knowledge to deal with certain situations occurring and I would think "hey I just learnt that, this is how we deal."

I have been in my workplace for 6 months and had I not had the chance to see the impact of these rules from more than one angle and apply in a more meaningful way, I would have left months ago.

The onus is on me: How to move beyond frozen states of forcing procedures on others without getting them involved in furthering the aim of these procedures.

I hope to spend some more time on how to become more plastic in my interpretations of what people around me are saying. I have learnt a lot—my approach in both change and management generally is already influenced by what everyone around me is saying.

Plasticity has a place in my life. Don't get me wrong, I still like to follow rules and procedures, but . . . in context, dialogue remains a blip on the overall change effort and environment.

Nikulin summarized the difference between dialectic and dialogue:

> dialogue clarifies and allows for *being* as pluralistic and as a live being with the other, whereas dialectic studies and orders the *meaning* of a particular thing or term, including the *meaning* of being as an abstract notion. Hence dialogue belongs to both anthropology and ontology, whereas dialectic belongs to logic. Dialogue and dialectic, therefore, have different spheres and rules of functioning, which some thinkers (most notably, Hegel) try to unduly match and identify.
>
> (Nikulin 2010, 89: italic in original)

Bakhtin commented on dialogue and dialectic:

> Take a dialogue and remove the voices . . . remove the intonations . . . carve out abstract concepts and judgments from living words and responses, cram everything into one abstract consciousness—and that is how you get dialectic.
>
> (Bakhtin 1986, 147)

Even with this distinction, the two concepts remain entangled, in that when voice and social representations are brought to bear, the two become more malleable and harder to separate. Such a reminder about the intractable limitations of relying on either dialogue or dialectic may seem self-evident. As anyone engaged in a conversation has experienced, however, leaders—especially in formal positions of authority—seem to believe more in the revelatory power of their utterances when they are supported by deduction. When an organization is committed to its own side of the story without reaching out for the other, the need for dialogue becomes evident, but it loses its power. It becomes a method of explanation rather than empathic understanding. It also loses its potential for transforming the conversation from monologism to polyphony.

In cases where we truly think that dialectic is the way to go but there is scope for dialogue, we will want to try using dialogue to enhance the reach of dialectic and to make up, as it were, for what we are 'missing' by not using dialogue. We can do that by listening to what the other has to say, learning from the other, and learning from those who have been suppressed or disadvantaged.

Both dialogue and dialectic have a crucial role in getting an organization to continue changing and to see what is coming. Plasticity also requires being aware of the limits of the authoritative discourse. It can help in getting the balance right as we negotiate the complex, dynamic interaction between a quick dictation of rules, and the willingness to share and make such rules open for change. We do not need to arbitrate between the two, because they are in fact supple and malleable to each other. We therefore see malleability of dialectic as a necessary part of the process of change. Dialectic can help in filtering the right reason, but for that reason to be conveyed, we need the right amount of dialogue. Seeing diagnosis as a collective project can prove useful for managing change and the leadership of those advising on it.

## ORGANIZATIONAL LEARNING AND EMBODIMENT OF THE CHANGE EFFORT

What do we know about polyphony as a condition that allows for the emergence of extraordinary learning, and the embodiment of the change effort? In the following chapters, each of these key areas will be discussed and elaborated upon. As a prelude to each of these areas, the rest of this section introduces the concepts necessary for their understanding. Each of these areas has important implications for managing change. In excess of seeing, for example, it is the new capacity for seeing and accepting things from another's point of view without relinquishing one's own point of view. The areas include:

- The role of polyphony in creating 'surplus of meaning' in organizational learning.
- The role of polyphony in embodying the change effort.

The choice of these areas is based on a close reading of Bakhtin. They constitute important motifs, adding to each other's relevance and importance. There is mutual accommodation between these areas in managing change and obtaining new insights into the process.

Chapter 6, on surplus of meaning, showcases the connections between polyphony and collective learning. Bakhtin believed that an excess of meaning was likely to accrue because human thought is truly genuine based on contact between people. Through utterances and their recursive aspect, we come to experience how surplus develops, which may be conscious or not. Bakhtin explored the notion of 'surplus of meaning,' noting that there has to be willingness to acknowledge the emergence of new ideas and that a new idea can only live by giving birth, or surplus, to more ideas. He explained 'surplus of seeing' as:

> The idea begins to live, that is, to take shape, to develop, to find and renew its verbal expression, to give birth to new ideas, only when it

enters into genuine dialogic relationships with other ideas, with the ideas of *others*.

(Bakhtin 1984, 88: italic in original)

Much of the way we conceptualize 'double loop' learning (Argyris 1993) appears to ignore Bateson's notion of "cybernetic circuits of interactions" (1980, 147), or the idea that dialogue gives us a better grasp because it stops us from overlaying a view with itself. Bateson (1980, 147) noted that "we have been taught to think of learning as a two unit affair." He thought that the model of the speaker and the listener was obsolete because it ignores the depth that characterizes the stereoscopic vision and the surplus of meaning it generates.

As binocular vision gives the possibility of a new order of information (about depth), so the understanding (conscious and unconscious) of behavior through relationship gives a new *logical typ*e of learning

(Bateson 1980, 143; italic in original).

Bateson's use of the term 'relationship' must be understood in quite a wide sense: not a passive relationship such as that of the speaker and listener, but more widely as active participants in a dialogic relationship. It is necessary to examine precisely how understanding, both 'conscious' and 'unconscious,' can be acquired through both external and internal speech. One interface is Bakhtin's notion of polyphony, where the thoughts of an individual can only be understood by taking on board consciousness in relationship to each other.

In Chapter 7, the aim is to showcase the connections between polyphony and the notion of embodying the change effort, and to note that change is also about raising awareness of those who suffer. Much has been written about embodiment of the change effort, but one aspect has not been given the attention I believe it deserves, despite its importance in cultivating advocacy for embodiment. This is about polyphony resonating with 'eventness' as the capacity for co-being (Bakhtin 1984). Bakhtin's use of the word 'event' has its own etymology in the Russian language. *Sobytie* can mean *"co-being"* or *"me being with you and you being with me,"* showcasing moments in time where there is a deep simultaneity of feelings with the other, as the other produces an utterance (Holquist 2002).

It is the notion of 'many voices' being present that enables people to relate to each other and to emerge as extraordinary advocates witnessing and feeling what the other is experiencing. Polyphony allows people to take turns in expressing advocacy, followed by the ability to listen to each other and to be aware and willing to care about things that touch on the lives of those suffering. Polyphony is the collective effort that could bring together two or more voices able to touch or at least to bring attention to the suffering of the other.

Finally, the aim of discussing embodiment of the change effort is to show-case the connections between it and polyphony. Embodiment of the change effort is deemed crucial because it is through embodiment that readiness for change effort is enacted and sustained. Lack of readiness insinuates its way into the body. Jung (1998) emphasized the importance of the body by noting that much of how we feel and experience ourselves is absorbed as embodied experiences. Polyphony plays an important role in liberating individuals from the authoritative discourse. When individuals interact and live their representations, a commonality of embodied experiences results in sharing of subjectivities, a sort of jointed awareness *between* organization members.

## REFERENCES

Argyris, Chris.1993 Knowledge for Action, San Francisco: Jossey-Bass.

Bakhtin, Mikhail Mikhailovitch. 1981. *The Dialogic Imagination*, edited by Michael Holquist, translated by Carey Emerson and Michael Holquist. Austin: University of Texas Press.

———. 1984. *Problems of Dostoyevsky's Poetics*, edited and translated by Carey Emerson. Minneapolis: University of Minnesota Press.

———. 1986. *Speech genres and other essays*, edited by Carey Emerson and Michael Holquist, translated by Vern McGee). Austin: University of Texas Press.

Bateson, Gregory. 1980. *Mind and Nature: A Necessary Unity*. London: Fontana.

Berger, Peter L. and Thomas Luckmann. 1966. *The Social Construction of Reality: A Treatise in the Sociology of Knowledge*. New York: Anchor/Doubleday.

Blake, Robert Rogers and Jane S. Mouton. 1976. *Consultation*, 2nd ed. Reading, MA: Addison-Wesley.

Bushe, Gervase R. and Robert J. Marshak. 2009. "Revisioning organization devel-opment: Diagnostic and dialogic premises and patterns of practice." *Journal of Applied Behavioral Science* 45 (3): 348–68.

Cassam, Quassim. 2014. *Self-Knowledge for Humans*. Oxford: Oxford University Press.

Colman, Felicity. 2005. "Affect." In *The Deleuze Dictionary*, edited by Adrian Parr, 11–12. New York: Columbia University Press.

Cooperrider, David, Frank Barrett and Suresh Srivastva. 1995. "Social Construc-tion and Appreciative Inquiry: A Journey in Organizational Theory." In *Man-agement and Organization: Relational Alternatives to Individualism*, edited by Dian Hosking, H. Peter Dachler and Kenneth Gergen, 157–200. Aldershot, UK: Avebury.

Cooperrider, David and Suresh Srivastva. 1987. "Appreciative Inquiry." In *Research in Organization Development*, edited by Richard W. Woodman and William A. Pasmore, Vol. 1, 129–69. Greenwich, CT: JAI Press.

Cooperrider, David L. and Diana Whitney. 2001. "A Positive Revolution in Change." In *Appreciative Inquiry: An Emerging Direction for Organization Development*, edited by David L. Cooperrider, Peter F. Sorenson, Diana Whitney and Therese F. Yeager, 9–29. Champaign, IL: Stipes.

———. 2005. "A Positive Revolution in Change: Appreciative Inquiry." In *Appre-ciative Inquiry: Rethinking Human Organization Toward a Positive Theory of Change*, edited by David L. Cooperrider, Peter. F. Sorensen, Diana Whitney and Therese F. Yeager, 3–26. Champaign, IL: Stipes.

126 *Styles of Engagement: Dialogue with Dialectic*

Cooperrider, David, Diana Whitney and Jacqueline M. Stavros. 2008. *Appreciative Inquiry Handbook*, 2nd ed. Brunswick, OH: Crown.

Crockett, Clayton. 2013. *Deleuze beyond Badiou: Ontology, multiplicity and event.* New York: Columbia University Press.

Cronshaw, Steven F. and Ashley McCulloch. 2008. "Reinstating the Lewinian vision: from force field analysis to organization field assessment." *Organization Development Journal* 26 (4): 89–103.

Cunliffe, Ann L. 2004. "On becoming a critically reflexive practitioner." *Journal of Management Education* 28 (4): 407–26.

Deleuze, Gilles and Félix Guattari. 1987. *A Thousand Plateaus: Capitalism and Schizophrenia*, translated by B. Massumi. Minneapolis: University of Minnesota Press.

Emery, Merrelyn. 1999. *Searching: The Theory and Practice of Making Cultural Change.* Amsterdam: John Benjamins.

Gergen, Kenneth. 2008. *An Invitation to Social Construction*, 2nd ed. London: Sage.

Holquist, Michael. 2002. *Dialogism.* New York: Routledge.

Jabri, Muayyad. 2012. *Managing Organizational Change: Process, Social Construction and Dialogue.* Basingstoke: Palgrave Macmillan.

Jung, Hwa Yol. 1998. "Bakhtin's Dialogical Body Politics." In *Bakhtin and the Human Sciences: No Last Words*, edited by Michael Mayerfeld Bell and Michael Gardiner, 95–111. London: Sage Publications.

Kirby, Vicky. 2011. *Quantum Anthropologies: Life at Large.* Durham: Duke University Press.

Leonard-Barton, Dorothy. 1992 "Core capabilities and core rigidities: A paradox in managing new product development." *Strategic Management Journal (1986–1998)* Summer 13: 111–26.

Ludema, James D., David Cooperrider and Frank Barrett. 2001. "Appreciative Inquiry: The Power of the Unconditional Positive Question." In *Handbook of Action Research: Participatory Inquiry and Practice*, edited by Peter Reason and Hilary Bradbury-Huang, 189–99. Thousand Oaks, CA: Sage.

Malabou, Catherine. 2005. *The Future of Hegel: Plasticity, Temporality and Dialectic*, translated by Lisabeth During. London: Routledge.

———. 2008. *What Should We Do with Our Brain?* translated by Sebastian Rand. New York: Fordham University Press.

———. 2010. *Plasticity at the Dusk of Writing: Dialectic, Destruction, Deconstruction*, translated by Carolyn Shread. New York: Columbia University Press.

Nikulin, Dmitri. 2010 *Dialectic and Dialogue.* Stanford: Stanford University Press.

Oswick, Cliff. 2009. "Revisioning or re-versioning? A commentary on diagnostic and dialogic forms of organization development." *The Journal of Applied Behavioral Science* 45 (3): 369–74.

Pondy, Louis R. and Ian Mitroff. 1979. "Beyond Open System Models of Organization." In *Research in Organizational Behavior, Vol. 1*, edited by Barry Staw, 3–39. Greenwich, CT: JAI Press.

Rapoport, Robert N. 1970. "Three dilemmas in action research." *Human Relations* 23 (6): 499–513.

Schein, Edgar H. 1988. *Process Consultation: Its Role in Organization Development*, Vol. 1, 2nd ed. Reading MA: Addison-Wesley.

Schwandt, Thomas A. 2000. "Three Epistemological Stances for Qualitative Inquiry: Interpretivism, Hermeneutics, and Social Constructionism." In *Handbook of Qualitative Research*, edited by Norman K. Denzin and Yvonna S. Lincoln, 189–214. Thousand Oaks, CA: Sage.

Shapiro Michael. 2013. *Studies in Trans-disciplinary Method: After the Aesthetic Turn.* Milton Park: Routledge.

Ulmer, Jasmine. 2015. "Plasticity: a new materialist approach to policy and methodology." *Educational Philosophy and Theory*, http://dx.doi.org/10.1080/00131 857.2015.1032188.

Vahanian, Noelle. 2008. "A Conversation with Catherine Malabou." *Journal for Cultural and Religious Theory* 9(1): 1–13.

Weisbord, Marvin R. 1993. *Discovering Common Ground*. San Francisco, CA: Berrett-Koehler.

Young, Michelle. 1999. "Multifocal educational policy research: Toward a method for enhancing traditional educational policy analysis." *American Educational Research Journal* 36 (4): 677–714.

# 6 Polyphony and Organizational Learning

And what is the word without its shadow of knowledge?

Kahlil Gibran (1923, 112)

This chapter is on 'organizational learning' and how Bakhtin's ideas about language and communication can be applied. What do we know about Bakhtin's ideas about language that will help with the emergence of organizational learning? What do we know about the materiality of language, a key phrase for Bakhtin, which allows new ways of thinking and enacting learning in words, or *parole*?

Over the past thirty years, many researchers have considered 'organizational learning.' Despite the massive proliferation of reviews and case studies offering useful insights and prescriptions, I believe that some of the simplest and most obvious elements have gone missing. In particular, we have lost a more involved consideration of the materiality of language (utterances) and how learning is dependent on words that provoke, tease, and generate thinking in and of organizational settings. In discussing learning, Shotter (2000, 129) suggested that "we do not need any new theories. We need to elaborate critically the spontaneous theory of language we already possess." I am, therefore, trying to show how the materiality of Bakhtin's world of language could contribute to our understanding of learning as something we already do, *as part of everyday life*, and building on the capacity of the 'other.'

This chapter starts by exploring the role of language (utterances) in our conceptualization of learning. Utterances have implications for making learning more plastic in that each one summons the 'other' to enter the learning process. That process of calling upon the other to respond is "plasticity itself" (Bakhtin 1981, 39). It is what lies between any two utterances and opens the space for learning to occur. Every experience, every thought, every suggestion from an organization member is internally dialogic, free-for-all, and filled with encounters and tensions. It is therefore open to variations in the way people discern patterns of significance within their workplace, and possibly alienation as well as inspiration.

I then outline Bakhtin's notion of surplus of meaning as a concept useful to illuminate the conceptualization of learning as 'triple loop,' or Learning III. The idea behind the phrase 'triple loop learning' is that learning goes beyond insights (the basis of 'double loop' learning) to examine the underlying principles and context. I consider the connection between Bakhtin's work on language and that of Gregory Bateson (1972, 1980). This is not about dovetailing their work, but about finding an interface that would implicate the importance of utterances in the way we think of triple loop learning, or learning about the context. Last but not least, I expand on the interpretive power that triple loop learning would have if we were to incorporate utterances, both internal and external, in the learning process in and about organizational settings.

There is extensive literature on organizational learning, and space constraints do not permit a full review. This should not, however, be construed as reflecting a lack of importance (see, for example, Argyris and Schön 1978; Fiol and Lyles 1985). The term 'organizational learning' is used in the sense of organizations being able to learn. The concept has a long and muddled history, however (Easterby-Smith and Lyles 2003; Fox 2009; Argote 2011; Tosey, Visser and Saunders 2011) and is far from consensual even though there has been an attempt to highlight issues of concern associated with anthropomorphism (e.g., Awieringa and Wierdsma 1992; Friedman, Lipshitz, and Popper 2005; Lipshitz, Friedman, and Popper 2006).

Recently, the phrase, and the ideas behind it, has started to acquire a more reflexive or dialogic emphasis (Cunliffe 2008) culminating in the idea of embodiment. Other authors have also mentioned important issues, including the embodiment of learning and the relevance of existential phenomenology (Küpers 2008). Relying on work associated with the existential philosophy of Merleau-Ponty (1962), Küpers (2008) called for more work on inter-relational and inter-subjective processes where embodiment is implicated.

## UTTERANCES

Bakhtin's idea of learning achieved through utterances is about their malleability, with their innate ability to become responses to previous utterances, and promote others in future. For Bakhtin, the word (*slovo*) is in the body (Morson and Emerson 1990, 133). That is whether it is communicated as utterances, through gestures, or by attention to visual, aural (hearing), and tactile (physical) modes of perception. Far from subordinating the body to the 'word' (*slovo*), the word is brought back to the body and its meaning is enhanced through sociality and people's relational exchange. Bakhtin's world of learning is neither one of reified treatments based on ascribing groups and organizations with human learning attributes (anthropomorphic), nor a '*socially constructed*' type of learning, absent of dialogue.

Instead, it involves the plasticity of everyday use of the *word* and the fact that every utterance we make, both external and internal, takes place in a social context. Bakhtin (1984) opposed smugness and aloofness, noting that a person has no internal sovereign territory, in the sense that they are always looking inwards and *"into the eyes of another or with eyes of another"* (1984, 287; italic in original). We can learn much each day through utterances mutating, because when we speak or think, the words we use, whether we like it or not, are filled with and draw on the words of others. This happens even though each person genuinely believes they have generated their own opinion or view.

As we saw in Chapter 2, an utterance can be a word or a sentence, spoken or written. It was defined by Bakhtin (1986, 67; italic in original) as a *"real unit of speech communication"* because it reflects a real speech situation. Each utterance is infused with intentions. To say that utterances are subjective (univocal) would be too limiting. Bakhtin's idea was that each utterance takes meaning from another. There must be other interpretations for one's own to exist. Every utterance has its own social theme, creating its own speech genre. Bakhtin observed:

> Genres correspond to typical situations of speech communication, typical themes, and consequently, also to particular contacts between the *meanings* of words and actual concrete reality under certain typical circumstances.
>
> (Bakhtin 1986, 87; italic in original)

An utterance, therefore, includes not only the words, but also the context or the situation in which it is uttered. Pending context, it summons action, and so an utterance is basically an invitation for answerability that takes place within a genre.

Consider the following example:

A: *G'day. How r u?*

Here we have an utterance but it is incomplete. Without understanding the style and context, there is no way to interpret it. It can only summon the 'other' once we know more about that other and the situation in which the utterance is made.

Along similar lines, Voloshinov (1986, 97), a member of the Bakhtin Circle, defined utterances as "a fact of the social milieu," in the sense that at any given point in time, the meaning attached to a word has its own social property. This may be different from the social meaning of the same word at a different time. Both definitions highlight the simple but stunning fact that utterances are an expression of social character even though they come through the subjective experience of the speaker. Every utterance is made in anticipation of a response and what the other has to say. Utterances therefore have their own social property, in that they look for the other to respond.

The prevailing view of the role of utterances in the literature on learning is *grammatical*—each utterance is treated as a sentence, and meaning is determined by the final sentence. This view is largely ethnocentric, even though it might call on the other to collaborate and respond to change. Much of the current viewpoint requires ideal statements centered on prescriptions for achieving and structuring the learning effort. Meaning is predominantly based on a Saussurean mode of transmission with 'organizational learning' used as code, without meaning-making (Jabri, Adrian, and Boje 2008). Such a viewpoint has become ingrained into mainstream managerial consultation and accreditation practices as well as in change agency through a worldview that ascribes groups with human learning properties.

As noted in Chapter 1, Ferdinand de Saussure, one of the founders of modern linguistic analysis, originally suggested that the study of language (*langue*) and speech (*parole*) should be separated (with signifier and signified being viewed as two separate but stable systems) and that emphasis should be placed on language as a social institution of the word (Saussure 1983). Saussure rejected the inclusion of actual speech as an investigation because of its infinite variety.

Bakhtin took issue with Saussure's rejection of speech. He felt that the variety of speech would explain the empowerment of the character. Bakhtin distinguished utterances from sentences—sentences being a linguistic, grammatical approach to language. Sentences are static, fixed in time and space. Utterances, in contrast, take on new meanings as they are embodied and exchanged with other people in the form of discourse. According to Bakhtin:

> The entire life of language, in any area of its use (in everyday life, in business, scholarship, art, and so forth) is permeated with dialogic relationships.
>
> (Bakhtin 1984, 183)

Bakhtin, therefore, objected to Saussure's approach in structuring language as an independent system of signs in which each reflects a ready-made code and signifies a definite concept, giving speech a fixed and stable meaning. Bakhtin (1986, 147) noted that the context of a conversation is always subject to change and plasticity, but a code must be finalized and that is because "[a] code is only a technical means of transmitting information; it does not have cognitive, creative significance. A code is a deliberately established, killed context." Bakhtin was really saying that the difference between systems (*langue*) and *parole* is the difference between dialectics and dialogue:

> Take a dialogue and remove the voices (the partitioning of voices), remove the intonations (emotional and individualizing ones), carve out abstract concepts and judgments from living words and responses,

cram everything into one abstract consciousness—and that's how you get dialectics.

(Bakhtin 1986, 147)

Many change agents today remain compulsively dedicated to organizational learning based on structures and systems of information transmission, reflecting ideas of change rooted in transmission of messages using ready-made codes. Bakhtin (1984, 182) was quite unequivocal in his view that in '*langue,*' as the object of linguistics, "there are not and cannot be any dialogic relationships: they are impossible both among elements in a system of language" and that "dialogic interaction is indeed the authentic sphere where language *lives*" (1984, 183).

Bakhtin's view was based on the idea that learning is and should be authentically *extralinguistic* and so at least double-voiced. Every speech act awaits another for more meaning. All utterances are humanizing, and human thought takes place both externally and as inner speech (Morson 2009). Bakhtin viewed even a simple utterance, such as thanking someone or requesting information, as a speech act that engages in a "plurality of consciousness, one that cannot in principle be fitted into the bounds of a single consciousness, one that is, so to speak, by its very nature *full of event potential* and is born at a point of contact among various consciousnesses" (1984, 81; italic in original).

For example, the two utterances '*This change is good*' and '*This change is good*' constitute an extralinguistic relationship only if they *enter* each other in the sense that they embody each other. The same applies with two non-identical statements: '*This downsizing exercise will work out well*' and '*This downsizing will not work out well.*'

These utterances would constitute a dialogic relationship only if we were to stop treating them as categorical judgements separate from each other, and if there is a genuine intent to relate to the feedback from the other, even though power relations might not be equal. Each utterance holds a unique place and yet remains open for the other, which is where utterances are simultaneously constituted and interpreted. An utterance responds to those that came earlier—in a sense, they come to be inhabited by others. Whether communicated aloud or in silence, utterances emerge as an active expression of meaning.

Deleuze and Guattari (1987) used the idea of a 'plateau' to show how concepts are often entangled with each other and the way in which they can produce continuity. In exploring the 'plateauing of concepts,' they defined 'plateau' by noting that Gregory Bateson "uses the word 'plateau' to designate something very special: a continuous, self-vibrating region of intensities whose development avoids any orientation toward a culmination point or external end." They advanced the idea of a 'rhizome' as a metaphor for the way concepts are entangled. A rhizome is a subterranean part of a plant, which sends up shoots (words) in new and often unexpected places, and through which new growth (ideas or excess of meaning) occurs. A rhizome, as with a 'stretch of utterances,' is unintentionally creative as it gives rise to new shoots (Deleuze and Guattari 1987). Even if an utterance is not merged with another, it "ceaselessly varies and alters its distance in relation to the others. These variable distances are not extensive quantities divisible by each other . . . they cannot diminish *without their elements changing in nature*" (Deleuze and Guattari 1987, 30–31).

Deleuze and Guattari's perspective is connected to the dialogic nature of utterances, namely how utterances are defined by others. Every utterance can be viewed as an output, but eventually becomes the input, or rhizome, for the next round of talk. Utterances, therefore, have profound rhizomatous implications because they produce what might be described as a stretch of interactions among people wanting to know through and from each other, whether intentionally or unintentionally. Importantly, Bakhtin as well as Deleuze and Guattari, and of course Bateson, viewed the flow of such utterances as being full of recursivity. In the example below, utterances continue to change and the change is recursively functional in the sense that meaning is carried over from one utterance to another, leading to some form of output. The output may be obscure or appear lacking in *form*, but that is often due to the fact that no utterance can ever be neutral.

B:   This merger will help us all.
A:   I don't think it will. I just don't see how.
B:   Hmmm well. . .
A:   If they are to hope that this merger will get them out of trouble then we will need some level of trust in those forcing this option.
B:   Let's hope they know what they are doing. It is a matter of trust. Don't you think so?
A:   I've never thought about trust being so much important, but something about the notion rings true for me.
B:   Yeah, trust is very hard to earn. . .
A:   And very easy to lose. I mean people expect the plan to have no gaps.
B:   If there are gaps then those at the top will invent data to fill in.
A:   They are good at this.
B:   Well . . . if people trust them then there is hope that things will work out . . . but if people don't trust you then they will find gaps.
A:   We've been driven by them. Change can still be achieved without trust . . . and this one is no different.
B:   You think so?
B:   We'll see . . . it is the erosion of trust that creates resistance. I know this from past experience. . .

Each utterance is infused with intentions. Every utterance spoken by A is infused with B's awareness of A, and vice versa. The awareness of both is also infused with the influence of other speakers that they have previously heard.

We also notice that the context within which their utterances are made remains subject to change and becoming as other utterances remain in a stretch of talk, and as the talk becomes 'populated' by words. Bakhtin (1981) stressed that no word can be neutral and the world of change in and of organizations is no different.

In summary, utterances shed new light on learning from at least two angles. First, they have the potential to transcend the organizing property of any single utterance even though a person's perspective is what they genuinely believe. Second, utterances have the potential to uncover a variety of meanings and suggestions from others. These have implications for building new scenarios and possibilities for learning in and of organizational settings and so determine how learning takes place.

## BAKHTIN'S NOTION OF OUTSIDENESS

Bakhtin (1981) advanced his notion of 'outsideness,' or 'transgredience,' as the act of stepping across, to emphasize the self as dialogical. It is saturated with and occurs through 'otherness.'

By 'outsideness,' Bakhtin (1981) meant that elements of the self, of one's own utterances, or the self's culture (identity) can cross over. That is, aspects of the self can cross over to other selves or identities. Each character takes an element of the other, and *illuminates* it. Applied to change, it leads to the phenomenon of being able to 'tele-transfer,' or 'commute' elements of one's way of thinking about and seeing change to social others (Jabri, Adrian, and Boje 2008). Learning can be cultivated in process terms based on a number of utterances mutating among each other and yet unmerging. This is basically co-creating everyday talk, by reaching back to the other's utterances. Bakhtin valued everyday talk, noting that:

> The idea begins to live, that is, to take shape, to develop, to find and renew its verbal expression, to give birth to new ideas, only when it enters into a genuine dialogic relationships with other ideas, with the ideas of *others*.
>
> (Bakhtin 1984, 88; italic in original).

Outsideness is a crucial concept for learning, and is both new and insightful. It re-envisions our location *vis-à-vis* the other. Bakhtin is not talking about focus groups, sharing of management talk, participation in conversation or transmission of messages in meetings or in emails. Rather, his emphasis or center of attention, is on the mutation of utterances embedded in the joint act of giving and taking, namely consciousness. Bakhtin believed that outsideness is likely to accrue even without equal power relations because human thought is truly genuine based on contact between people (see Figure 6.1).

*Figure 6.1*   Unmerged voices with each side taking aspects of each other

Through utterance, as with plasticity, it is possible to destroy as well as to create. A team leader 'outside' the team members is likely to see things about them that they cannot see. Likewise, because a team member is outside the team leader, they will see things about the leader's style, strengths, or weaknesses that are invisible to the leader.

Outsideness is significant for change because it sees change as transgressions of utterances that are simultaneously constituted and interpreted. Change achieved through the transgression of utterances is, therefore, not an immutable substance, nor an auto-immune structure (Jabri 2004). It is continuously influenced by the surplus of insight achieved through seeing what the other cannot see.

Under outsideness, recursivity is ongoing and cannot be finalized. A recursive statement aims to create an exchange of meaning-making. Meaning is not black and white, and it is not Cartesian, as if my meaning and yours are separate. Instead, it builds on what has taken place before. The output of one round of talk continues to change because it promotes a surplus of meaning, and is enriched by insights brought to bear from more than one angle. It gives way to a new output on top of what has already been achieved, allowing new ideas and learning to emerge.

## CONSCIOUSNESS AS A PROPERTY OF THE SOCIAL

We now turn to the social aspect of consciousness, through the utterances we make, both external and internal. Bakhtin's (1993) idea of consciousness comes from seeing utterances, both external and internal as social. Bakhtin spoke several languages, including Latin, Greek, German, and Russian and from his understanding of Latin, saw 'consciousness' as knowledge that is inherently social, because it is produced through the presence of and with the other (*con* as in *togetherness*; *scio* as in *to know*).

Bakhtin's (1984, 287) point is that every thought, every experience, every utterance has its own unique social dimension: "I am conscious of myself and become myself only while revealing myself for another, through another, and with the help of another." Clearly, Bakhtin did not see consciousness as some kind of single, unabridged undifferentiated whole, but a simultaneous unity of differences in the interpenetration of utterances (Baxter 2004). Consciousness is about considering, accepting, or rejecting the utterances of the other.

Based on this social meaning, Bakhtin approached almost every thought, experience, conversation, and everyday utterance as internally dialogic, in the sense that it remains open to inspiration from outside itself. "To live means to participate in dialogue: to ask questions, to heed, to respond, to agree, and so forth" (1993, 293).

Bakhtin's point about the social nature of consciousness echoes Bateson's (1972, 306) idea of the unity between mind and matter (nature), where "personal identity merges into all the processes of relationship in some vast ecology or aesthetics of cosmic interaction." Bakhtin's view of the self is also aesthetically relational, as well as materialistic. It is neither self-contained nor independent of the other. Both Bateson and Bakhtin put emphasis on the meaning brought by the other, enabling the capture of moments of meaning-making, and the emergence of successive realizations.

Bakhtin noted that even a very simple conversation can be new because it summons one party to a sudden and more conscious realization that was not previously there. This may be, for example, a sudden understanding of why someone else holds a different viewpoint, and a grasp of that point of view (Morson and Emerson 1990). Each participant becomes aware that their utterances are an important theme in the other's consciousness, and vice versa. The actual facts discussed may not be new to either participant, but they may come to a different understanding by making sense of their experiences together, even if neither changes their views.

Each participant comes to discuss their view (realization) with the other. Each sees their lives being made more visible through what the other has said, even though they may opt to keep their individual stance. Such an unmerged realization is more about consciousness being "never self-sufficient; it always finds itself in an intense relationship with another consciousness" (Bakhtin 1993, 41). Bakhtin (1993) believed that such hybridity came from seeing an utterance, external or internal, as having an imaginative sociality. Bakhtin's idea is that consciousness of self is mediated by the other. Pollard (2008) suggested that consciousness under Bakhtin is social, in that utterances, even in silence, are made within a social context. Lazzarato (2009) explained that in Bakhtin's conception of consciousness, the characters are in fact not first and foremost linguistic or psychological subjects, but 'possible worlds' in the sense that they occupy 'chronotopes,' or blocs of space-time, as 'existential territories.' This is similar to the work of Deleuze and Guattari, and makes Bakhtin's idea even more interesting because it implies that the characters are aware of their unmerged voices coming to relate to each other.

Bakhtin's viewpoint is important because it construes learning as dependent on the other, and contingent on words that provoke, tease, and create dialogue. My learning comes into the picture once I see myself through the other's words. To be aware, and particularly to be aware reflectively, I need the other. Bakhtin's ideas suggest that it would be reckless of me not to seek the other, because I need them to become self-conscious and internalize the intra-personal. In other words, self-consciousness is about the awareness of another's awareness of oneself. One becomes aware of oneself by seeing oneself through another's words. Interestingly, Broks noted:

> The notion [phenomenal consciousness] will remain invisible to conventional scientific scrutiny and will forever remain so . . . Science can study the neural activity, the bodily states, the environmental conditions. . . but the quality of—the feel—of our experiences remain forever private and therefore out of bounds to scientific analysis.
>
> (Broks [2003, 140], quoted in Pollard 2008, 124)

The inner speech we have as we listen to someone talking in a meeting could only be construed and *lived* through language (speech), for how could we come to account for any internally persuasive utterance or some authoritative discourse without an awareness expressed in inner talk?

## BAKHTIN'S NOTION OF THE SURPLUS OF MEANING

Commenting on Bakhtin's notion of 'outsideness,' Morson and Emerson (1990, 185) noted that, as each side takes on aspects of the other, a 'surplus' is obtained that allows each side "to complete and finalize an image of each other." Bakhtin (1984, 110) put this as vision being born "between people" collectively.

In *Author and Hero in Aesthetic Activity*, Bakhtin explored the notion of surplus by offering a description of how we encounter one another:

> When I contemplate a whole human being who is situated outside and over against me, our concrete, actually experienced horizons do not coincide. For at each given moment, regardless of the position and the proximity to me of this other human being whom I am contemplating, I shall always see and know something that he, from his place outside and over against me, cannot see himself: parts of his body that are inaccessible to his own gaze (his head, his face and its expression), the world behind his back, and a whole series of objects and relations, which in any of our mutual relations are accessible to me but not to him. As we gaze at each other, two different worlds are reflected in the pupils of our eyes.
>
> (Bakhtin 1990, 22–23)

Further on, Bakhtin noted:

> It is possible, upon assuming an appropriate position, to reduce this difference of horizons to a minimum, but in order to annihilate this

difference completely, it would be necessary to merge into one, to become one and the same person.

(Bakhtin 1990, 23)

Bakhtin explored the notion of 'surplus of meaning' as an *overflow*, noting that there has to be willingness to acknowledge the emergence of new ideas and that a new idea can only live by giving birth, or surplus, to more ideas. Bakhtin described surplus of meaning as two unmerged tendencies arising in self-consciousness, between the moment when the self and the other come together in speech, which makes self-consciousness possible. There is also the moment of difference arising when one is conscious of the other. These arise because, for Bakhtin, learning lies on the borderline between oneself and another, and each has to recast the other's ideas in the process of sense-making.

Much of what Bakhtin said appears obvious at first sight, namely that our awareness of the physical and spatial materiality of our bodies remain limited. Of course, we could fix this problem by having a digital camera on our back, but such knowledge, or so-called feedback, would remain constrained by what we could see through the gadget. Consciousness here is singular, even though it receives its own feedback. Even if we were to gaze at ourselves in the mirror, we would remain limited by ourselves. In other words, the knowledge we have of *ourselves* stays limited by what we see. Without the other, the knowledge we have of ourselves remains singular.

There is more to the accrual of such surplus of meaning than a single-minded vision, way of thinking or ideology found inside the head of an individual leader, or manager. When I see things only from my own point of view, from the point of the truth I hold, I can argue with you but I cannot enter into a genuine dialogue. Our debate will always tend towards defensiveness and perhaps lack of compassion for each other. If I have no point of view of my own, I may not argue with you, but I will not care either, and will, therefore, be easy prey for those who want to impose their own point of view.

Morson and Emerson (1990, 185) noted that under Bakhtin's idea of surplus, there is a deep sense of involvement based on each side being willing to take on aspects of the other. A luminous (creative) flux is shed, which allows each side "to complete and finalize an image of each other." This produces the "surplus of meaning," a surplus of seeing or capability that manifests itself through speech. Identities are enriched by insights being unveiled in the light of simultaneous differences (outsideness) through utterances set in context. The worst that can happen is a defensive response, which purges the creativity that would have emerged. Such surplus develops in a back-and-forth manner as people exchange utterances, and as words are transposed among contexts and situations.

Bakhtin noted that the dialogic self, or inner world, is never self-sufficient. As Pollard pointed out, the polyphonic or dialogic self has no central 'I' in the centre or in charge and is therefore a decentred or even fragmented self, as well as being a thoroughly social self suffused with the voices of others.

(Pollard 2008, 35)

A thought is an utterance, and is answered by another based on the willingness to acknowledge. Whenever a new idea emerges, it comes to live as it is sustained, and then gives a new meaning, or surplus, to other novel ideas. Surplus has important implications:

* To listen to others' points of view, we do not have to abandon our own (Harris 1997).
* If we want to learn, then an awareness of the importance of the 'other' becomes essential for getting change to take root. We cannot change our views until we come to know the views of others.
* Our views remain temporary and tentative until we recognize that other views are possible.

## DOUBLE AND TRIPLE LOOP LEARNING

In this section, I wish to go back to some of the ideas we often teach, and disrupt our knowledge about double and triple loop learning by asking what might appear to be the *unaskable*. Double loop learning (Learning II) is a useful concept, especially on feedback, but what is the prospect for extending our knowledge of the double loop through simultaneity of utterances?

According to Argyris (1993), there are at least two ways of thinking and acting on a problem or mismatch. The first, or first loop, relies on correcting it using an equivalent mode of action, under an existing set of governing values (master program), or prevailing assumptions. The double loop, by contrast, requires a look at the set of governing assumptions or values (master program) with a view to reviewing and revising them and/or replacing them with a new set more likely to resolve the mismatch or problem.

Most definitions of the double loop see changes in the master program as crucially important in reshaping or altering the mismatch and informing strategy (Argyris 1993). To change the master program is a huge undertaking, because management is often only interested in what it wants to hear. Pursuing the double loop involves revisiting the prevailing assumptions to build new capabilities. Regrettably, the model used to communicate the double loop is largely one based on the monologic transmission of systematic feedback between a speaker and a listener, rather than one based on a holistic affirmation and the role of the other in co-constructing knowledge.

The focus on capability and actionable knowledge sees learning as rooted in the pooling of resources and other changes in the master program. Change in the master program, however, is about consciousness, only found in intense relationship with another consciousness. Every change in the master program, every experience, every thought is internally dialogic, and obtained through interanimating utterances mutated from diverse points.

There is, however, one important aspect of double loop learning which has not been given the attention it deserves, despite its importance in cultivating learning in organizational settings. This is the way that utterances predict and relationally change those that follow. Consider the following points which are often viewed as essential for learning to take root:

- Learning needs to be visibly valued and reflected in the vision and corporate plans. Leadership needs to show commitment to learning through clear communication at all levels of the organization. Leadership must practice what they preach before they can expect anyone else in the organization to do so.
- Communication and information systems need to be in place to ensure the information is received at all levels of the organization, before rumors reach individuals. Information can be disseminated very easily and quickly, using electronic mail, bulletin boards, and focus groups.
- People need to receive timely feedback about performance. Appraisal systems, therefore, need to incorporate feedback not only on actions, but also on learning from the process.
- There needs to be a balance between performance outcomes and learning outcomes. Innovation, questioning, risk-taking, and self-development need to be encouraged and rewarded appropriately.

There is little in the above about utterances. People are seldom given the opportunity to discuss what is happening, what is not happening, or what is likely to happen. In the quest for prescriptions and as we feign objectivity, we undermine our capacity for dialogue, losing the surplus of meaning.

All of the statements above are prescriptive, and often endorsed and repeated in an authoritarian (monologic) manner. None of them constitutes mutuality and responsiveness through talk. Paying continual attention to people's interrelated utterances remains very important for explaining how an organization can expand its capability to learn and innovate, and how it could emerge as polyphonic, with un-merged utterances surfaced and used for learning. None of the statements makes reference to context. Each and every one stops short of describing how and under what conditions each can inform meaning-making through utterances.

Building on the work of Bateson (1972) and Bakhtin (1984), we see the need to explore how language informs learning and how things are enriched by insights being brought to bear from more than one person.

One interface is that of consciousness having its social property achieved through the utterance of one person revealing themselves to another, through another, and with the help of another. Once such revelations are made, then that is the beginning of the idea of polyphony, as long as people are protected from being judged from an authoritative position or by 'someone' dialectic, aloof, or indifferent. Having obtained such excess of capability through the other, the onus is on recursive talk to continue building on what has been achieved. An interface here is that of Bateson (1972, 304; capitalization in original) noting that "If Learning II is a learning of the contexts of Learning I, then Learning III should be a learning of the contexts of those contexts."

## BATESON MEETS BAKHTIN: LEARNING III AND THE MUTATION OF UTTERANCES

So far, triple loop learning or Learning III lacks a dialogic property, in terms of exhibiting resonance to utterances and consciousness. In this section, I propose to focus on the capacity of utterances, both external and internal, to transform monologue and to displace it with dialogue in ways that promote excess of learning. Bateson noted:

> *Learning the contexts of life* is a matter that has to be discussed, not internally, but as a matter of the external relationship between two creatures. *And relationship is always a product of double description.*
> (Bateson 1980, 146; italic in original)

Bateson's comment echoes Bakhtin's viewpoint that:

> When we select words in the process of constructing an utterance, we by no means always take them from the system of language in their neutral, *dictionary* form. We usually take them from *other utterances*, and mainly from utterances that are kindred to ours in genre, that is, in theme, composition, or style.
> (Bakhtin's 1986, 87; italic in original)

In exploring triple loop learning, which is in essence what Bakhtin sought in his idea of utterance and consciousness, Bateson noted:

> To the degree that a man achieves Learning III, and learns to perceive and act in terms of the contexts of contexts, his 'self' will take on a sort of *irrelevance*. The concept of 'self' will no longer function as a nodal argument in the punctuation of experience.
> (Bateson 1972, 304; italic is mine)

Bateson believed that the self would start lessening its degree of containment and move away from smugness, and towards the other, attaining 'irrelevance' or Bakhtin's sociality of consciousness.

Bateson's idea of the self attaining 'irrelevance' is deeply fascinating and something that is profoundly echoed in Bakhtin's view that "the very being of man (both external and internal) is the *deepest communion*" (1984, 287; italic in original). There is always a moment in time, a sideways glance at what the other is saying, based on utterances made in anticipation of the other's active response.

Bateson believed that Learning III starts to lead to greater relevance and flexibility when considered in the context of the other and their consciousness. But then what happens when the other is not there, or not willing or able to listen? That is when Learning III, the learning about Learning II, stops. Smugness and petrification of systems and people starts to characterize learning in and of organizational settings at this point, and people are left disheartened and with little option but to exit the organization altogether or agree to some learning outlet of a trivial nature that would circumvent the purposeful nature of Learning III.

Bateson believed that all conversations are woven from the tissues of other conversations. It is through the medium of talk and listening that learning can be expressed through the understanding of another's thoughts and feelings. Much of Bateson's emphasis on talk is evident in the daughter–father conversations in Chapter 8 of *Mind and Nature: A Necessary Unity*:

> DAUGHTER: So what? You tell us about a few strong presuppositions . . .
> FATHER: Oh, no. I also told you something about the limitations of imagining.
> DAUGHTER: Is that evolution, then?
> FATHER: Yes, indeed. It all shifts and swirls around the verities. . .
> DAUGHTER: Yes, I know you love reciting that sentence.

An important interface is that of plasticity. Malabou suggested that we should understand plasticity as the "spontaneous organization of fragments" (2010, 7) and "the excess of future over the future" (2005, 6). Learning III requires a plastic reading, one that challenges forms, rules, and paperwork. It can illuminate elements of the dialectic that we rarely see, shaping, reshaping, and even destroying the monologic utterances that often pervade the operation of the double loop and the way the assumptions and values that govern the master program are reinforced through managerial logic.

As we saw in Chapter 5, Malabou (2005, 5–6) posited that the future can be thought of instead as 'that which is now to come.' The future lies in the seizing its excess now, rather than waiting for it to occur. To seize "that which is now to come," we would need to destroy the operation of the double loop and its master program through the spontaneity of utterances and the excess of seeing likely to emerge through expanding to larger networks, even though they appear to have their own counter narratives.

The constraint on Learning III is that the double loop is considered to be an object to be judged based on external criteria, rather than a way of getting people to relate without having to give in. How would we ever be able to restore the learning potential if we were not willing to destroy the rules, and respond plastically to the dominant dialectic governing the future of the organization and its capacity for learning?

In destroying the double loop, people will be enabled to move to a new situation where they can see for themselves how their utterances, reflecting their embodied insights into the change situation, "teem with the consciousness of others" (Clark and Holquist 1984, 241). It should enable organizations and the people in charge to move away from the pursuit of rules, paperwork, and adherence to fixed systems of accreditations.

A treatment of Learning III could benefit from looking at Bateson and Bakhtin. A meeting between these two could prove useful in shifting to the transpersonal dimension, to see learning from an utterance angle but also to engage consciousness as a social property. Bateson (1980, 147) noted that "we have been taught to think of learning as a two unit affair: The teacher 'taught', and the student 'learned'. But that lineal model became obsolete when we learned about cybernetic circuits of interaction." In his view, the old mode is obsolete, because it ignores interactions and the surplus generated.

Since Bateson (1980) wrote his book *Mind and Matter: A Necessary Unity*, there has been a marked increase in our awareness of matters related to representation of the voice of the other, as in our awareness of the plight of minorities, their employment, the plight of refugees, and those innocent people who have been disadvantaged due to wars, etc. It is not only the freedom of speech but it is also the 'fairness of speech' that matters. This is how we can better change towards a greater understanding of mutual differences, where multiplicity and inclusivity are responsibly bounded and mutated through utterances (Kakabadse and Jabri 2015). The fact remains, however, that despite such marked awareness, we remain tied to ways of thinking largely aimed at managing people as *objects* and *indicators* rather than *relationships* based on what the other sees and has to say.

To break the habit of reflecting on objects, we need the other but not his or her political subservience. Without the other, it is difficult to fully arrest strategic inertia in an attempt to manage. Bateson (1972, 304) elaborated on the importance of flexibility that should inhere the double loop by noting that "I once heard a Zen master stat[ing] categorically: To become accustomed to anything is a terrible thing." Bateson observed that we are almost unaware of trends in our change of state, requiring the other to help us see what we cannot see. It might well be the case that learning in and of organizations is no exception. We need, therefore, to focus on genuine relationships and connections, thinking aloud with the other.

Accommodation becomes problematic when we try to intervene in a change that has become habituated or is being sustained through adjustment or adaptation. According to Bateson,

> There is a quasi-scientific fable that if you can get a frog to sit quietly in a saucepan of cold water, and if you then raise the temperature of the

water very slowly and smoothly so that there is no moment *marked* to be the moment at which the frog should jump, he will never jump. He will get boiled.

(Bateson 1980, 109)

The question we are asking is: are our organizations sitting too quietly and dwelling on the smugness of strategies, procedures, petrified adherence to rules, objectivity of accreditation standards, and large data sets? If we are not plastically changing or *relational*, then are we *deliberately* deteriorating?

Learning is achieved not just in going back and taking corrective action. It is also in the way we relate to the other and how we accelerate the sharing of moments where surplus of meaning is foreshadowed, or guessed ahead. This takes us back to Malabou's point about the future and the plastic capacity to receive and give new structures or directions, or to understand plasticity as "the excess of future over the future" (Malabou 2010, 6). It is the "future of the future of learning" in and of organizational settings that is at stake. Malabou viewed the future as "yet-to-come," but what happens when such learning or future remains absent of Learning III, described by Bateson as being learning about the 'contexts of all contexts,' including the double loop?

When those with managerial logic achieve what they can by devaluing 'non-standard' and more novel contributions or structures, in favor of more secure repetitive designs and procedures, what is 'yet-to-come' will be dysfunctional to the learning future of the organization. It will be particularly damaging to the need for the organization to establish a strong and unique niche in which it is not seeking to compete with other organizations on what might well be their turf. There is also a problem that such 'yet-to-come,' even under its revised dialectic, tends to discourage the pursuit of innovative practice in favor of managerial logic driven by ticking boxes, paperwork, graphs, and measures, and reasoning based on quantifiable indicators.

## LEARNING III INFORMED THROUGH UTTERANCES

As with Bateson's aesthetic notion and enactment of Learning III, Bakhtin constructed his model of polyphony as an aesthetic act through which outsideness, in relation to the other, provides the ground for triple loop learning, or Learning III, to occur. These two ideas support each other. Learning III needs outsideness to support polyphony, as much as polyphony supports Learning III. For surplus of learning to take place, we would need to be outside the other to see what they cannot see, as much as we need the other for what they see. If we were to utter 'what we see' to the other, being outside, there will be an excess of seeing obtained through the utterance of the other.

Bakhtin talked about the surplus of meaning without calling for the merger of voices or for utterances to be finalized. The idea of many voices foreshadowing different consciousnesses being shared, and yet without being merged, provides a genuine opportunity for Learning III to occur, based on seeing things from another's point of view without relinquishing one's own point of view.

Morson and Emerson (1990) emphasized that Bakhtin's notion of polyphony is at the heart of creative thinking, in the sense that it provides the platform through which surplus of meaning is generated between self and other. Using the metaphor of a choir, each member is outside the others, yet can relate to each of them in the act of organizing the performance. They combine their performances, but remain independent, answerable to themselves as well as each other.

Rather than seeing change as a set of emails or messages, announcements, or plans of action to be communicated, we need to focus more on how such messages are made more malleable, in terms of changing our power to persist with the other (see Johnston and Malabou 2013). Malabou's idea of plasticity is about imagining and producing new forms of meaning, reinforcing the power of the brain to persist. Malabou (2005, 62) talked about imagining plasticity as the capacity to receive form, transgress our own limits, and respond to what is occurring from the outside. She said that "if repeated change produces a difference in the subject experiencing it, this means that change coming from the outside has altered into a change emerging from the inside." A change emerging from the inside takes on a recursive form and is, therefore, plastically never-ending at the boundaries of selfhood and otherness. There is no limit to the extent to which utterances cannot be finalized 'plastically,' leading to an ever-changing view.

Many organizations fail to achieve the surplus of insights that could emerge as connections are made and that is one reason why some strategies backfire. Training, rewards, performances, and competences need to be linked and smoothed with the aim of fostering the creation of triple loop learning. Consider the importance of a plan to enhance the capability of staff through training. Training on its own is not a panacea, as we cannot force people to embrace specific competencies unless attempts are made to take on board what they have to say.

Through otherness, learning is revealed as dynamic rather than static. If we seek to learn, then an awareness of the importance of the role of the 'other' becomes essential for getting change to take root. We cannot change our views until we know the views of others. Our views remain temporary and tentative until we can recognize that other views are possible.

A person or a group has no alternative but to 'bring forth' other selves (person, group, organization). It is not only 'I-for-myself' but also 'I-and-the-other,' and this is accomplished through more than one round of recursive story-telling as surplus is produced and imagined. An actor does not necessarily arrive at *the* meaning, but continues to learn new meaning through ongoing interaction with others (Oswick et al. 2000). This meaning comes from the "contact between the word and the concrete reality" (Bakhtin 1986, 87), and reality is shaped and reshaped through utterances made by other actors at more than one level (Gergen and Thatchenkery 1996; Kellett 1999).

As the top management group of an organization develops its bearings from conversations with change recipients, so change recipients develop their bearings from conversations with top management. Lacking an awareness that utterances have a social property can lead those in authority to assume, mistakenly, that change recipients will be bound to accept what is expected of them.

## STORYTELLING CHANGE AS A SOURCE FOR UTTERANCES LEADING TO SURPLUS

Several scholars (e.g., MacIntyre 1984; Bruner 1990) have gone as far as to argue that one of the essential characteristics of being human is to tell stories. We turn to storytelling to bring on board additional surplus of meaning, as the other wishes to bring their story, or even stories. This helps us to understand and learn about the world around us (Boje 2008). If change is to achieve a surplus of meaning, however, each needs to invite the other to tell their story and then relate to it. In doing so, the timing and location of events remain crucial.

Boje (1995, 1000) defined a story as "an oral or written performance involving two or more people." When two or more people become engaged in storytelling, they are interpreting the past or anticipating changes for the future. Past events are revealed as having significance for future changes. Although stories can be either fictional or derived from real-life situations, they are all ultimately based on narrations derived from human experience of life. Brockelman (1992, 1) noted that "we not only tell stories but are our stories." Our 'being' and 'method' work together and this is at the heart of storytelling.

Considering the role stories play in the world around us, Gabriel noted:

> If human action always achieved the results it intended, there would be no space for stories. Nor would there be a space for stories, if we lived in a perfectly ordered and rational world, like Plato's Republic.
>
> (Gabriel 2000, 239)

Stories are not only utterances recited for their own sake, or facts about a certain event, such as learning from a recent downsizing, but they also "enrich, enhance and infuse facts with meaning" (Gabriel 1998, 136). They change the way we view the world around us.

Bakhtin (1986) equated narratives with utterances (conversations) from people coming to talk with each other. There is an ongoing process of narration with a constant theme. The outcome is seen in the making, and the process is unfolding all the time. Building on Bakhtin (1986), one could argue that there is nothing said about change that does not already have a 'form' or a 'structure' similar to that of narrative. Every change and the direction it takes originate in narration. Every conversation in corridors and meeting rooms could easily be treated as a narrative in the making, unfolding in time.

The act of narration is crucial for getting surplus of meaning to flow through utterances. Pollard (2008) argued that the 'I' can speak from different 'selves' in different positions and with different experiences and stories to tell about those experiences at different times. It follows that consciousness and the capacity of the person to comprehend reality is also facilitated by storytelling. It helps us to see reality not only as about experiences and stories encountered by ourselves, but also happening to the other. Nikulin (2010, 87) elaborated on the property of narration as it relates to dialogue by noting that "the person in dialogue is not established theoretically through logical argument, but instead is revealed through narration."

Time can be chronological or narrative. For example, looking back on a downsizing exercise, the actual time is in the past. When we recall a story about it, however, and attach it to events in the present, its new time is no longer where downsizing has occurred in the past. Rather, it becomes narrative time. To obtain surplus, historical events are recalled and simultaneously combined with present utterances. Surplus and the transitory nature of every human experience emerge as mutually constitutive. According to Ricoeur (1991), this mutuality remains fluid and dynamic as it is shaped and reshaped through ever-changing meanings, desires, and aspirations.

Some narrative theorists (for example, Ricoeur 1991; Richardson 1995) have treated 'narrative' and 'story' as almost synonymous and suggested that selfhood is achieved through narrative. Others have maintained that there is a difference between story and narrative. For example, Leitch (1986) maintained that the element of 'closure' is a distinguishing characteristic of stories as opposed to narratives. According to this view, for a surplus to be achieved, a story is judged to be 'good' or 'poor' on the basis of how well it delivers its theme or lesson as utterances are made, whereas a narrative simply recounts a sequence of events. This might or might not have a surplus that is evident in the first place.

Stories typically have a definite ending and bring about some meaningful lesson. Most stories, however, can be interpreted in various ways, and some of these lessons or conclusions can actually be at variance with each other. People can construct apparently incompatible stories, or bring about the recital of counter-stories. A marketing department might tell one story and the R&D people another about the same events. One surplus can outperform another as talk is recursive. Meanings, therefore, emerge from storytellers' own preferred interpretations of events and their context (Boje 2001).

Baskin (2008) explained that stories and counter-stories have the ability to 'push' and 'pull.' The fact that a story can be co-constructed or recited in different ways actually provides ample scope for surplus to emerge. That is because it invests the act of storytelling with even greater scope for polyphony. For Baskin (2008), it also means that storytelling can help people to respond to the inherent complexity of the situation. Reciting counter-stories is a manifestation of polyphony (Bakhtin 1984). The fact that a story can be co-constructed in different ways actually provides ample scope for multiple representations.

Stories enable people to cope with the complexity of change (Boje 2001). A single coherent story that is agreed or recited by everyone does not exist. People chase different stories and explore different plots and counter-stories as they seek to make sense of their unfolding experience. Boje (1995) conceived storytelling as a house where people in different 'rooms' or 'corridors' recite and tell their common experiences differently. Importantly, they have little choice but to negotiate such shared reality. In the same way, sharing stories of change provides people with a variety of options. More than one meaning can emerge from a single story, and this is multiplied as other storytellers share their stories and understanding of the world.

Cohen (2003; quoted in Baskin 2008, 3) believed that "this ability to create somewhat contradictory meanings from the same reality is a central quality of all complex systems." Organizations are no exceptions. Williams (2004, 168) commented that reality makes storytelling polyphonic, in helping us to get various stories to work together and "to focus the process of dialogue and communication" by looking at the broad systems that influence and shape variations in our stories.

Despite the multiplicity of meanings that can be derived from a single story, a story has the power to lead to more than one meaning, in much the same way as a logical argument. For example, one consultant might advocate the adoption of total quality management (TQM) by telling success stories of organizations that have used it to pursue quality accreditation. Another might advocate a different perspective and provide examples of organizations that have pursued TQM unsuccessfully.

Stories, therefore, have the capacity to 'adjudicate' surplus between ideas and bring diverse perspectives together. Stories provide an account of what is working and what is not. As a consequence, change is not imposed from above or 'outside.' Instead, the recital of stories enables change to be shaped and reshaped from 'within.'

Stories not only unite the present with the past, but are also used to link the present with the future. People recite stories to obtain meaning as they reflect on past events, like looking through an album and then turning to take a snapshot. Stories from the past also influence people's aspirations, hopes, and fears as they contemplate the future. In listening to these stories, change agents have an opportunity to look into the future to see how issues and concerns are gathering pace. This knowledge can be used to defuse critical situations before they cause trouble or get out of control.

We develop a passion for stories not because we are fond of storytelling events but to inform ourselves and others around us. Morson and Emerson (1990, 185) noted that, as each chronotope takes on aspects of the other, an "illumination" is achieved, and each comes to illuminate the other. A story about a merger in one organization crosses over to another organization and takes on new elements. In time, and through our utterances, new elements of learning are illuminated, creating 'surplus in meaning' (Jabri 2005). Stories form and showcase movements and transitions as we tell of their themes and lessons, to provide insights. The transformative ideas associated with storytelling may be conceptualized as transgressing the bounds that separate (Küpers 2008). A story relating to a change situation, such as that of a forced merger or downsizing, is tied to the present in the sense that it could easily affect the lives of others and how they see downsizing.

Interestingly, Tattam (2013) saw narrative time as about anticipating the future and yet at the same time recalling the past in relation to the present. As an example, I might narrate how fellow organization members found their way around the last time a merger took place at my place of work. As I recall the merger in the past, and the problems it caused, I might recall the downsizing exercise that followed. To talk about the downsizing, however, is not the same as talking about the merger itself.

My recital will, therefore, capture the existential tension between one story and another. The meaning attached to the merger will assume an immediacy that is grounded in the 'here and now' in the way it affects the people around me. That is because there is more than one temporality, even though the previous merger has occurred in the past. This brings us to a temporal multiplicity where "every attempt to articulate a 'new' meaning already carries within it references to a dense network of past ideological struggles" (Sandywell 1998, 200).

## CONCLUSION

As it stands, learning conceived in terms absent of outsideness and surplus of meaning clearly limits the horizon of the scholarship on learning in and of organizational settings. Bakhtin's alternative, in contrast, draws on the role of utterances between people as promoting more possibilities for surplus of meaning to be achieved, constituting the basis upon which learning might progress.

Each of us has the skills to learn and cope but such coping can only be rendered in time and space. We need others to help us to turn back inwards and improve on the surplus next time we approach reality. The "I" needs narration to come to grips. For this to happen, we need the other to be able to remain in a state of grasping, clutching, and charging oneself.

Polyphony helps with this. It allows both change agents and change participants to reflect on three important issues: (i) that change efforts need an ontological position where consciousness is seen as a social property contingent on the boundary between selfhood and otherness; (ii) that the boundary between selfhood and otherness provides focus and content for change achieved through utterances; and, (iii) most importantly, that it is only through otherness that Learning III can be defined as learning in all contexts. All three issues presume a continuing self-awareness and awareness of others, their subjectivities, and their sensibilities. For all three issues to succeed in providing effective interventions, it is necessary to presuppose an equal partnership between change agents and change participants. This is necessary if identity is not to be subordinated to coherence and order.

Change management must cast off not only the dualistic idea of the word as immutable code, but also unhelpful dualistic concepts of relationship. Bateson, Malabou, and Bakhtin all have something to offer. An emphasis on change conceived as surplus will motivate managers to become more open and responsive in involving themselves in self-analysis. Rather than encoding "sameness" and assuming conformity of the self with social others, learning would need to include the other, contest coherence and synthesis, and enfranchise those change participants whose voices have previously been silenced.

Change conceived as surplus of meaning offers an opportunity to expand the horizon for empowerment and for control to be located at the level of coordination. A surplus of meaning achieved through the other provides the possibility of change. It also provides more options and opportunities, which is in itself empowering.

Organizational change is constructed by the richness of the word (dialogue). In polyphony, the word brings knowledge and insight into the situation. As Gibran (1923, 112) asked, "And what is the word without its shadow of knowledge?" Such a view encapsulates the central theme of this chapter, that the challenge for change agents is to work through the utterance of the word and the way in which words are made meaningful through both dialogue and dialectics. A change that is led through both is more likely to take root.

## REFERENCES

Argote, Linda. 2011. "Organizational learning research: past, present and future." *Management Learning* 42 (4):439–42.

Argyris, Chris. 1993. *Knowledge for Action*. San Francisco: Jossey-Bass.

Argyris, Chris and Donald Schön. 1978. *Organizational Learning: A Theory of Action Perspective*. Reading, MA: Addison-Wesley Publishing Company.

Awieringa, Joop and André Wierdsma. 1992. *Becoming a Learning Organization: Beyond the Learning Curve*. Reading: Addison-Wesley.

Bakhtin, Mikhail Mikhailovitch. 1981. *The Dialogic Imagination*, edited by Michael Holquist, translated by Caryl Emerson and Michael Holquist. Austin: University of Texas Press.

———. 1984. *Problems of Dostoyevsky's Poetics*, edited and translated by Caryl Emerson. Minneapolis: University of Minnesota Press.

———. 1986. *Speech Genres and Other Late Essays*, edited by Caryl Emerson and Michael Holquist, translated by Vern McGee. Austin: University of Texas Press.

———. 1990. *Art and Answerability: Early Philosophical Essays*, edited by Michael Holquist and Vadim Liapunov, translation and notes by Vadim Liapunov. Austin: University of Texas Press.

———. 1993. *Toward a Philosophy of the Act*, edited by Michael Holquist and Vadim Liapunov, translated by Vadim Liapunov. Austin: University of Texas Press.

Baskin, Ken. 2008. "Storied spaces: the human equivalent of complex adaptive systems." *Emergence: Complexity and Organization* 10 (2): 1–12.

Bateson, Gregory. 1972. *Steps to an Ecology of Mind: Collected Essays in Anthropology, Psychiatry, Evolution and Epistemology*. Chicago: The University of Chicago Press.

———. 1980. *Mind and Nature: A Necessary Unity*. London: Fontana. First published in 1979 by Wildwood House, London.

Baxter, Leslie A. 2004. "Relationships as dialogues". *Personal Relationships* 11:1–22.

Boje, David. 1995. "Stories of the storytelling organization: a postmodern analysis of Disney as Tamara-land'." *Academy of Management Journal* 38 (4): 997–1035.

———. 2001. *Narrative Methods for Organizational and Communication Research*. London: Sage.

———. 2008. *Storytelling Organizations*. London: Sage.

Brockelman, Paul T. 1992. *The Inside Story: A Narrative Approach to Religious Understanding and Truth*. New York: State University of New York Press.

Broks, Paul. 2003. *Into the Silent Land*. London: Atlantic Books.

Bruner, Jerome S. 1990. *Acts of Meaning*. Cambridge, MA: Harvard University Press.

Clark, Katerina and Michael Holquist. 1984. *Mikhail Bakhtin*. Cambridge, MA: Harvard University Press.

Cohen, Jack. 2003. "Why is negentropy, like Phlogiston, a privative?" International Nonlinear Sciences Conference, Vienna, Austria, 9–11 February.

Cunliffe, Ann L. 2008. "Orientations to social constructionism: relationally responsive social constructionism and its implications for knowledge and learning." *Management Learning* 39 (2): 123–39.

Deleuze, Gilles and Félix Guattari. 1987. *A Thousand Plateaus: Capitalism and Schizophrenia*, translated by B. Massumi. Minneapolis: University of Minnesota Press.

Easterby-Smith, Mark and Marjorie A. Lyles. 2003. The Blackwell Handbook of Organizational Learning and Knowledge Management. New York: Wiley.

Fiol, C. Marlene and Marjorie A. Lyles. 1985. "Organizational learning." *Academy of Management Review* 10: 803–13.

Fox, Steve. 2009. "This interpreted world: two turns to the social." *Management Learning* 40 (4): 371–78.

Friedman, Victor J., Raanan Lipshitz and Micha Popper. 2005 "The mystification of organisational learning." *Journal of Management Enquiry* 14: 19–30.

Gabriel, Yiannis. 1998. "The Use of Stories." In *Qualitative Methods and Analysis in Organizational Research: A Practical Guide*, edited by Gillian Symon and Catherine Cassell, 135–60. Thousand Oaks, CA: Sage.

———. 2000. *Storytelling in Organizations: Fact, Fictions, and Fantasies*. Oxford: Oxford University Press.

Gergen, Kenneth J. and Tojo J. Thatchenkery. 1996. "Developing dialogue for discerning differences." *Journal of Applied Behavioral Science* 32: 428–33.

Gibran, Kahlil. 1923. *The Prophet*. New York: Alfred A. Knopf.

Harris, M. R. (1997). "The Surplus of Seeing: Bakhtin, the Humanities, and Public Discourse." In *Standing with the Public: The Humanities and Democratic Practice*, edited by J. F. Veninga and N. McAfee, 136–68. Dayton, Ohio: Kettering Press.

Jabri, Muayyad. 2004. "Change as shifting identities: a dialogic perspective." *Journal of Organizational Change Management* 17: 566–77.

———. 2005. "Narrative identity achieved through utterances: the implications of Bakhtin for managing change and learning." *Philosophy of Management* 5 (3): 83–90.

Jabri, Muayyad, Allyson Adrian and David Boje. 2008. "Reconsidering the role of conversations in change communication: a contribution based on Bakhtin." *Journal of Organizational Change Management* 21: 667–85.

Johnston, Adrian and Catherine Malabou. 2013. *Self and Emotional Life: Philosophy, Psychoanalysis, and Neuroscience.* Columbia University Press.

Kakabadse, Nada and Muayyad Jabri. 2015. "Freedom of speech: the role of organizations in influencing socio-organizational change." *Call for Papers. Special Issue. Journal of Change Management.*

Kellett, Peter M. 1999. "Dialogue and dialectics in managing organizational change: the case of a mission-based transformation." *The Southern Communication Journal* 64 (3): 211–31.

Küpers, Wendelin. 2008. "Embodied 'inter-learning'—an integral phenomenology of learning in and by organizations." *The Learning Organization* 15 (5): 388–408.

Lazzarato, Maurizio. 2009. *Bakhtin's Theory of Enunciation*, translated by Arianna Bove. Presentation made at the Department of Fine Arts, Norwegian University of Science and Technology, 16 May.

Leitch, Thomas M. 1986. *What Stories Are: Narrative Theory and Interpretation.* University Park: Pennsylvania State University.

Lipshitz, Raanan, Victor J. Friedman and Micha Popper. 2006. *Demystifying Organizational Learning.* Thousand Oaks, CA: Sage.

MacIntyre, Alasdair. 1984. *After Virtue: A Study of Moral Theory.* London: Duckworth.

Malabou, Catherine. 2005. *The Future of Hegel: Plasticity, Temporality, and Dialectic*, translated by L. During. London: Routledge.

———. 2010. *Plasticity at the Dusk of Writing: Dialectic, Destruction, Deconstruction*, translated by Carolyn Shread. New York: Columbia University Press.

Merleau-Ponty, Maurice. 1962. *Phenomenology of Perception.* London: Routledge and Kegan Paul.

Morson, Gary S. 2009. "Addressivity." In *Concise Encyclopedia of Pragmatics*, edited by Jacob L. Mey, 13–16. Oxford: Elsevier.

Morson, Gary S. and Caryl Emerson. 1990. *Mikhail Bakhtin: Creation of a Prosaics.* Stanford: Stanford University Press.

Nikulin, Dmitri. 2010. *Dialectic and Dialogue.* Stanford: Stanford University Press.

Oswick, Cliff, Peter Anthony, Tom Keenoy, Iain L. Mangham, and David Grant. 2000. "A dialogic analysis of organizational learning." *Journal of Management Studies* 37: 887–901.

Pollard, Rachel. 2008. *Dialogue and Desire: Mikhail Bakhtin and the Linguistic Turn in Psychotherapy.* London: Karnac.

Richardson, Laurel. 1995. "Narrative and Sociology." In *Representation in Ethnography*, edited by John Van Maanen, 198–221. London: Sage.

Ricoeur, Paul. 1991. "Narrative Identity." *Philosophy Today* 35 (10): 73–81.

Sandywell, Barry. 1998. "The Shock of the Old: Mikhail Bakhtin's Contributions to the Theory of Time and Alterity." In *Bakhtin and the Human Sciences*, edited by Michael Mayerfeld Bell and Michael Gardiner, 196–213. London: Sage.

Saussure, Ferdinand de. 1983. *Course in General Linguistics*, translated by Roy Harris. London: Duckworth.

Shotter, John. 2000. "Inside dialogical realities: from an abstract-systematic to a participatory-holistic understanding of communication". *The Southern Communication Journal* 65 (2/3): 119–32.

Tattam, Helen. 2013. *Time in the Philosophy of Gabriel Marcel*. London: Modern Humanities Research Association.

Tosey, Paul, Max Visser and Mark Saunders. 2011. "The origins and conceptualizations of 'triple-loop' learning: a critical review." *Management Learning* 43 (3): 291–307.

Voloshinov, V. N. 1986. *Marxism and the Philosophy of Language*, translated by Ladislav Matejka and I. R. Titunik. Cambridge, MA: Harvard University Press.

Williams, Bronwyn T. 2004. "The truth in the tale: race and the 'counterstorytelling' in the classroom." *Journal of Adolescent and Adult Literacy* 48 (2): 164–69.

# 7 The Verdict: Embodying Change through Polyphony

*For God's sake shut your eyes and consider how your experiences are arriving from the antecedent state of mind and body.*

Alfred North Whitehead in lecture, Harvard, 23 March 1937; quoted in Johnson (1983, 9)

As the title of this book suggests, Bakhtin was always keen to distinguish dialogue from dialectics. For example, in *Speech Genres*, he noted:

"Take a dialogue and remove the voices (the partitioning of voices), remove the intonations (emotional and individualising ones), carve out abstract concepts and judgements from living words and responses, cram everything into one abstract consciousness—and that's how you get dialectics"

(Bakhtin 1986, 147).

In distinguishing dialogue from dialectics, Bakhtin was also very careful to avoid the trap of treating language as a system of linguistics. He therefore noted the difference between language as a self-constrained system, which he identified as a codification, and "a feeling for utterance." The former is centered on a Cartesian separation. It is about positing the self against monologic truth treated as objective truth, upon which much of the ideology of managerialism is based.

The latter, namely "a feeling for utterance" suggests that utterances are part of the body, whether they are communicated through speech, gestures, or attention to visual, aural, and tactile modes of perception. Far from subordinating the body, the word is brought back to the other, generating feelings of embodiment and making our experiences more concrete (co-being with the other). Meaning is enhanced through sociality and relational exchanges. Underlying polyphony is the idea of many voices coming together without merging. These include our own inner affirmation of ourselves, which we can project through inner talk, and projections of ourselves into others to experience their lives. Bakhtin noted,

I must experience—come to see and to know—what *he* experiences;
I must put myself in his place and coincide with him, as it were.

(Bakhtin 1990, 25; italic in original)

That projection can only be attributed to a polyphonic reliance on dialogic sense of truth. It cannot be monologic as the projection is more likely to be enacted where there is a system of thought reflecting organizational practices not requiring plurality of consciousness. It is possible that management's rather indecisive attitude towards polyphony can, to a large extent, be attributed to the viewpoint that consensus is important, and that merging voices is appropriate. In other words, there is a belief that this is how organizations *should* be managed and that merging of voices is crucial, even if in fact it is not.

Imagine a meeting of a CEO with organization members, in which those leading the meeting allow people to bring many voices to co-exist, including those of the organizers and the CEO. Even though meetings between CEO and organization members are often designed to achieve consensus, they may ignore a sense of truth that is dialogic, in that they ignore individual differences within and beyond what has been prescribed in rules and formalization. Such meetings often rigidly follow an agenda, rather than allowing alternatives to be discussed in a truly many-voiced way, where everyone has equal right to speak.

Polyphony is an ontology based on *sobytie* being translated as *co-being* (Morson and Emerson 1990). I define *sobytie* as energy derived from being with the other. It is saturated with eventness where it gets harnessed into a new state, or surplus, or excess of meaning. In Figure 7.1, I attempt to show how such an energy is harnessed through utterances and their malleability as well as embodiment that is inter-corporeal. Most importantly, it is *sobytie* that places us in the world with other people, in nature, and other things.

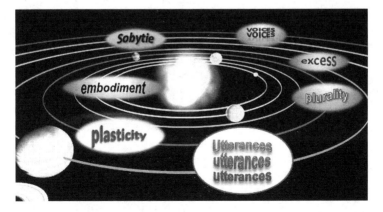

*Figure 7.1*   *Sobytie* applied to polyphony

Polyphony is also about 'eventness' as the capacity for co-being (Bakhtin 1984). Bakhtin's use of the word 'event' has its own etymology in the Russian language. *Sobytie* can mean "*co-being*" or "*me being with you and you being with me*," showcasing moments in time where there is a deep simultaneity of feelings with the other, as the other produces an utterance (Holquist 2002). We all encounter such events in time, and they bring us into that '*co-being*' with the other, whether that other is human or perhaps another form of the post-human, such as pets or nature.

It is my personal feel that *sobytie* might be close in meaning to Whitehead's (1956) notion of prehensions. A prehension is a realization, a moment of affective knowing, or some experiencing of Bakhtin's *sobytie* as co-being (Jabri 2012). Of course, our grasp is of something that has already passed but the realization is—in the feeling of it—abrupt and instantaneous. These become embodied in the '*in-between-ness*' with the other. They affect both self and other. They resonate as events develop through that glance, or flash of sudden realization calling for embodiment of some new and immediate improvement. They can be understood as a glance in a rearview mirror but one that brings the future to the present.

The transformation from a managerialist ideology to polyphony has to retain plasticity. It is a transformation from an idealism fixed and repressed through the dialectics of Hegel into the sort of realism accomplished through an ontology of being with the other. It resolves dialectics through structures of transformation achieved through plasticity and hence having the capacity to switch over to simultaneity of voices without ignoring what the other is saying. In the dialogic, language and polyphony are intertwined. There is no point in calling for *becoming* or developing more process-related theories of change unless the call for processual thinking is substantiated through Malabou's (2005) plastic reading of the future to come.

How could 'becoming' ever accrue under dialectics and in the absence of polyphony? The prevailing notion of 'becoming,' absent of polyphony, has made it much more difficult for organizations to embrace continuity in the true sense of the word. My 'impossibility theorem' here is that without polyphony and plasticity, the possibility of 'becoming' is highly debatable, because it is only through simultaneity of talk and the malleability of utterances that the prehension of 'changing' becomes feasible.

We need to think of an organization as 'becoming' through polyphony as well as plasticity, rather than 'being,' otherwise we are thinking only in the here and now. In other words, without simultaneity and Malabou's notion of plasticity, there will be no sense of continuity because everything will be finalizable through synthesis. It is polyphony *itself* and the unfinalizability of utterances that give and sustain 'becoming.' This is where plasticity is linked to a state of 'becoming' and the notion of the future being 'here and now' (Malabou 2005). In many ways, this is as much to do with Alfred North Whitehead's (1956) notion of prehensions as with Malabou's (2005) notion that plasticity includes both malleability and the giving of form, like an artist shaping and re-shaping forms as they are destroyed one after the other. Whitehead's use of prehension is centered on the notion that "experience involves becoming, that becoming means that something becomes, and that what becomes involves repetition transformed into novel immediacy" (Whitehead 1978, 136–7).

What Bakhtin has to say about polyphony and about consciousness having a social property may be interesting in its own right, but the crucial issue here is using it in leadership of change. Polyphony makes us more willing to lead through unmerged perspectives, not by a monologic sense of truth, or single voice. More importantly, Bakhtin's call for polyphony is not so much about being the leader as about the *sobytie* or *co-being* with the other (Morson and Emerson 1990). This makes us fully appreciative of plurality of consciousnesses resonating and turning into surplus, and is, therefore, about embodiment and the celebration of inter-subjectivity as a relational attunement. This notion of *sobytie* is felt deeply as it has a striking power leading to a quality of leadership based on genuine consensus.

## MERLEAU-PONTY MEETS BAKHTIN

As Hirschkop (1999) noted, Bakhtin never wrote in solitary confinement, away from other thinkers. In the rest of this chapter, I attempt to bring the thinking of Bakhtin into a dialogical relationship with that of the French existential philosopher Merleau-Ponty (1908–1961).

The affinity between Bakhtin and Merleau-Ponty has been noted by a number of scholars, including Holquist (1990), Gardiner (1998), Dufva (2004), Küpers (2005, 2008), and Boje (2008). They all agree that overcoming the Cartesian duality of mind versus body is crucial. Descartes's (1969) dictum is centered on *cogito, ergo sum* ("I think, therefore I am"). It is based on the separation of the mind from the body, putting the onus on the mind. It disembodies the mind and confines it to a largely monologic 'I.' The body is almost ignored and treated as secondary to the person doing the thinking.

Both Bakhtin and Merleau-Ponty were influenced by the existential philosophy of the nineteenth century German philosopher Friedrich Nietzsche (1844–1900). Both called for a reversal of the isolation of the mind from the body. Both wanted to recognize the power of feeling the lived body in ways that can facilitate reciprocity between self and other, and remake relations. Merleau-Ponty noted that "our [twentieth] century has wiped out the dividing line between 'body' and 'mind'" (1964, 226; quoted in Nagataki and Hirose 2007, 223). Both developed a line of analysis that highlights the importance of embodiment of our subjective bodily experiences in understanding ourselves and the way in which people are envisioned in polyphony.

Gardiner (1998) presented an account of how the respective intellectual projects of Bakhtin and Merleau-Ponty display a number of remarkable affinities, in terms of reversing the separation between the self and other and between body and world. He went on to show how both Bakhtin and Merleau-Ponty were able to adopt a more dialogical world-view to capture the open-ended interactive nature of bodies and selves.

Gardiner (1998) stated that Merleau-Ponty objected to distancing of the mind from the body. Both he and Bakhtin called for a phenomenology of the body. Merleau-Ponty went as far as replacing 'I think' with 'I can; we can,' which means that the social 'we' forms the basis for polyphony and reciprocity. New powers are, therefore, given to us through the human body, including sociality. As Jung (1998, 96) noted, "sociality is inconceivable without bodies-in-relation (that is inter-corporeality). The body is the living site of sociality, it actively places us in the world with other people and other things."

## EMBODIMENT AS AN INHABITATION

The notion of embodiment is centrally important as a manifestation of polyphony. Polyphony is contingent on maintaining a dialogic sense of truth, with consciousness having its own social dimension. Bakhtin understood embodiment thriving on the tension between a dialogic and a monologic sense of truth. A dialogic sense of truth contributes to embodying the change effort via the habitual understanding of the reality we experience in how the body structures our experiences.

Without the centrality of consciousness having its own social property, polyphony crumples into homophony. It depends on simultaneity to make the inter-corporeal meaningful for people as they come to relate to each other and embody the change around them, and as change is announced and sustained through building readiness. We all have the capacity to embody our *lived* experiences, felt meanings, change, compassion, and perceptive awareness.

At the very beginning of this book I made the point that for Bakhtin, polyphony was about simultaneity and the presence of multiple voices. The essence of this is reality expressed as utterances that are inter-corporeal, in that my voice and that of the other are embodied and expressed by and through the other. We could explain the 'inter-corporeal' as 'habitations' with oneself and with the other. We dwell, we 'live' in our utterances, and as we do so, we use them to reconstruct the way we see the other. Mair, for example, described this inhabitation as follows:

> We inhabit the great stories of our culture. We live through stories. We are lived by the stories of our race and place . . . It is this enveloping and constituting function of stories that is especially important to sense more fully. We are, each of us, locations where the stories of our place and time become partially tellable.

(Mair 1988, 127)

As we inhabit change around us, utterances come to the fore. In the desire to understand change and what needs changing, we ask questions such as how far from change should we be? This question is linked to asking how deep we should be and how far we should embody change. Change in my organization is not far from me. I experience change on a daily basis, and have to decide how near I should be to what is happening around me. Each quality speaks to my body and my daily inhabitation, my living of change. Unity or disunity of such qualities can be a great concern to me, as it might be for others around me.

## PHENOMENAL BODY AND COPING WITH CHANGE

Polyphony and embodying the change effort are both about the phenomenal body, the tacit knowledge or surplus of meaning we have of ourselves, and our feelings and emotions. It is how we go about 'becoming,' knowing who we are and how we relate to the phenomenal bodies of the change participants around us. It therefore includes how we see, or are conscious of, our capacity in relation to theirs; how we see their dreams and aspirations changing over time; how we see performance; and how we learn through them and they through us.

Whether transitional or transformational, change is about the process of destruction, modification, adjustment, shifting, or adaptation. Our body is led by change, as is the body of the 'other.' It can react to change but can also assume an active role in it. I understand the situation through my body, as it grasps the way change is affecting me and how I can affect or influence the change effort. My body can detect phenomena (physical, biological, and psychological) and integrate them in ways that enable it to cope and try again even when it fails.

The same is true of the 'other,' who also has the skills to cope and to grasp the path of change. The other may be able to cope in the same way as me, or may differ in the degree and nature of coping. The degree of difference is not important. What *is* important is my recognition that I have my body in me, and others have their bodies in them, and yet we are connected: the beginning of inter-corporeality.

Such properties have an important role in helping us obtain an optimal grip on reality. I obtain my grip, as does the other. For Merleau-Ponty, our bodies are led by changing, and move and are led by what is visible and invisible (Dreyfus and Dreyfus 1991). Through my body, my coping and inhabitation of change are made more meaningful. It helps me see the other. The dialogical other is encouraged to express individual and personal thoughts, rather than being reified or treated as an object. For such an expression to take shape and form, narratives depicting our own inhabitations assume a special place.

Merleau-Ponty asked us to take a step back and reflect on our existence as a phenomenon searching for the pre-consciousness of our lived bodies.

This is not the physical body but the phenomenon of each one of us having an experience of the body. It is through the phenomenal body that utterances are made. Bakhtin (1984, 17) noted "each opinion really does become a living thing and is inseparable from an embodied human voice." Both Bakhtin and Merleau-Ponty invited us to think of how we are immersed through the self (consciousness), and that of the other. The thinking that produces the voice and the desired action are existentially felt and experienced in ways that make the body polyphonic to every other body.

Farnell (2003) and Gardiner (1998) demonstrated that it is not surprising that the mind has been accorded pride over the body and the body has been largely neglected. Cartesian modes of thinking lead us to believe that the body is unrelated or has little to do with the mind, especially in terms of capacity to contribute to the power of the mind. Polyphony plays an important role in achieving simultaneity, liberating individuals from the authoritative discourse, even though under simultaneity there is no merging of voices.

Our body, in the phenomenal sense, is the most important site of awareness, compassion, comprehension, and utterances. It is through the body that we utter and enact a grip on reality. The body is the first and foremost source of information about any object. It drives the flow of our utterances not as mere words, but as powerful expressions providing energy as we inter-animate our utterances with those of others.

It is not surprising that Merleau-Ponty viewed the Cartesian mode with contempt, because he did not wish to confine or contain the body. He also did not wish to see duality failing to recognize the interactive unity in the body-mind relationships. Bakhtin disliked the Cartesian mode because its separation prevents the heart and soul of consciousness being a social property. A Cartesian mode relies on the subject being responsible for all the reasoning. The subject has the power to reason (all through thinking by the 'I') and to make judgements in a state largely independent of the other, and then transmit that decision to the other. Strictly speaking, there does not need to be any responsiveness, as almost all the thinking is done by the 'I.'

Gardiner (1998, 128) explained that both Bakhtin and Merleau-Ponty aimed to "reverse this alienation between self and other (alterity), and between body and world." Such a reversal is vital for embodiment, defined as engagement with the world achieved through lived experiences, felt meanings, and perceived awareness of the world around us in ways that bring our body much closer to our own existence.

Merleau-Ponty distinguished between the objective body, or the body in its physicality as a *physical* unit, or object, and the *phenomenal* body. This is the human body in the way we experience it existing and come to be conscious of its existence. The physical unit is the material, occupying its own space. Merleau-Ponty (1964) noted that the phenomenal relates to perception. It is lived and experienced from within, without excluding the body of the other as it is being experienced through consciousness. Importantly, Merleau-Ponty (1964, 431) noted that the physical body "is not the true version of the phenomenal body, that is, the true version of the body that we live by. It is no more than the latter's impoverished image."

Nagataki and Hirose (2007) were keen to caution against regarding these distinctions as in opposition. It is true that the phenomenal body cannot be reduced to a mere thing in Cartesian meaning, "but it has the same properties that a thing has." They explained that "the phenomenal body implies some aspects of the objective one," and so one should not assume that Merleau-Ponty has committed to some kind of ontological dualism in distinguishing one form the other.

Embodying the change effort is also about that inter-subjective element, *sobytie*, and yet not merging. Our changing existential condition is largely connected in time and space and has its own relation to the changing existential condition of those around us. Such 'co-being' (in Bakhtin's terms) or the 'inter-subjective' (Merleau-Ponty's word) between one person and another provides fertile ground for affects (feelings) and compassion achieved by letting the other talk and at the same time the other letting me talk: what the other wants to say of their experience and challenges and what I want to say about mine.

Jung (1998, 95) pursued this point by noting that this aspect of co-being with the other matters and "matters deeply" in the sense that the mind is in the body but the body is also in the mind. He noted that the body is the living site of sociality. Without the body, real or imagined, there is neither sociality nor inter-subjectivity, and so the body "actively places us in the world with other people and other things."

Jung (1998, 95) described Descartes as the philosopher who fastened a "clamp on the interpretive art of the body" by treating the mind as independent, undermining the role of the body when "the visible body is the true *soulmate* of the invisible mind" (italic mine). Jung considered the body as connected to everything we do. Nietzsche also reprimanded those who despised the body, and censured those who saw the body as simply less important than the mind (Kaufmann 1977).

---

I want to speak to the despisers of the body. I would not have them learn and teach differently, but merely say farewell to their own bodies—and thus become silent . . . [t]he body is a great reason, a plurality with one sense, a war and a peace, a herd and a shepherd . . . [b]ehind your thoughts and feelings, my brother, there stands a mighty ruler, an unknown sage—whose name is self. In your body he dwells; he is your body.

There is more reason in your body than in your best wisdom. And who knows why your body needs precisely your best wisdom? . . . The self says to the ego, "Feel pain here!" Then the ego suffers and thinks how it might suffer no more—and that is why it is *made* to think. The self says to the ego, "Feel pleasure here!" Then the ego is pleased. And thinks how it might often be pleased again—and that is why it is *made* to think.

*Source:* Nietzsche (quoted in Kaufmann 1977, 146–7).

Nietzsche's sharp yet insightful account of the body brings on board new possibilities or ways of thinking about sociality. These have their own implications for determining inter-corporeality applied to managing and communicating change. In the next section, we will consider why embodiment is important for moderating our experiences of change.

## EMBODYING OUR UTTERANCES

How does Merleau-Ponty describe the body as the primary site of knowing? For him, we can connect to the material world and intertwine with other selves through relational existence. In elaborating on this notion, Mensch (2010, 450) explained that it is through perception that we obtain evidence that the world is within us and that our being is within the world. This intertwining is an output of "perceptual faith" because that is how our perception is achieved. Merleau-Ponty noted:

> When I see an object, I believe that my vision terminates in it, that it holds and stops my gaze with its insurmountable density . . . as soon as I attend to it, this conviction is just as strongly contested by the very fact that this vision is *mine*.
>
> (Merleau-Ponty 1968, 4–5)

Merleau-Ponty asserted, "our flesh lines and even envelops all the visible and tangible things" (1968, 123; quoted in Mensch 2010). Thus, we "line" the world with visual qualities through our eyes, with tactile qualities through our sense of touch, and so on. In doing so, our embodied being provides measures "for being, dimensions to which we can refer it" (Merleau-Ponty 1968, 103; quoted in Mensch 2010).

Merleau-Ponty's view of the body as the primary site of knowing accords with Bakhtin's in many respects, but Bakhtin took this one step further through his notion of consciousness relating to the other. Bakhtin saw the body as immersed in what is largely relational, and believed we are all joined through the corporeal. Utterances bring us together and establish our material connection with each other and with the world at large, including our organizational life. When I feel the impact of rules, the rules can speak to me.

Change has its own sensations. At one level, it is within me. On another level, it is outside. When a new rule, system, or change strategy is imposed on me, my body has a sense of such imposition. That sense remains mine until it is shared with others. Then, and only then, will I be able to connect to the material world of the organization and to other selves. Bakhtin described this as co-authoring whilst Merleau-Ponty saw it as the universal flesh of the world we all share. When such authoring is disclosed, and, therefore, becomes co-authoring, we start to feel a sense of relatedness to our immediate world.

## ORGANIZATIONAL CHANGE: MULTIPLICITY AND TENSIONS

Multiplicity of forces is a central characteristic of organizational life. There will always be centripetal as well as centrifugal forces, and they will always be in tension with each other. Out of these forces, certain objects are likely to be formed. An object, such as a strategy, will include an entangled set of plans, intentions, and moves.

Strategy has been defined as diagnosing patterns in observable activities, events, or behaviors over time (Ferrier 2001); reliance on chronological order of events as data (Pettigrew 1992; Van de Ven 1992); and searching for logical patterns based on consistencies in streams of behaviors (Mintzberg and Waters 1985). Mitroff and Emshoff (1979) called for a dialectical approach with an explicit emphasis on clarifying assumptions in the formulation of options. However we define strategy, the notion itself remains complex. Its implementation is accomplished through a range of methods. The meaning we attach to it tends to vary across organizational settings.

We have our own sense of the object (in this case, strategy). My sense of strategy is within me. It is already there in what I have in mind when I see what needs to be done or what could have been done. Much of what we know about strategy also applies to structure and systems.

To engage in strategy, we use language to describe how we diagnose patterns in observable activities, events, or behaviors. We might also rely on some chronological order of events as data. Whatever meaning or method we use in formulating a strategy, each meaning gives another sense of what strategy actually means on an individual level. Are such senses within or without? On one level they are within. They are what I have in mind when I employ various aspects of strategy. They are within my perceptual awareness, but start to assume new external meaning as my conversation is entangled with other conversation through utterances. This is related to what we mean by sociality. The problem with strategy is that it is always argued and presented as real objective plans. There is a tendency to see people as detached subjects, where the role of the change agent or manager is to move in and treat an issue with objectivity and detachment.

To grasp and agree on what is real would require people to be willing to relate to it. When I talk about strategy to make my point, the sensible meanings I assign to the strategy are apparent to others. The body-project that is guided by these senses affects what others perceive. I can ask others if they see what I see, and they may or may not confirm that.

People are often asked to doubt their perceptions. What is real is embedded in language. Utterances share in the intertwining that characterizes our perceptions of strategy. We can perceive an object such as strategy but without relating to it (monologic) or we can relate to it by sharing its attributes. Strategy itself as a body project can intimidate when not shared through what others have to offer. Lived experiences, felt meanings and perceptual awareness all play an important role in making strategy meaningful or daunting.

The term 'real' assumes special meaning in the work of Merleau-Ponty. Mensch (2010, 253) observed, "When we say that something objectively exists, we assert that it is there not just for us, but for everyone else." For Mensch, this basic sense of the real appears whenever we doubt our perceptions. To resolve this doubt and to obtain some confirmation, we probe the perceptions of others. We judge things to be real when others confirm our perceptions.

As such, what is real takes its place within the world. It assumes a public presence. We can grasp it through inter-subjective understanding. Stawarska's (2008) research provided evidence that we are literally born into inter-subjectivity. According to her, there is strong evidence that verbalized interaction between addresser and addressee emerges out of the earliest pre-linguistic relations between self and other. Todres (2008, 1569) talked about embodiment as " 'being with that' we are not, as human beings, originally nonparticipant observers processing things deep inside. We are more immediately responsive, before distancing ourselves from the 'being with.' "

Making it real is not the same as reification. Reification of strategy is about locating it somewhere outside our own being. Making it real is achieved through relating to it. This is not the same as top management announcing a five-year strategy and making it publicly available. That is reification, and does little but to make us contemplate an external world of facts. It makes the strategy distinct and separate, a static and self-contained object. There is no point in touching that object because it is already there. We can see the object and all that we are required to do is follow its dictate.

## EMBODIMENT IS ABOUT ENERGY

Embodiment is a process but it is also about enthusiasm and energy, gearing the body and making our experiences more concrete and meaningful. Küpers (2008, 391) noted that embodiment "does not simply mean physical manifestation. Rather, it means being grounded in everyday, mundane experience and integrally connected to the environment, including also a social community and a structural system, in an on-going interrelation." The body moderates our location in view of the world around us, and also searches and connects, seeking knowledge and the *sobytie* (the event of *being* with the other) as it continues becoming aware of the changing settings. Thus, the body acts as an intermediary between my experience and what is external.

Embodiment is about what is real and the way we go about expressing that 'real' in our utterances. It may be like a smoker, whose body says "You are doing no good to me or to the neighbors," or like a non-smoker valuing clean air. It has its own axiology or value system, in the sense that it can explain the *why* or *why not* that Bakhtin (1990, 30) said was "founded in emotional and volitional terms *out* of the other and *for* the other human being" (italic in original). By 'volitional,' Bakhtin means the act of choosing or resolving, thus exercising free will. There is a prospect of a conscious (free) choice but not everyone will find making such a choice easy. Some would prefer to adopt the prevailing paradigm of searching for objectifying knowledge through reason and cognition, with little reference to the body. Some might prefer to respond through embodiment, yet remain constrained by not wishing to bring the other on board.

For example, as an organization member participating in change in my organization, I can read a document about the organization's strategic plan. As I read, I try to attribute, through my body, not only my own lived experiences, but also those of the other. In dwelling on how I see myself relating to that plan, I might seek the view of the other. That other exists in materiality to me, as well as in relation to the materiality of the object, in this case the strategic plan. I therefore start to move from my self-centered axiological plane to the social axiological plane. I do so because I seek to renew and bring life to my conception of strategy by supplementing my understanding and adding a newer dimension.

My intention might or might not be to 'personify' the strategy. Having read the strategy document, I want my phenomenal embodiment to relate to that strategy, not necessarily as part of me but as something I can relate to and comment on, without having to objectify it as something external. When talking about embodiment, we need to erase the boundary that separates the Cartesian subject from the object. Embodiment is about collapsing the Cartesian subject-object binary. It is about enacting the stream of thoughts to allow for more overflow of meaning where the body is brought to bear on how I view organizational life.

In order to vivify my own outward image and make it a part of a concretely viewable whole, the entire architecture of the world of my imagining must be radically restructured, by introducing a totally new actor. This new actor results in my outward image being affirmed and founded in emotional and volitional terms "*out* of the other and *for* the other human being" (Bakhtin 1990, 30–31; italic in original).

I then start looking through the other subsystems, simultaneously inside and outside one another. My awareness runs back to me, as I become the object, even though I am also the subject. As I bring my experiences to the fore, I feed my knowledge back to others.

## EMBODIMENT AND SOCIALITY

As we perceive and deal with change, we soon become aware of the perceptions and feelings of others. That is quite usual in itself, as emotions and new sensations often generate more energy for change. Through gestures and bodily expressions, as well as language, we begin to know more of what the other is thinking. When we perceive that they perceive things as we do, we build on their agreement as they build on ours. Through utterances, both we and they realize our responsiveness.

Embodiment entails building and developing a relationship with the world (Bakhtin 1993). Applied to organizational life, it is how we use our awareness through utterances and lived experiences, and relate to what might be. Todres (2008, 1568) saw the other as indicating "some phenomenon, person, or situation beyond oneself . . . If we are open to it, 'that' is in excess of what we know because it is alive in time and can always surprise with something new, some new nuance, meaning, or texture."

Whether change is top-down, center-out, or bottom-up, how we relate in our *sobytie*, or co-sociality with others, has an important role in polyphony and the simultaneity of perceptions of situations. For example, consider how new formations of sociality are likely to emerge as a new system for staff performance is launched with little consultation. Under such a situation, it is not unusual for people to react and respond to the new order differently. Some might prefer to keep watching, to see what is coming next. Others might prefer to withdraw, in anticipation of the imposition of other new decisions, or simply wait. In an organizational setting, we are related to other bodies and it is not unusual for people to relate to each other.

Under an authoritative discourse, the emergence of new types of negative socialities and dysfunctional inter-bodily relationships is not unusual. Levels of collaboration start to diminish and people carry 'grudges' as a new order takes over. Their bodies are unable to cope because of authoritative discourse, so they start to protect and guard themselves, forming new socialities alongside new change cultures. Some will avoid cooperation, and an 'everyone for themselves' attitude often emerges. Hermans et al. reminded us:

> We need to recall that the Cartesian expression '*I* think' assumes that there is one '*I*' responsible for all the reasoning. Second, the Cartesian '*I think*' is based on a disembodied mental process assumed to be essentially different from the body and other material extended in space.
>
> The dialogical [polyphonic] self, in contrast with the individualistic self, is based on the assumption that there are many *I* positions that can be occupied by the same person. The *I* in one position can agree, disagree, understand, misunderstand, oppose, contradict, question, and even ridicule the *I* in another position.
>
> (Hermans et al. 1992, 29: italics in original).

## IMPORTANCE OF EMBODIMENT IN MANAGING CHANGE

Why is the notion of embodiment important in managing change? And, by the same token, what is the connection between embodiment and the need to create a climate ripe for change? The answer lies in the ingenuity and resourcefulness required to capture the lived experiences of organization members and the willingness to view these experiences as knowledge in ways that would encourage relational understanding between people. Merleau-Ponty noted that:

> At the root of all our experiences and all our reflections, we find, then, a being which immediately recognizes itself, because it is its knowledge of itself and all things, and which knows its own existence, not by observation and as a given fact, nor by inference from any idea of itself, but through direct contact with that existence.
>
> (Merleau-Ponty 1962, 432)

The ability to cope and manage change in a way that would enable it to take root is an added reason. Merleau-Ponty notes that "the body is the mirror of our being" (1962, 198). The body carries, absorbs, and turns to itself, in a kind of reflexivity. That takes place through bodily senses, as the body changes and adjusts itself to coping with what needs changing. This recalls the idea of Hermans et al. (1992) that the Cartesian "I *think*" is based on a disembodied cognitive mental process assumed to be essentially different from the body, and that the organization is a reified entity, no matter what anyone happens to think.

We rely on the physical (material) body of the organization and its corporeality. Our experiences of working in organizations provide us with an awareness of a co-constitutive relationship between self, organization, and people. For example, we do not look at ossified rules and regulations without recalling those wanting to enact them. We are dependent on having to follow these rules, each developed by one or more individuals. The body works its way *through* and *within* these rules and the people around them. We get a grip on reality and we are always moving to develop an optimal understanding of the rules. We experience them as if we are *in* them and yet *outside* them (Merleau-Ponty 1968). Organizations, their rules (written) and norms (unwritten), and the people who put these rules and norms into practice, do not exist in a vacuum.

As I see the other, I am taken out of my body, yet remain within it. My body transforms the view of the other to be larger than any other foreground figure. I encounter the inverse perspective of the other as my body transforms their linear view into an inverse perspective (Hutchings 1999). This turns my linear perspective of that person back on itself, and brings it to the fore. I accept, contest, or even rebut the other and the other's decision-making. The other will see me in exchange. My body traverses the visual to reach what is invisible.

For Bakhtin (1986, 120) the word is "inter-individual." Every utterance is relational, in the sense that:

> Everything that is said, expressed, is located outside the soul of the speaker and does not belong only to him. The word cannot be assigned to a single speaker. The author (speaker) has his own inalienable right

to the word, but the listener has his rights, and those whose voices are
heard in the word before the author comes upon it also have their rights
(after all, there are no words that belong to no one).

(Bakhtin 1986, 121)

Bakhtin therefore concluded that sociality and understanding can only
occur through the body. How do we go about embodying change? Bakhtin
argued that all dialogue is interdependent, always changing, and that we
are, in fact, living in and through our relationships with one another. This
provides a useful way of understanding organizations in ways that embody
diversity, pluralism, polyphony, and the interdependence between individuals working within the organization, as well as the interdependence of an
organization and its wider community setting.

Embodiment has important implications for understanding polyphony.
Csordas argued:

If embodiment is an existential condition in which the body is the subjective source or inter-subjective ground of experience, then studies
under the rubric of embodiment are not 'about' the body per se. Instead
they are about culture and experience insofar as these can be understood from the standpoint of bodily being-in-the-world.

(Csordas 1999, 143)

Farnell and Graham (1998, 411) suggested that embodiment provides
"inter-subjective means by which persons, social institutions and cultural
knowledge are socially constructed, historically transmitted and revised and
so are constitutive of culture and self."

The objective (cognitive) is often captured through descriptions and
questionnaires from external systems that do little but ask us to respond to
what is non-sentient. Even though changing has become part of my perceptive body, emotions, and activities, they neither take us inside our bodies
and then outside into the organization, nor bring us back, as they consist of
mere descriptions with no consciousness of their own. Such descriptions are
imposed on us even though change has done little but stretch our existence
out of shape and annex our bodies. For Merleau-Ponty (1968), my way of
seeing change should be centered on change about me, but it is also my own
or in me.

Monologism becomes the dominant trait characteristic of the organizational setting. The organization, therefore, is not altered by what organization members see. The radiance of their vision fails to reach the top. Often,
what they see is blocked by fortifications meant to distance organization
members from the center. There is little dynamic intertwining and sharing
of perceptions at more than one level. The gaze fails to reach the top and
so members give up hope of using their vision to influence the status quo.

Applied to change, strategy is treated as an objective entity to be talked about as separate and independent. We describe the 'object' as we see it. There is no intertwining between self and the object. What we see does not take us into the self. The organization is also well outside us, as is our seeing.

We are altered by changes in themselves and so should we not consider them? The answer is that we do, and yet we often end up ignoring the issue, or belittling important concerns. We end up saying to ourselves that these concerns will sort themselves out even though we know that this is not the case.

We describe as we see. Merleau-Ponty built on the idea that the body is a hyphen that connects the self and the object. For Florensky (1997), as for Bakhtin (1984), the body is pivotal in connecting our selfhood with the world around us. We experience the body as both subject (for itself and the self) and object (for the other). We need the body for the self to move on and connect with the outside world, as the body acquires a "halo of *visibility*" (Merleau-Ponty 1968, 244; italics in original) and the interior world recedes.

Merleau-Ponty (1962) argued that the phenomenon of human perception demonstrates the inseparability of subject and object. He added (1962) that the phenomenon of human perception demonstrates that the subject and object are not alien to one another, but are closely associated and even incapable of being separated. Opposing the union of the two does little but obliterate it, but is often attempted. We try to portray the subject (addressor) as pure consciousness and see the approaching object, whether strategy or structure, as *in itself*.

## LOOKING TO THE FUTURE

I could not speak of polyphony without discussing managerialism. Central to managerialism is a Cartesian view of the world predicated on separating body and mind. It assumes the mind has power to objectify rules and procedures outside the body by making them external elements, objects that can be controlled by or through a person. It compels us to work in contexts that discourage us from relating to the other, hence preventing us and our organizations from progressing into genuine inclusiveness of change effort and the simultaneity of voice (polyphony).

I have stressed that there is no point in allowing polyphony, unless the issue with dialectics is resolved. Much of the work on Bakhtin applied to organizational studies has shunned the full impact of dialectics, to the extent of making Bakhtin's work on polyphony almost inapplicable. Tracking the threats to polyphony is crucial, as there is no point in calling for polyphony unless we can monitor conventional managerialism and the way it manifests through formalization, dialectics, and managerial logic.

There is also no point in calling for polyphony unless we can see the difference between a monologic and dialogic sense of truth, and no point in talking about a dialogic sense of truth unless we move the monologism of dialectics to a polyphonic context. Once rules are laid down and managerial logic takes precedence, polyphony is internally compromised. It is further stifled by the introduction of more rules and reviews which codify language even more, moving away from change and becoming inherent in utterances.

Malabou suggested that in managing change, we should understand plasticity as "the capacity to receive form and a capacity to produce form" (2005, 9). This is to show that we can be more genuinely open to the future than we have ever been led to think, thus able to move away from the imposition of prevailing forms and the sort of dialectics leading to closure and stagnation. Organizations reproduce the reason for their own demise because of their fixed mindset, rigidities of dialectics, and lack of malleability. There is no point in a treatment centered on polyphony unless it is preceded by a plastic reading of dialectics.

It takes a while to see the reason for lamenting celebrated acts of managerialism and managerial logic, as much as it takes time to understand the pitfalls of managerialism. That is because understanding managerialism requires a close examination of rules and procedures and how these evolve in time towards stagnation, demise, and destruction. It is hard for simultaneity of talk to replace monologic sense of truth unless plasticity comes to our aid. Malabou believed that plasticity is indeed disruptive and the beauty of her conception of what is 'disruptive' is the capability of plasticity for disruption, enabling single-hearted monologic truth to be destroyed. Reflecting on her own experiences of Hegelian Dialectics and Heidegger's reading of Hegel, Malabou (2010, 9; italic in original) elegantly proceeded by noting "plasticity thus appeared to me from the outset as *a structure of transformation and destruction of presence and the present.*" We all have examples of organizations that have reached their demise because it was too late for them to be destroyed in time to save their heritage (e.g., Enron).

I see Bakhtin's notion of polyphony as providing an olive branch to help us reconsider the task ahead of us. It shows that there can be more than one way of thinking about change and changing. At the same time, I also see the need for Malabou's (2005) notion of plasticity, and, therefore, for dialogue between Bakhtin, Bateson, and Malabou in the hope that our organizations and the lives we inhabit could be sculpted through polyphony and the associated notion of *sobytie*.

## REFERENCES

Bakhtin, Mikhail Mikhailovitch. 1984. *Problems of Dostoyevsky's Poetics*, edited and translated by Carey Emerson. Minneapolis: University of Minnesota Press.
———. 1986. *Speech Genres and Other Essays*, edited by Carey Emerson and Michael Holquist, translated by Vern McGee. Austin: University of Texas Press.

————. 1990. *Art and Answerability: Early Philosophical Essays*, edited by Michael Holquist and Vadim Liapunov. Austin: University of Texas Press.

————. 1993. *Toward a Philosophy of the Act*, edited by Michael Holquist and Vadim Liapunov, translated by Vadim Liapunov. Austin: University of Texas Press.

Boje, David. 2008. *Storytelling Organizations*. London: Sage.

Csordas, Thomas. 1999. "Embodiment and Cultural Phenomenology." In *Perspectives on Embodiment*, edited by Gail Weiss and Honi Fern Haber, 143–164. London: Routledge.

Descartes, René. 1969. *The Philosophical Works of Descartes*, translated by E. S. Haldane and G. R. T. Ross. Cambridge: Cambridge University Press.

Dreyfus, Hubert L. and Stuart E. Dreyfus. 1991. "Towards a phenomenology of ethical expertise." *Human Studies* 14 (4): 229–50.

Dufva, Hannele. 2004. "Language, Thinking and Embodiment: Bakhtin, Whorf and Merleau-Ponty." In *Thinking Culture Dialogically*, edited by Finn Bostad, Craig Brandist, Lars S. Evensen and Hege C. Faber, 133–46. London: Macmillan Publishers.

Farnell, Brenda. 2003. "Kinesthetic sense and dynamically embodied action." *Journal of Anthropological Study of Human Movement* 12 (4): 132–44.

Farnell, Brenda and Laura R. Graham. 1998. "Discourse-centered methods." In *Handbook of Methods in Cultural Anthropology*, edited by H. Russell Bernard and Clarence C. Gravlee, 411–57. Thousand Oaks, CA: AltaMira Press.

Ferrier, Walter J. 2001. "Navigating the competitive landscape: the drivers and consequences of competitive aggressiveness." *Academy of Management Journal* 44 (4): 858–77.

Florensky, Pavel. 1997. *The Pillar and Ground of the Truth: An Essay in the Orthodox Theodicy in Twelve Letters*, translated by Boris Jakim. Upper Saddle River, NJ: Princeton University Press.

Gardiner, Michael. 1998. "'The Incomparable Monster of Solipsism': Bakhtin and Merleau-Ponty." In *Bakhtin and the Human Sciences: No Last Words*, edited by Michael Mayerfeld Bell and Michael Gardiner, 129–45, Theory, Culture & Society. London: SAGE Publications Ltd. doi: http://dx.doi.org/10.4135/9781446278949.n9.

Hermans, Hubert J. M., Harry J. Kempen and Rens J. van Loon. 1992. "The dialogical self beyond individualism and rationalism." *American Psychologist* 47 (1): 23.

Hirschkop, Ken. 1999. *Mikhail Bakhtin: An Aesthetic for Democracy*. Oxford: Oxford University Press.

Holquist, Michael 1990. *Dialogism*. London: Routledge.

————. 2002. *Dialogism*. New York: Routledge.

Hutchings, Stephen. 1999. "Making sense of the sensual in Pavel Florenskii's aesthetics: the dialectics of finite being." *Slavic Review* 58 (1): 96–116.

Jabri, Muayyad. 2012. *Managing Organizational Change: Process, Social Construction and Dialogue*. Basingstoke: Palgrave Macmillan.

Johnson, Allison H. 1983. *Whitehead and His Philosophy*. New York: University Press of America.

Jung, Hwa Yol. 1998. "Bakhtin's Dialogical Body Politics." In *Bakhtin and the Human Sciences: No Last Words*, edited by Michael Mayerfeld Bell and Michael Gardiner, 95–111. London: Sage Publications.

Kaufmann, Walter. 1977. *The Portable Nietzsche*. Middlesex: Penguin.

Küpers, Wendelin. 2005. "Phenomenology of embodied implicit and narrative knowing." *Journal of Knowledge Management* 9 (6): 114–33.

————. 2008. "Embodied 'inter-learning'—an integral phenomenology of learning in and by organizations." *The Learning Organization* 15 (5): 388–408.

Mair, Miller. 1988. "Psychology as storytelling." *International Journal of Personal Construct Psychology* 1 (2): 125–38.

Malabou, Catherine. 2005. *The Future of Hegel: Plasticity, Temporality and Dialectic*, translated by Lisabeth During. London: Routledge.

———. 2010. *Plasticity at the Dusk of Writing: Dialectic, Destruction, Deconstruction*, translated by Carolyn Shread. New York: Columbia University Press.

Mensch, James. 2010. "The temporality of Merleau-Ponty's intertwining." *Continental Philosophy Review* 42 (4): 449–63.

Merleau-Ponty, Maurice. 1962. *The Phenomenology of Perception*, translated by Colin Smith. London: Routledge and Kegan Paul.

———. 1964. *Signs*, translated by Richard C. McCleary. Evanston, IL: Northwestern University Press. (Original work published in French in 1960 under the title *Signes*).

———. 1968. *The visible and the invisible*, translated by Alphonso Lingis. Evanston, IL: Northwestern University Press.

Mintzberg, Henry and James A. Waters. 1985. "Of strategies, deliberate and emergent." *Strategic Management Journal* 6: 257–72.

Mitroff, Ian I. and James R. Emshoff. 1979. "On strategic assumption-making: a dialectical approach to policy and planning." *Academy of Management Review* 4 (1): 1–12.

Morson, Gary S. and Caryl Emerson. 1990. *Mikhail Bakhtin: Creation of a Prosaics*. Stanford: Stanford University Press.

Nagataki, Shoji and Satoru Hirose. 2007. "Phenomenology and the third generation of cognitive science: towards a cognitive phenomenology of the body." *Human Studies* 30 (3): 219–32.

Pettigrew, Andrew M. 1992. "The character and significance of strategy process research." *Strategic Management Journal* 13 (S2): 5–16.

Stawarska, Beata. 2008. "Feeling good vibrations in dialogical relations." *Continental Philosophical Review* 41 (12): 217–36.

Todres, Les. 2008. "Being with that: the relevance of embodied understanding for practice." *Qualitative Health Research* 18 (11): 1566–73.

Van de Ven, Andrew H. 1992. "Suggestions for studying strategy processes: a research note." *Strategic Management Journal* 13 (5): 169–88.

Whitehead, Alfred North. 1956. *Modes of Thought*. Cambridge: Cambridge University Press.

———. (1929/1978). *Process and Reality*. Corrected Edition. Boston: The Free Press.

# About the Author

**Muayyad Jabri** MSocSc (*Birmingham*), PhD (*Manchester Business School*)

Muayyad's research focuses on the philosophy of management and the management of organizational change. As a Visiting Professor in a number of universities in Europe and the People's Republic of China (1997–2001), he has developed a keen interest in the philosophy of change as inspired by the work of Catherine Malabou, Merleau-Ponty, Alfred North Whitehead, and Mikhail Bakhtin. Before joining the University of New England in Australia, Muayyad held teaching positions in the University of Wollongong and the Manchester Business School.

Muayyad's work has focused on the philosophy of management, management education, cross-cultural management, and the management of organizational change. His current research is in philosophical and dialogic approaches to change management. His work on modes of innovation has been translated into Japanese, German, and Spanish. His research work has received the best paper award at the American Academy of Management.

Professor Jabri's research output has appeared in leading journals in management, including: *Philosophy of Management, Journal of Organizational Change Management, Journal of Management Education, Journal of Organizational Behavior, and the British Journal of Management,* He has consulted on team design and the management of organizational change with several organizations, including Amersham International, Pfizer, and ICI Pharmaceuticals.

# Index